# Bridging the Transition from Pr
# to Secondary School

The transition from primary to secondary school can often be a difficult time for children, and managing the transition smoothly has posed a problem for teachers at both upper primary and lower secondary level. At a time when 'childhood' recedes and 'adulthood' beckons, the inequalities between individual children can widen, and meeting the needs of all children is a challenge.

*Bridging the Transition from Primary to Secondary School* offers an insight into children's development, building a framework for the creation of appropriate and relevant educational experiences of children between the ages of 10 and 12. Based on the five 'transition bridges' – administrative, social and personal, curriculum, pedagogy, and autonomy and managing learning – this book is a complete guide to the primary–secondary transition.

Chapters cover:

- a review of the issues and challenges of transition and school transfer;
- management of physical, intellectual, social and emotional changes;
- issues of changing self-identity;
- approaches to ensure curriculum progression and continuity;
- ways to develop cooperation between primary and secondary schools;
- alternatives to traditional primary–secondary systems and pedagogy.

This book will be essential reading for all trainee teachers, undergraduate and postgraduate education students, and those working with children over the transition. The contributors offer a wealth of guidance and insight into meeting the educational and social needs of children through early adolescence.

**Alan Howe** is Senior Lecturer and Programme Leader in Education Studies at Bath Spa University. He specialises in Primary Science Education.

**Val Richards** is Senior Lecturer in Education Studies at Bath Spa University, specialising in Psychology.

# Bridging the Transition from Primary to Secondary School

Edited by Alan Howe and
Val Richards

Routledge
Taylor & Francis Group

LONDON AND NEW YORK

First published 2011
by Routledge
2 Park Square, Milton Park, Abingdon, Oxon OX14 4RN

Simultaneously published in the USA and Canada
by Routledge
711 Third Avenue, New York, NY 10017

*Routledge is an imprint of the Taylor & Francis Group, an informa business*

*British Library Cataloguing in Publication Data*
A catalogue record for this book is available from the British Library

*Library of Congress Cataloging in Publication Data*
Bridging the transition from primary to secondary school / edited by Alan Howe and Val Richards.
p. cm.
Includes index.
1. Education, Primary. 2. Education, Secondary. 3. Classroom management.
4. Motivation in education. I. Howe, Alan. II. Richards, Val.
LB1737.A3B69 2011
370.15'4–dc22
2010052664

ISBN: 978-0-415-57546-1 (hbk)
ISBN: 978-0-415-57547-8 (pbk)
ISBN: 978-0-203-81871-8 (ebk)

Typeset in Bembo by Prepress Projects Ltd, Perth, UK

MIX
Paper from
responsible sources
FSC
www.fsc.org  FSC® C004839

Printed and bound in Great Britain by
TJ International Ltd, Padstow, Cornwall

# Contents

# Illustrations

# Contributors

**June Bianchi** is Leader of the Centre for Research in Arts Education at Bath Spa University, a National Teaching Fellow and visual artist; her artwork and research explore the construction of socio-cultural identity through the arts. June co-ordinates arts education at undergraduate, postgraduate and Master's level as well as lecturing in diversity education and co-ordinating the Erasmus programme for the School of Education. June exhibits, publishes and facilitates collaborative interdisciplinary arts educational projects across a range of national and international contexts.

**Dan Davies** is Head of Applied Research and Consultancy in the School of Education at Bath Spa University. He is Professor of Science and Technology Education and leader of the Centre for Research in Early Scientific Learning. He has taught in primary schools, worked as an education officer for the Design Council and been involved in teacher education at all levels in two universities. He has researched and published widely in the fields of science and technology education.

**Alan Howe** is Programme Leader for undergraduate Education Studies at Bath Spa University. He has over 25 years of experience of teaching in primary and higher education. He has published on a range of topics associated with teaching, creativity and science education.

**Mim Hutchings** is Senior Lecturer in Education Studies at Bath Spa University with a specialist interest in inclusion and diversity. She has taught in a range of schools (nursery, primary, secondary and specialist settings) and acted as an advisor for special educational needs. Her research interests are in learning in higher education and social and educational inclusion.

**Rachael Jefferson-Buchanan** is Senior Lecturer in Physical Education, Dance, Education Studies and Primary Professional Practice at Bath Spa University. She is also the UK consultant for Fundamental Movement Skills (Steps PD). She has more than 20 years of teaching experience in primary and secondary education, both nationally and internationally. She publishes regularly in the area of dance, primary physical education, early movement skills and young children's health. Her PhD focuses on a critical analysis of primary movement programmes and initiatives.

**Kendra McMahon** is Senior Lecturer at Bath Spa University. Formerly a primary school teacher, she now researches and teaches primary science education at undergraduate and postgraduate level, with a particular focus on the later primary years and on the role of talk.

**Stephen Miles** currently teaches English in north Somerset and was formerly Senior Lecturer in English Education at Bath Spa University. He has been involved in English teaching one way or another for nearly 20 years. His passion is children's literature.

**Tilly Mortimore** is Senior Lecturer in Inclusion and Education Studies at Bath Spa University. She also runs the Master's degree in SpLD/dyslexia. After more than 25 years teaching in settings for learners with SpLD/dyslexia, she moved into higher education and now researches, publishes and lectures internationally on inclusion and SpLD/dyslexia. Her most recent project focuses on dyslexia and multilingualism.

**Anny Northcote** has been teaching in higher education for 15 years after spending 17 years in primary education in the east end of London as a class teacher, language co-ordinator and advisor for bilingual learners. She is currently teaching at Bath Spa University on Education Studies, including a module on children's literature. She also teaches modern languages to primary PGCE students and supervises professional practice in schools. She has contributed to publications on linguistic diversity and is currently engaged in a Big Lottery-funded project on multilingualism and dyslexia in collaboration with the British Dyslexia Association.

**Val Richards** is Senior Lecturer on the Education Studies undergraduate programme at Bath Spa University. She has extensive teaching experience across a range of educational contexts including primary, secondary, adult distance learning and higher education at undergraduate and postgraduate level. Her specialist area is psychology and she teaches adolescent development, learning through life, health, education and behaviour.

**Hilary Smith** is Senior Lecturer in Early Years Education at Bath Spa University, teaching at both undergraduate and postgraduate level. She is also a Behaviour Consultant for Bristol Local Authority, specialising in the social, emotional and behavioural needs of young children.

**Marcus Witt** teaches mostly on the Primary PGCE course at Bath Spa University as well as contributing to undergraduate Education Studies modules. He has over 15 years of experience teaching in primary and higher education both in the UK and abroad. His main research interests are in mathematics anxiety and in the role of working memory in children's mathematics.

# Abbreviations

| | |
|---|---|
| AKSIS | Association for Science Education and King's College London Science Investigations in Schools |
| AZSTT | AstraZeneca Science Teaching Trust |
| BME | black and minority ethnic |
| CPD | continuing professional development |
| CST | Council for Science and Technology |
| DCFS | Department for Children, Families and Schools |
| DEA | Development Education Association |
| DES | Department of Education and Science |
| DfEE | Department for Education and Employment |
| DfES | Department for Education and Skills |
| ECM | Every Child Matters |
| FMS | Fundamental Movement Skills |
| HMSO | Her Majesty's Stationery Office |
| ICT | information and communication technology |
| IST | Improving Science Together |
| ITE | Initial Teacher Education |
| KS | Key Stage (of the National Curriculum) |
| MFMC | My Future My Choice |
| NC | National Curriculum |
| NCETM | National Centre for Excellence in Teaching Mathematics |
| NEET | not in employment, education or training |
| NLS | National Literacy Strategy |
| OAA | outdoor and adventurous activities |
| OECD | Organisation for Economic Co-operation and Development |
| Ofsted | Office for Standards in Education |
| ORACLE | Observational Research and Classroom Learning Evaluation |
| PIRLS | Progress in International Reading Literacy Study |
| PSHE | personal, social and health education |
| QCA | Qualifications and Curriculum Authority |
| RAiS | Restorative Approaches in Schools |
| SAT | Standard Assessment Test |

SEAL      Social and Emotional Aspects of Learning
SENCO   special educational needs co-ordinator
SEPT      Scientific Enquiry Progression Task
STAY      Science Transition AstraZeneca York
UNESCO United Nations Educational, Scientific and Cultural Organization

# Introduction

## Exploring the great divide

*Alan Howe*

## Chapter summary

This chapter introduces the key themes of the book. It begins by exploring the reasons for the existence of an education system that has, inherent in its structure, a deep discontinuity. After a brief examination of the aims of primary and secondary education in the UK and the problems associated with a divided education system and a divided teaching profession, it introduces a permeating theme of the book – the 'bridging' of the gap that exists between the two phases of schooling.

## The great divide

It is a bizarre thing about state education in the UK: when children are 11 they have to go to a new school. Every autumn, over half a million children find themselves heading off to an institution that is quite different from their small, local, non-specialised, non-selective primary school. The children may be well equipped by their family to start their first day – confident and happy, with a new uniform and shoes, some new pens and pencils, perhaps some sound advice from older siblings. Others may be ill-equipped materially, academically and emotionally to cope with the upheaval. Research shows that a move from primary to secondary school can lead to children's levels of attainment being held back or even reversed (Galton *et al.* 1999). Evangelou *et al.* (2008) reports that out of 16 per cent of children who did not feel prepared for transition only 3 per cent were worried or nervous a term after they started secondary school. To put it another way, that's approximately 80,000 children in England worrying about transition during their summer holiday, with 15,000 admitting to still being worried 4 months later. Why do we put children through this trauma? Is the disruption necessary? Does the education they receive until this moment prepare them for this major life event?

This book explores an important phase in a child's education – the transition between primary and secondary education. From a child's perspective it is both an end and a beginning. From an educator's perspective the child is somewhere in the middle of a very large and complex system, and there is a danger that he or she may get lost. By the time these children make the journey to secondary school they may have already made a number of transfers and transitions. They have a clear idea what schooling is like. They may have a view of themselves as a learner: a winner, a struggler or a loser. Will they be required to remember all they have learned or perhaps 'move on' and start learning in a new way? For many children, this transition is full of exciting possibilities, but there is no guarantee that a 'high flyer' will continue to fly high. A child full of confidence may find his or her inner resources considerably drained by the experience. Can schools and teachers make a difference or make things better? How should they ensure that the transition is a confident step forward rather than a stumble or fall into the gap between schools that are miles apart? Before looking at some of the answers to these questions, it is worth considering why the divide is there.

## Why a divided schooling system?

In the nineteenth and early twentieth centuries, it was only the children of the wealthy who tended to continue in education after the age of 11, at a grammar school or at one of the renowned 'public' schools such as Eton, Harrow or Rugby. Most children completed their schooling before they were teenagers. A framework for schooling of all children between the ages of 5 and 12 was set out by the Elementary Education Act 1870, commonly known as Forster's Education Act. The establishment of universal elementary education was driven by economic concerns of the Victorian age. Britain was competing in a world market for the manufacture and trade of goods and needed a workforce that was literate and numerate. Elementary schools gave these workers the basic education required. Few working families could afford the option of keeping their children in education after they had attained this rudimentary education and were old enough to earn a wage (Simon 1965).

In some cases, however, particularly centred on the industrial towns of the Midlands and the north, children did stay on in elementary schools. These 'Higher Grade' schools took children of ages 12, 13, even 14, and gave them a sound grounding in maths, science and languages useful to the skilled worker who would join the lower ranks of trade and industry. Furthermore, a few pupils were successfully prepared by these 'all age' schools for university entrance. Here the schools performed a function of the previously unchallenged private secondary education sector. This provision, by enlightened providers of education for the workers, met with opposition from the 'somewhat stagnant' grammar schools (Simon 1965), which saw it as a challenge to their monopoly on the schooling of the adolescent. A long ideological battle ensued. It was fought over the question of whether secondary education should be available to the masses. The battle lasted for half a century. The secondary school system that emerged was built on an educational ideology that had at its heart the view that education should contribute to the maximum efficiency of the state, and that that aim would be served by channelling children into post-elementary educational provision appropriate for their intellect and aptitudes. The prevalent thinking of the time suggested that the best moment to achieve this refocus of educational purpose was at the age of 11:

There is a tide which begins to rise in the veins of youth at the age of eleven or twelve. It is called by the name of adolescence. If that tide can be taken at the flood, and a new voyage begun in the strength and along the flow of its current, we think that it will 'move on to fortune'. We therefore propose that all children should be transferred, at the age of eleven or twelve, from the junior or primary school either to schools of the type now called secondary . . . central, or to senior and separate departments of existing elementary schools.

(Hadow 1926: xix)

Although the Hadow Report proposed the establishment of a new, more appropriate, type of school for adolescents, it didn't go as far as recommending the closure of the successful 'all through' elementary school. This happened later, when state secondary schools were finally brought into existence in the UK by a 1944 Education Act, often called the 'Butler Act' after the Secretary of State of the day. The act established (albeit implicitly) that the state would provide secondary schools of three sorts to meet the needs of three types of pupil: elite grammar schools for those with academic aptitude, technical schools for those capable of joining the skilled labour force and the 'secondary modern' for those who didn't show potential for either of the other two options. Furthermore, the act confirmed that the time to direct a child down one path or another was at age 11.

In the UK, children needed to pass the 'eleven-plus' test to gain a place at a grammar school (many children were age 10 when taking it). Although increasingly seen as extremely unfair and divisive, the test was administered to millions of children during the twentieth century and into the twenty-first century. Gardner and Cowan (2000) found the test administered in Northern Ireland at that time to be seriously flawed and to fall short of international standards for educational testing. In England during the period 1950–1975 there were places in grammar schools for the top 10–30 per cent of children, depending on the number of places available in the region. There were more grammar school places for boys than for girls. The system favoured those children from higher socio-economic groups. Children from well-off and smaller families had a much better chance of passing the eleven-plus than those from poor backgrounds (Halsey and Gardner 1953). The test was not reliable, with up to 25 per cent of candidates wrongly placed. Siblings, even twins, could be sent to separate schools at age 11 because one failed to perform well on the day of the test. Those children who attended grammar schools had a fair chance of going on to university and joining a well-paid profession. There were very few technical schools established and those who attended the secondary modern had limited opportunities to access higher education. Secondary modern schools were often housed in inadequate buildings and taught by poorly trained, demotivated teachers (Newsom 1963). A 1963 report to the Ministry of Education highlighted the plight of the 'average' and 'below average' child:

Our anxiety is lest the relatively unspectacular needs of the boys and girls with whom we have been concerned should be overlooked. They have had far more than their fair share of thoroughly unsatisfactory buildings and desperately unsettling changes of staff. Given the opportunities, we have no doubt that they will rise to the challenge which a rapidly developing economy offers no less to them than to their abler brothers and sisters.

(Newsom 1963: xiii)

Because of the flaws of the tripartite (in effect bipartite) system described above, many believed it should be replaced by one school type for all – the *comprehensive* school. These were non-selective state-funded secondary schools that admitted any child from the local area. It was believed that such schools would ensure that all children would have the opportunity to fulfil their potential, whether they were quick learners or slow burners. In 1965 the Labour government passed a motion in the House of Commons:

That this House, conscious of the need to raise educational standards at all levels, and regretting that the realisation of this objective is impeded by the separation of children into different types of secondary schools, notes with approval the efforts of local authorities to reorganise secondary education on comprehensive lines.

(DES 1965: 1)

In effect, the belief that it was necessary to judge the potential of children at age 11, and then make decisions on their behalf about the kind of school that would prepare them for adulthood, was called into question. The need for secondary schools to exist as discrete from primary schools was not widely disputed, although at this point it is worth acknowledging the existence of 'middle schools' in England and Wales. As left-wing politicians and educationalists campaigned for an end to the 'eleven-plus' and the establishment of fully comprehensive schools, local authorities baulked at the enormous cost of providing large purpose-built schools to replace the small existing ones. Some local authorities made use of the available premises by establishing comprehensive high schools for 11- to 14-year-olds, leading on to community colleges for those aged 14–18. In 1964 legislation was introduced that allowed local education authorities to establish middle schools that bridged the primary–secondary divide. Some local authorities reorganised their schools into three tiers, first, middle and upper schools, with justification provided by the influential Plowden Report (Central Advisory Council for Education 1967). By the end of the reorganisation process there were 1,500 middle schools in England and Wales (National Middle Schools' Forum 2010). Since the Education Reform Act of 1999 leading to the establishment of a National Curriculum and assessments organised around Key Stages (children aged 7–11 are in Key Stage 2, those aged 11–14 in Key Stage 3) the number of middle schools has halved. Although proponents of middle schools argue that they solve many of the problems of transfer highlighted in this book (National Middle Schools' Forum 2010), there is no evidence that they are likely to become a significant option for England and Wales in the near future.

Since 1975 the majority of children educated in England by the state have been obliged to attend a secondary comprehensive school, although whether so-called comprehensives are really that is strongly contested. Ward and Eden (2009) contend that the model of comprehensive education advocated by early pioneers is further away now than it was 40 years ago. At the time of writing, secondary schools can be academies, trust schools, community schools, specialist schools, grammar schools, religious in character, non-denominational, co-educational or single sex – and the list is not exhaustive. Ward and Eden suggest that the present diversity of secondary schools is more likely to lead to social division, inequality and substandard education than the tripartite system of the 1950s.

The current debate about secondary education is focused on power and control. Who should control the schools? Who should hire and fire teachers? Who should control the curriculum? During the last 70 years the very existence of secondary schools has not been seriously questioned during these debates. It is a taken for granted assumption that they should exist as separate and distinct from primary schools because they have a different role and different aims. We might then ask: What are our schools for? Do primary and secondary schools have distinctively different aims? This assumed difference in purpose between these two phases of education will now be considered.

## The purpose of primary schools

In questioning the purpose of primary schools, debates are had about three aims: the need to ensure that all children gain a command of 'the basics'; how schools can enable individuals to be creative, critical thinkers; and the need to prepare the child for the next stage of education (Alexander 2009). In other words, primary education can be elementary, developmental or preparatory. (For a more complete discussion of the formative traditions of primary education see Alexander 2000.) For Alexander, the 'elementary' strand is the most permanent and pervasive of the competing traditions and influences he identifies.

The structural arrangements that stem from the elementary tradition include:

- funding;
- a distinct and coherent phase requiring a uniform approach to the education of children aged from 5 to 11, identified by a rigid and extensive 'primary curriculum' and primary teaching strategies;
- the curriculum with a 'core' of the basics of mathematics and mother tongue and the rest, which might include a smattering of the arts and humanities;
- the class teacher – with an assumption that a single teacher is best placed to teach the whole curriculum to a full year group, or across year groups (Alexander 2000).

Alexander comments further on these arrangements:

> Each of these reinforces the other. The funding arrangements make alternatives to the class teaching system impossible to implement . . . This system, by taxing teachers' subject expertise and ingenuity to the utmost, creates problems of curriculum manageability. [This] is resolved by reducing the curriculum.
>
> (Alexander 2000: 148)

Since 2000 there has been much discussion of the curriculum – in particular the curriculum has been reviewed both 'officially' (Rose 2009) and unofficially (Alexander

2009) yet the recommendations of neither review have been accepted by the current government at the time of writing. Funding for primary education has improved in relation to secondary education although a gap still exists. In 2009–2010 the standard allocation for a Year 6 primary pupil in Birmingham was 78 per cent of that for a Year 7 secondary pupil (Birmingham City Council 2009). The 'elementary' nature of primary education is still very much in evidence, with literacy and numeracy still a priority and the class teacher in a central role. In short, the primary school might be said to be the most cost-effective way to ensure that the majority of children achieve a basic level of literacy and numeracy.

An alternative way to view the purpose of primary education is to see it as providing all children with the opportunity to grow and develop in their own way, according to their own needs. The progressive and developmental purposes of primary education are a complex amalgam of philosophical and psychological perspectives. On the one hand, the philosophy of the likes of Rousseau, Montessori and Dewey informed a 'child-centredness' which recognises the rights of the child as central and that provision should be determined by a child's needs. Psychological theories of Piaget and Vygotsky informed pedagogical approaches that are consistent with progressive thinking (Alexander 2000, 2009).

Those familiar with state primary education in the UK will recognise that these elementary and developmental strands are still present, and co-exist in tension. In England, the 2003 Primary National Strategy emphasised that, at the same time as focusing on excellence, attainment and standards, primary education should also be concerned with enjoyment and a child's individual needs. Many commentators have difficulty with today's hybrid, viewing it as contradictory (Shuayb and O'Donnell 2008).

The 'preparatory' function of primary education, that is, preparation for the next phase of schooling, is clear in traditional independent education. In fact, 'preparatory' (or 'prep') school is the preferred terminology for the sector. It can be argued that, structurally and philosophically, state primary schools make little attempt to fulfil a preparatory function until children are very near the end of their primary schooling. Classes continue to be led by a class teacher although some schools begin to make use of specialist teachers at the end of Key Stage 2. Primary school children usually have little access to specialist expertise, facilities or resources. The curriculum has more in common with that for 5-year-olds (Key Stage 1) than with that for 12-year-olds (Key Stage 3), with much more time devoted to English and mathematics than to foreign languages or science. It is possible that the teachers will have been trained by a university or college in which a progressive philosophy and developmental psychology are espoused but have little or no understanding of the secondary curriculum or the pedagogy or the aims of secondary education. We might say that primary teachers see their specialism as 'children' or 'learning and teaching' rather than mathematics, history or science. Sutherland *et al.* (2010) go as far as to characterise the two groups of teachers as 'two tribes', identifying

> continuities and discontinuities of culture, ethos and learning across primary and secondary schools. We suggest that the dominant education system in England has resulted in the creation of 'two tribes', namely primary teachers and secondary

teachers. In general there is very little understanding and valuing of the diversity of experience and expertise across these 'two tribes'.

(Sutherland *et al.* 2010: 62)

If this is the case nationally, then it is clearly worrying that such a discontinuity exists within a profession.

Parents seem to recognise the limitations of the preparatory function of primary education. Those who wish their children to obtain a place in a selective secondary school will often feel the need to supplement their child's education with private tuition. Ireson (2004), examining the phenomenon of additional private tuition of state-educated primary pupils, found that tutoring of Year 6 pupils was often targeted at getting children into their chosen secondary school. Where there is competition for places, for example in a region where there are entrance examinations for grammar schools, extra tuition is widespread.

## The purpose of secondary schools

State-funded secondary schools are for the majority of the population. Beyond that statement it is again difficult to find a consistent and uncontested answer to the question of the purpose of secondary schools.

The features that define 'elementary' education, particularly the monolithic curriculum (i.e. one that allows no choices or selection of subjects), the focus on 'the basics' of reading, writing and arithmetic and the central role of the class teacher, have all been dispensed with in secondary schooling. There is an underlying belief that subjects should be at the centre of a secondary education. The curriculum as experienced by the child is dominated by subjects. At the end of their schooling children will sit exams in each subject. The success of secondary schools has largely been judged by the proportion of children who gain subject-related qualifications (e.g. Department for Education 2009), rather than by the number of children who gain employment or a university place, which rarely feature in such 'league tables'. Teachers are usually appointed as subject specialists and introduce their pupils to the particular methods and knowledge base of 'their' subject. Children are increasingly encouraged to choose between subjects and specialise in a few.

The aims of the current National Curriculum for England give an indication of the aims of secondary education, that is, 'to develop a coherent 11–19 curriculum that builds on young people's experiences in the primary phase and that helps all young people to become successful learners, confident individuals and responsible citizens' (QCA 2007). The aim is developed with a number of bullet points:

Specifically, the curriculum is intended to help young people to:

- achieve high standards and make better progress;
- narrow the gap and enable those not achieving age-related expectations at age 11 to catch up with their peers;
- have and be able to use high-quality personal, learning and thinking skills (PLTS) and become independent learners;
- have and be able to use high-quality functional skills;

- be challenged and stretched to achieve their potential;
- have increased commitment to and enjoyment of learning leading to participation to 19 and beyond.

(QCA 2007)

The first five points are clearly focused on academic and personal development, while the sixth suggests that the curriculum will prepare students for further or higher education.

Has this brief discussion of primary and secondary schooling helped answer the initial question: Why is the system divided? The institutions were separated at the outset by their aims and methods and it seems that the rationale for a continued divide has not been seriously contested – it hasn't been 'on the agenda' for discussion for 70 years. A historical perspective provides evidence that our current system has emerged from ideological battles over the purposes of secondary education in relation to the needs of the state, particularly of the economy. The notion of selecting adolescent children for one educational path rather than another has, however, been somewhat discredited. The aims of primary and secondary schools are in many ways common – the development of personal and academic knowledge and skills is paramount in both, and in both phases the curriculum is organised around 12 or 13 subjects, although the secondary curriculum arguably provides a much broader education, beyond basic literacy and numeracy.

## Bridging the divide

Although we might recognise that it is difficult to construct an educational justification for the continued division of primary and secondary education, that does not help address the needs of those young people who will cross the divide in the middle of their schooling. Meanwhile, the body of evidence suggesting that the divide is damaging children's education has been growing steadily over the decades (Galton *et al.* 1999, 2003) and subsequent chapters explore this evidence in depth. The attention of educators and researchers has therefore been focused on how schools can 'bridge the gap' to ensure at least 'damage limitation' and at best that the transition is harmless or even beneficial.

In 1999 Galton and colleagues, in a report commissioned by the Department for Education of the time, provided evidence to show that considerable progress had been made in preceding decades to improve the transitional and transfer experiences of school children. They suggested that the transfer arrangements made by schools had begun to consider the needs of children and parents, becoming more 'user-friendly' and giving less cause for anxiety. The report did, however, identify that an estimated two out of every five pupils failed to make expected progress during the year immediately following the change of schools, pointing to a small range of research data to support this. Although schools had worked hard to settle children into their new school by attending to the social and emotional aspects of their lives, Galton *et al.* suggested that attention should be focused on curriculum continuity and widening the scope of their activities beyond a few weeks before and after transfer:

Schools will need to redirect some of their present efforts towards achieving a better balance between social and academic concerns at transfer as well as at various transition points, and in the process, give greater attention to pupils' accounts of why they lose ground or lose interest at these critical moments. The focus of activity in the past has been on the 'exits and entrances years' but the review suggests that in future attention needs to be directed more evenly across the whole of the middle years of each phase of schooling as pupils move from one year to another.

(Galton *et al.* 1999: 5)

Four years later Galton and colleagues (2003) revisited the topic and identified that further progress had been made in gathering evidence to help understand the reasons and remedies for the 'dips' in attainment and attitude identified after transfer. The report reiterated earlier recommendations that schools need to pursue initiatives that place increased emphasis on the academic rather than the social aspects of transfer and that more attention needs to be paid to pedagogic strategies known to improve both pupil attainment and intrinsic motivation. The consensus that emerged from the literature on transfer and transition is that, in order to prevent problems arising, a number of strategies need to be employed. A number of reports and authors have referred to the metaphor of 'bridging' the gap, and Barber (1999) suggested that five bridges can be identified:

- the bureaucratic bridge;
- the social bridge;
- the curriculum bridge;
- the pedagogical bridge;
- the management-of-learning bridge.

Barber echoed Galton *et al.* (1999) by suggesting that, although many schools had the first two bridges in place, only a relatively small proportion of schools were building the other three bridges:

the curriculum bridge was more or less in place in only about a third of schools. This meant that the schools exchanged information about the curriculum, how they organised it and sometimes schools co-ordinated what they taught. The pedagogic bridge was only to be found in one school in twenty, and a bridge which focused on how pupils should manage their learning in just one school in fifty. In other words, hardly any schools were engaged in serious dialogue about their core business.

(Barber 1999: 12)

Bore and Fuller (2007) develop the notion of five bridges in Figure 1.1 and the subsequent chapters discuss the bridges from the perspectives of the authors' areas of specialism.

| Administrative | The administrative bridge involves formal liaison between schools, usually at senior management level, in order to establish effective and robust administrative arrangements to support transition, such as pupil records transfer, including performance data management, administrative meetings between key school staff and common procedures |
| --- | --- |
| Social and personal | The social and personal bridge focuses on the development of social links between pupils and parents/carers and the new school prior to, and immediately following, transfer and induction into the new school. An example of this is improving primary pupils' and their parents' familiarity with the school layout and atmosphere. This bridge ensures that effective pastoral support is in place |
| Curriculum | The curriculum bridge involves sharing plans for the content to be taught on either side of the transition point, improving the continuity in the curriculum between the different phases to ensure that teachers build on the curriculum covered to date and seek to teach to pupils' strengths |
| Pedagogy | The pedagogy bridge deals with how teachers teach. A shared understanding of how students are taught and not just what they are taught will improve the continuity in teaching and classroom practice between phases. It seeks to counter stereotypes held by teachers in each phase and to encourage cross-phase professional support and dialogue |
| Autonomy and managing learning | The autonomy and managing learning bridge emphasises how each pupil can be encouraged to manage the transition. This would entail empowering the student with information about achievement and needs and the confidence to articulate these needs in the new environment, ensuring that pupils are seen as active participants in the transition process and in their own learning |

**FIGURE 1.1** Five bridges. Source: Bore and Fuller (2007).

The focus of this book, therefore, is wider than the 'exits and entrances', although they still continue to be vitally important. In Chapter 2 Hilary Smith will argue that much can be learned from early years education, in which the social and emotional effects of change on children, and the need for stable, resilient adults to support the process of transition, has been recognised for decades. Hilary will also explore the social and personal bridge to be crossed and will include current thinking on the link between 'emotional intelligence' and educational achievement. In Chapters 3, 4 and 5 Val Richards considers the wide range of physical, intellectual, social and emotional changes that occur during puberty/adolescence – changes that often coincide with the transition from primary to secondary school. The chapters look at how adolescents adapt to these changes and how they impact upon their self-image and self-identity.

Chapters 6–10 use the lens of school subjects to explore the transitional bridges, particularly those concerning curriculum and pedagogy. In Chapter 6, Dan Davies and Kendra McMahon explore the post-transfer 'dip' in enthusiasm for and attainment in science and associated discontinuities in curriculum and pedagogy and evaluate some of the initiatives that have attempted to address children's changing attitudes towards science. In Chapter 7 mathematics educator Marcus Witt explores the implications of research which suggests that (1) mathematics comes top of the list of subjects that children do not look forward to on transfer from primary to secondary school and (2) many children experience a 'hiatus' or even a dip in performance in mathematics on transfer. The chapter also explores research into the reality of children's mathematical experiences in secondary school and whether this reality lives up to the negative expectations of many children in upper Key Stage 2.

There is much debate around the different literacy practices encountered at home and at school. In Chapter 8, Anny Northcote and Stephen Miles investigate some of the issues around reading in the 'transition' years between Key Stage 2 and Key Stage 3. They consider the range of literature and other texts that children may encounter at this age and the relationship between children's choices in their reading and expectations on them as readers and producers of texts. The chapter also includes a discussion of issues of pupil diversity, inclusion and achievement with specific reference to gender.

It is important that children entering adolescence have positive attitudes towards physical activity to ensure their lifelong continuation in activities that might contribute to their health and well-being. Towards the end of Key Stage 2, the majority of children will have strong perceptions about their competence in physical education and sports activities. Children with low motor skill levels avoid and eventually drop out of such activities because of negative expectations about their ability to participate successfully. In Chapter 9 Rachael Jefferson-Buchanan reviews compelling research from Australia and Canada which has concluded that the Fundamental Movement Skills (FMS) resource, developed in Western Australia, can address such issues.

In Chapter 10 June Bianchi proposes that participation in arts and cultural education at transition effectively promotes social cohesion and global citizenship. She suggests that not only does an understanding of global perspectives equip children at the transitional stage to take their place as citizens within local, national and international contexts, but also sharing cultural experiences fosters appreciation of pluralist values and facilitates tolerance and cultural inclusion. The principles are demonstrated through case studies drawn from recent initiatives.

In Chapter 11 Tilly Mortimore and Mim Hutchings take an 'ecological' perspective to discuss the impact of the types of vulnerabilities that can emerge during this period. They explore how the school and wider community might respond and adjust to support youngsters to develop their resilience and reduce the risk of their becoming disaffected or excluded. They also consider how policies attempt to address this particular transition time and suggestions for action.

School leaders and managers have a key role in ensuring that children's experiences of transfers are positive ones. In the final chapter Alan Howe summarises the challenges that the transfer of children presents for schools. He discusses what we have learned about the management of primary–secondary transition by drawing on the previous chapters and other published reports and sources and identifies where there is a consensus on the direction of future 'good' practice, and considers what can be learned from practice elsewhere in the world, including those education systems that do not have a primary–secondary divide. The chapter concludes by exploring some alternatives to the current structure of the education system in the UK.

## Questions to consider

- In what way might the aims of primary and secondary education be different?
- Can you suggest reasons why it might be a good idea for children to go to a new school when they are 11?
- In your own education, what was good or bad about the transitions you experienced?

## Suggested further reading

Sutherland, R., Ching Yee, W., McNess, E. and Harris, R. (2010) 'Supporting learning in the transition from primary to secondary schools'. University of Bristol. Online. Available http://www.bristol.ac.uk/education/news/2010/transition-bristoluniversity.pdf (accessed 10 June 2010).

An excellent review into the transition arrangements in Bristol. The authors are very critical of a divided schooling system that has resulted in a divided teaching profession.

## References

Alexander, R. (2000) *Culture and pedagogy: international comparisons in primary education*. Oxford: Blackwell.

Alexander, R. (ed.) (2009) *Children, their world, their education: final report and recommendations of the Cambridge Primary Review*. London: Routledge.

Barber, M. (1999) 'Taking the tide at the flood: transforming the middle years of schooling'. *Education Today*, 49 (4), 3–17.

Birmingham City Council (2009) 'School budgets 2009/10'. Online. Available from http://services.bgfl.org/cfpages/budgetnew/s52_2.cfm?SchoolID=388&TypeID=3&fundyear=0910&block=2 (accessed 15 July 2010).

Bore, K. and Fuller, K. (2007) 'Crossing bridges: ready for transfer'. *CB*, 5 (3), 17–20, 64–65. Online. Available from http://www.eduwight.iow.gov.uk/curriculum/transition/.../TransitionCBarticleKBKF.pdf (accessed 28 February 2011).

Central Advisory Council for Education (1967) *Children and their primary schools ('the Plowden Report')*. London: HMSO.

Department for Education (2009) 'Achievement and attainment tables'. Online. Available from http://www.education.gov.uk/performancetables/schools_09.shtml (accessed 17 February 2011).

Department of Education and Science (DES) (1965) 'The organisation of secondary education'. London: DES.

Evangelou, M., Taggart, B., Sylva, K., Melhuish, E., Sammons, P. and Siraj-Blatchford, I. (eds) (2008) 'What makes a successful transition from primary to secondary school?'. London: DCSF.

Galton, M., Gray, J. and Rudduck, J. (eds) (1999) 'The impact of school transitions and transfers on pupil progress and attainment'. Research report RR131. Nottingham: DfEE.

Galton, M., Gray, J. and Ruddock, J. (eds) (2003) 'Transfer and transitions in the middle years of schooling (7–14): continuities and discontinuities in learning'. Nottingham: DES.

Gardner, J. and Cowan, P. (2000) 'Testing the test: a study of the reliability and validity of the Northern Ireland Transfer Procedure Test in enabling the selection of pupils for grammar school places (full report)'. Online. Available from http://arrts.gtcni.org.uk/gtcni/bitstream/2428/6312/1/Testing%20the%20Test.pdf (accessed 20 July 2010).

Hadow, S. W. (1926) 'The education of the adolescent: report of the consultative committee'. London: HMSO.

Halsey, A. H. and Gardner, L. (1953) 'Selection for secondary education and achievement in four grammar schools'. *British Journal of Sociology*, 4 (1), 60–75.

Ireson, J. (2004) 'Private tutoring: how prevalent and effective is it?'. *London Review of Education*, 2 (2), 109–122.

National Middle Schools' Forum (2010) Online. Available from http://www.middleschools.org.uk/content.php?page=archive (accessed 20 July 2010).

Newsom, J. (1963) 'Half our future: a report of the Central Advisory Council for Education (England)'. London: HMSO.

Qualifications and Curriculum Authority (QCA) (2007) 'National Curriculum – aims, values and purposes'. Online. Available from http://curriculum.qcda.gov.uk/key-stages-3-and-4/aims-values-and-purposes/index.aspx (accessed 14 July 2010).

Rose, J. (ed.) (2009) 'Independent review of the primary curriculum'. Nottingham: DCFS.

Shuayb, M. and O'Donnell, S. (eds) (2008) 'Aims and values in primary education: England and other countries'. Primary Review Research Survey 1/2. Cambridge: University of Cambridge Faculty of Education.

Simon, B. (1965) *Education and the labour movement 1870–1920*. London: Lawrence & Wishart.

Sutherland, R., Ching Yee, W., McNess, E. and Harris, R. (2010) 'Supporting learning in the transition from primary to secondary schools'. University of Bristol. Online. Available from http://www.bristol.ac.uk/education/news/2010/transition-bristoluniversity.pdf (accessed 10 June 2010).

Ward, S. and Eden, C. (2009) *Key issues in education policy*. London: Sage.

# The emotional impact of transfer

## What can be learned from early years practice

*Hilary Smith*

## Chapter summary

This chapter will argue that the socially constructed, holistic pedagogy commonly practised in early years settings has much to offer and inform the transitions experienced by older children. It will discuss how early years practitioners help children cope with three universal experiences: separation and loss, being overwhelmed by strong emotions and conflict. It will examine three significant aspects of practice: the key person role, creating an emotionally enabling environment and conflict resolution. It will demonstrate how this practice supports emotional resilience and consider how this can be transferred to Year 6/7 transition.

## Introduction

> It is not the event itself but the coping process that makes it a transition.
>
> (Neisel and Griebel in Dunlop and Fabian 2007: 23)

Sonya is 3 years old. She arrives at the nursery holding on tightly to her mum's hand, a small blue action figure clutched just as tightly in her other hand. This is not her first time at the nursery but this is a special day; today her mum needs to leave her there for the whole morning as she is returning to work. As soon as Sonya is led through the door she is greeted warmly by Julie, her key person, who crouches down, tells her how glad she is to see her and talks to her about the action figure she has brought with her. When her mum says goodbye and tries to leave, Sonya's face crumples; she begins to howl and cling to her mum's legs. Julie gently strokes her back and tries to reassure her but Sonya's howling increases; she looks and sounds as if she is in agony; her pain is palpable. Her mum carefully prises her away and Julie holds Sonya gently but firmly as her mum goes, closing the door behind her. Now Sonya feels completely bereft; she pulls away from Julie and bangs her fists on the door, screaming and sobbing. A few other children approach, looking at Sonya, standing close by, curious, fascinated. Julie explains that Sonya is sad and angry because her mum had to leave and she misses her but that she will be back later. Julie remains calm amidst Sonya's continued distress; she is patient, understanding, unobtrusive and available. From her experience as an early years practitioner she knows that Sonya is securely attached to her mum and, although she may take a long time to adjust to the new environment, and new people, she is confident that, with the right support, this crucial transition will be a positive one and Sonya's resilience will be strengthened by it.[1]

This story is real; taken from an observation at Hartcliffe Children's Centre in Bristol, it is a typical example of scenes that occur in early years settings at times of transition, as young children cope with the discontinuity between home and setting, or between setting and school. The complex process of absorbing a new cultural context has a powerful impact on children and their parents, an impact that is likely to have long-term consequences as it becomes the emotional benchmark for future transitions. The transition itself is often inevitable; the coping strategies employed to manage change successfully are affected by developmental and ecological factors and, in educational settings, strongly influenced by pedagogy.

First, though, the holistic approach that is commonly cited as fundamental to early years pedagogy needs a brief explanation. The philosophy and practice of holism in an educational context aims to value the whole child; it is a personalised approach that combines care, well-being and learning. It recognises each child's context, taking account of their family circumstances, and the community and culture they come from, as well as their individual personality. In practice, the holistic approach requires professionals to view children's learning and development 'in the round', including physical, cognitive, social, emotional, cultural, moral and spiritual needs. This is visible in early years settings by learning opportunities being available either as adult-directed tasks or as child-initiated activities, ideally open-ended and exploratory in nature. This allows children to discover and learn at their own pace, in their own way, and avoids promoting any one area of development above, or at the expense of, another. Through this approach, practitioners support and extend children's knowledge and skills by close observation, interpretation and reflection, taking a broad view of the learning that takes place. It is also through this approach that emotional resilience and coping strategies are developed and supported.

## Coping with separation

During the transition from primary to secondary school, children are separated from the familiar. Not only their understanding of rules, routines and systems, but also, more crucially, relationships with adults and children that have developed over a number of years are altered. Research suggests that children who are emotionally resilient are more able to cope with separation and loss than others, and two of the most significant factors that are associated with emotional resilience are secure attachment to significant adults and a strong self-concept (Bunce and Rickards in Harvey 2004).

Since Bowlby (1969) identified patterns of attachment in infants, advances in neuroscience and a number of longitudinal studies seem to confirm his theory that secure attachment in early childhood is essential for the successful development of social and emotional competencies in later life (Gerhardt 2004). This knowledge and further understanding of separation anxiety, which begins to occur at about 9 months old, informs much of current early years practice, most significantly the development of the Key Person Approach (Elfer *et al.* 2009).

From birth to 5 years old, every child in an early years setting in England is entitled to a *key person*, a named member of staff who takes care of their well-being, development and learning while they are in the setting/school. This person's role is to develop a close, trusting relationship with the child and their family. Through day-to-day personal interactions, planning learning opportunities, recording and assessing progress and being the first port of call for primary caregivers, it is a role that aims to provide a secure secondary attachment figure for each child. Dorothy Selleck expands on this in her advice for reception teachers:

> The key person will respond to a child at times of stress or challenge – for example, separation from home attachment figures at the beginning of the day, providing physical care for their small group of children (comforting, accidents, emotional holding for a child who may be enraged or frightened). The key person will ensure that each child in their group is equally valued and included to take account of social and family background, gender or disability. The key person will nurture the child's sense of identity as a family child, as well as enabling them to participate and belong in the school.

> (Selleck 2008: 2)

The following example, taken from an observation at Filton Avenue Nursery School and Children's Centre in Bristol, demonstrates how a key person supported a child having difficulties adjusting to a new setting.

---

Jake has been attending the children's centre for a number of weeks now but is still having difficulties adjusting. He does not make a fuss when his mum leaves him in the morning, in fact he barely glances at her when she says goodbye, keeping his head down, but neither is he really engaging with any of the adults or children in the centre, or showing much interest in the activities on offer. He tends to gravitate outside to the garden area and often sits by the fence just watching what's going on. His key person, Angela, always welcomes him warmly and encourages him to join in but so far he has remained silent and disengaged. Today Angela tries a different approach; as Jake heads outside to the garden she follows with a magnifying glass and a trowel. Without looking at Jake, she begins to dig a small patch of soil around the plants near

---

to him. Shortly she announces, 'Aha! Here's one', as she uncovers a worm and looks at it through the magnifying glass. 'Do you want to have a look?' she asks Jake, holding out the magnifying glass to him, but he shakes his head; this is clearly too direct. Angela patiently continues with her search and before long Jake has edged a little closer and even puts his hand on her arm. Angela finds another worm and this time Jake tentatively holds the magnifying glass with her. He says quietly, almost in a whisper, 'this one for Mia'. This is a small but significant breakthrough, as Angela knows that Mia is the name of Jake's baby sister and from this she can begin to connect with his world.

As this example illustrates, the role of the key person involves more than providing educational experiences and a link between home and setting; it requires identified adults to build trusting relationships with children through patience and persistence, and often subtle interactions, getting to understand and know them well, becoming attuned to their needs and available to provide emotional support. A skilful key person is pivotal in enabling young children to cope with separation from their main carer and in providing parent-like guidance throughout times of transition. The statutory guidance for early years settings in England (the Early Years Foundation Stage) is based on four key principles, the second of which, 'Positive Relationships', asserts that 'children learn to be strong and independent from a base of loving and secure relationships with parents and/or a key person' (DCSF 2008a: 5). This statement informs the key person role, which includes carrying out tasks that range from providing intimate care to planning learning and development opportunities.

Elfer (2008: 27) refers to this as a relationship of 'professional intimacy', and, although older children may not want to be seen by their peers as having such a close association with one adult in school, having an identified person whose role it is to build positive, empathic relationships with a group of children and their parents during Year 6/7 transition can have a powerful influence on whether pupils are well motivated or disaffected in Years 8 and 9 (Ainscow and Humphrey 2006).

The challenge for schools is to provide adequate staffing for this, and there are significant cost and capacity issues to consider. It is a role that often falls to the class tutor, or head of Year 7, who is often beset by conflicting demands and is not always best placed, or qualified, to support the needs of individuals experiencing an emotional rollercoaster. This role requires much more than just ensuring academic continuity; it is about providing an attuned, sensitive response to children's needs, knowing individuals well and being emotionally available to them. It is a relationship that takes time to develop and requires skilled adults, either those with well-established relationships with Year 6 pupils, who continue working with them into Year 7, or identified secondary school staff who build significant relationships with children throughout Year 6. Guidance for this, and examples of models of practice, consider the role of non-teaching staff in providing transition support (DfES 2005a). It is often the case that a troubled child in a primary school will turn to a trusted teaching assistant or dinner supervisor for help, and they need to know who they can turn to in the less intimate and more impersonal setting of a secondary school.

Another crucial aspect of emotional resilience is having a strong self-concept. This can be defined as the ability to mentally represent oneself without distortion (Harvey 2004), a process that begins in early childhood and continues into adulthood. Maines and Robinson (1997) argue that children's self-concept is determined by their interactions with significant others, and emphasise the responsibility educators have in helping children develop a positive view of themselves. In early years practice, particularly when working with infants who are not yet verbal, practitioners use the process of observation, interpretation and documentation to help young children make sense of their thoughts, feelings and behaviours (Dahlberg et al. 2007). This involves a non-judgemental, optimistic approach and is a key component in enabling children to construct a positive self-concept; it is through this consistent reflection and acknowledgement by skilled, sensitive adults that children come to know themselves as capable and competent.

Early years pedagogy helps children to develop a strong self-concept by recognising their natural curiosity, exploration and inventiveness; the environment is designed to support this by providing opportunities for creativity through play-based learning. Children can discover and express their sense of self by designing, building, storytelling, role-playing, mark-making, exploring text, and making art, music or dance. Adults in early years settings are trained to scaffold children's self-knowledge and self-efficacy throughout this process. This often contrasts strongly with teaching and learning in primary schools where a more prescriptive approach is usually prevalent. Concerns about raising standards have often resulted in schools focusing more on narrowly defined subjects than on open-ended creative endeavours; until recently, that is, when the Rose Review (DCSF 2009) recommended an overhaul of the primary curriculum, suggesting a more flexible, cross-curricular approach. The review took account of a number of creative programmes already being used in schools, promoted by Creative Partnerships (2004) and supported by the National College of School Leadership (2004). It remains to be seen whether these 'creative curriculum' initiatives, which are more akin to the holistic pedagogy practised in the early years, and which could significantly enhance children's self-concept, will survive the current political and economic agenda.

Meanwhile, creativity continues to be an integral part of early years practice. Child-initiated exploration is balanced with adult-directed activities to help give children a 'voice' and affirm their self-concept. Some examples used at times of transition include each child compiling an 'all about me' book; using small-group time to explore individual likes and dislikes; and giving children cameras to record their views and document their own learning journey (Clark and Moss 2001). Enabling children to articulate their self-view is less evident in schools as children get older, but St Werburgh's Primary School in Bristol has used it to good effect for Year 6/7 transition, with each child compiling a transition 'passport' to pass on to their secondary school. This child-friendly document includes their photograph and personal details as well as their thoughts, ideas and opinions, giving particular emphasis to the things they have an emotional response to. Although some of the receiving secondary schools have failed to take up and extend the use of these passports, the children have responded enthusiastically to creating them and have expressed a sense of pride and enjoyment through the process of self-reflection.

## Coping with strong emotions

Change of any kind can evoke strong emotions and witnessing this can be very frightening (Sharp 2001). Goleman (1996: 14) refers to emotional explosions as 'neural hi-jacking', describing it as a process when the thinking brain shuts down as we are flooded with feelings. Much has been written and advised in recent years on how to help children understand and manage these experiences; transition is a particularly sensitive time when the brain is more than usually susceptible to being 'hijacked' and adults need to be proficient in offering coping strategies. No number of school maps, timetables, uniform lists and glossy personal planners are going to alleviate children's fears and confusion when they arrive at their secondary school; in fact, they can result in feelings of panic. Being self-aware, having practised ways of managing feelings throughout their school lives to date, and being offered more opportunities to do so, is more likely to help children cope successfully.

In early years settings, helping children manage strong feelings is fundamental to the process of learning; the affective and cognitive curricula are inseparable. This is achieved through skilled spontaneous responses to child-initiated behaviours, but is also developed through adult-directed activities. The following example, taken from an observation at Ilminster Avenue Specialist Nursery School in Bristol, demonstrates the use of a self-registration system with inbuilt opportunities for children to recognise and express their feelings as they arrive.

---

As soon as the door is opened, Troy runs in, pushing past others to get the attention of Claire, his key person. He holds a small toy car up to her face. 'Look! Look! It does this!', he exclaims, then focuses very intently on manipulating the parts of the car, trying to change it into an action figure. Claire expresses her interest and says, 'You're very excited this morning, Troy!', but then turns to greet other children and their parents. She encourages them to find their photo on the self-registration board and place it by the picture that best describes how they are feeling; there is a choice of 'happy', 'sad', 'angry', 'excited', 'tired' and 'don't know'. This is part of the daily routine and the children are now familiar with it and place their photos on the board to show the mood they have come in with. Meanwhile Troy is becoming increasingly frustrated; he is struggling with the transformer and is upset that he is unable to show off to Claire his new-found skill. In desperation and anger he throws the toy on the floor. Claire calmly goes over to Troy and puts her arm around him, picking up the transformer as she does so. She says, 'Troy, I can see you're really upset and you want to show me how your transformer works but you're having difficulty'. Troy shrugs her off, goes to the board, finds his photo and presses it firmly by the angry picture. It takes a while longer before he is prepared to accept Claire's help and talk about his feelings but using the self-registration board has enabled him to discharge some of the emotion in a safe way.

---

Other ways of enabling young children to understand and express their feelings include providing accessible, interactive, multimedia displays showing particular emotions; exploring emotional responses to events through narrative, during group work; reading and enacting well-known stories and acting out the feelings of the characters. Three- and four-year-olds are able to recognise and make connections between feelings and behaviour, and can also understand and practise calming down techniques, such as yoga and peer massage, with adult support. Many early years settings are now focusing attention on creating an emotionally enabling environment (DCSF 2008b) and provide resources such as music to affect mood and a separate 'calming down' area within the work room. Having a well-equipped outdoor space, with opportunities for free-flow play, is also universally recognised as essential for supporting young children's development and learning, and can be a particularly useful resource when helping children to cope with strong feelings; simply being outside is proven to have a beneficial effect on emotion management.

Similar strategies are evident in primary classrooms in England, partly as a result of the upsurge of interest in emotional literacy within education generally, but more specifically as a result of the dissemination of the resource Social and Emotional Aspects of Learning (SEAL) (DfES 2005b). The SEAL materials are based on the premise that emotional understanding and regulation can be learned and, if taught consistently, will improve behaviour and raise academic standards (Weare 2004). Within the SEAL materials are activities designed to help children cope with change, for example a task intended for Year 6 pupils identifies potential fears about moving to secondary school and suggests that participants predict the thoughts and behaviours that may occur as a result of those fears.

Recent evidence suggests that programmes such as SEAL are enabling children to manage their feelings and cope with stressful situations more effectively than before and have a strong preventative effect (Bolton *et al.* 2008; Hallam 2009). It is partly as a result of this success that a SEAL programme for secondary schools was launched in 2008. Evidence shows that strategies learned for managing difficult feelings at times of change are more effective if they are reinforced and developed throughout the transition period; however, the uptake of secondary SEAL has been less widespread than for primary schools, resulting in a significant discontinuity for some children.

It is also recommended that for SEAL to be most effective it needs to be embedded in a whole-school approach to emotional literacy (DfES 2005b). It is worth noting, however, that successful emotion management in early years settings is achieved through a holistic, whole-child approach. These two perspectives (whole-school and whole-child) are distinct but often mistakenly interpreted as one and the same. A potential improvement of the prescriptive, adult-directed methods apparent in the SEAL materials could be to include a more child-initiated focus, which could be drawn from early years pedagogy.

## Coping with conflict

Transition can be emotionally traumatising as strong internal feelings compete: excitement and fear, anticipation and anxiety, enthusiasm and apathy. Conflicting emotions can quickly and easily result in 'fight or flight' behaviours, and some children either retreat into themselves, becoming withdrawn or sullen, or begin challenging authority figures such as parents and teachers or get into fights with siblings or peers.

The following example, taken from an observation at St Paul's Nursery School and Children's Centre in Bristol, demonstrates how conflict is often managed in early years settings.

It is some weeks into the new school year and the majority of the children have settled well. However, Abdi is still rather quiet and solitary in his play and is taking longer than others to adjust to the rules and routines that are unfamiliar to him. He enjoys playing with the set of plastic dinosaurs and today he is focused on burying them in the sand tray, then slowly making them re-emerge as he digs them out with his hands. Abdi is so engaged with his task that he does not immediately notice Charlie join him at the sand tray and plunge his hands into the sand, but when Charlie finds one of the dinosaurs and holds it up, Abdi quickly snatches it from him, shouting: 'No! MINE!'. Charlie is startled but grabs the dinosaur back, saying just as vehemently: 'You have to share!'. This soon escalates into pushing each other and Abdi falls backwards. However, he quickly regains his balance and retaliates by biting Charlie on the arm. It is at this point that the teacher becomes aware of the commotion and intervenes. She approaches calmly saying, 'I can see there's a problem here', and using the conflict resolution steps helps Abdi and Charlie to discharge their feelings in a safe way, explain their version of events and problem-solve solutions. By using the conflict resolution approach, the teacher is helping Abdi to experience acknowledgement, feel 'heard' and begin to see the social and emotional benefits of co-operation; in this way he learns that sharing resources is not just an arbitrary rule and need not threaten his sense of self. A more punitive approach, e.g. giving him 'time out' for biting Charlie, would have reinforced a feeling of threat, lack of belonging and isolation; it would have impeded his adjustment to school and been likely to result in further anti-social behaviours.

As illustrated in this example, one of the ways that adults in early years settings help children make sense of conflicting emotions within themselves is by practising conflict resolution; this approach is based on the High/Scope method (Evans 2002) (see Figure 2.1).

Learning and using this process enables children to develop the competencies of listening to others, expressing feelings appropriately, co-operation, problem-solving and, above all, empathy. It also helps children to experience being restored to a place of emotional safety after feeling distressed, which, if they are fortunate enough to have been securely attached as a baby, will resonate with their early infant experiences of an attuned carer restoring them to a feeling of equilibrium after a feeling of terror and panic.

Evidence shows that even children as young as 2 years can engage in the process of conflict resolution as they are already capable of empathic responses (Dowling 2010). It is not unusual to see a child in an early years setting approach another who is crying, displaying an expression of sympathy and making physical contact to reassure them with a pat or a kiss. The drive to communicate and connect with others is well established from an early age, and observations of children's play reveal sophisticated and complex patterns of social interaction. Young children develop a sense of self

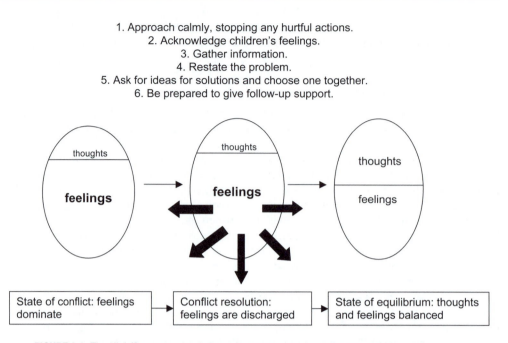

1. Approach calmly, stopping any hurtful actions.
2. Acknowledge children's feelings.
3. Gather information.
4. Restate the problem.
5. Ask for ideas for solutions and choose one together.
6. Be prepared to give follow-up support.

| State of conflict: feelings dominate | Conflict resolution: feelings are discharged | State of equilibrium: thoughts and feelings balanced |

**FIGURE 2.1** The High/Scope approach to conflict resolution. Source: Evans (2002).

through these interactions, making sense of who they are, often by exploring who and what they are not; this inevitably leads to clashes with peers as part of discovering their 'otherness'. As a consequence, social conflict is a necessary and everyday occurrence in an early years setting. Skilled practitioners capitalise on this to support and develop children's social and emotional competencies.

Other methods of conflict resolution have been developed for older children but all are broadly similar to the original High/Scope approach and can be universally applied. Some methods are specifically designed for children to practise independently from adults, for example peer mediation (Tyrrell 2002). This has been used to good effect in primary schools to help reduce aggressive incidents in the playground and the role of peer mediators is often given to Year 6 pupils to provide status and responsibility. Where this is the case, children also have the task, towards the end of Year 6, of training Year 5 pupils to become mediators the following year. This process of continuity combined with the explicit teaching and the practice of conflict resolution methods can be particularly useful during transition; it supports children's social and emotional development and helps build emotional resilience. Participating in a process in which feelings of distress are transformed into an experience of calm, focused action enables children to have a sense of self-efficacy and empowerment, which is essential for coping well with the emotional turmoil prevalent during times of change.

Embedding the practice of conflict resolution at every stage of schooling could have a powerful impact on reducing some of the disturbances experienced by children at transition, but currently there are few secondary schools that consistently use problem-solving methods for disputes. If a child becomes involved in a conflict at secondary school they are more likely to encounter disciplinary procedures and punitive methods, such as detentions, than conflict resolution. However, Restorative

Approaches in Schools (RAiS) is a recent project that has successfully brought a version of conflict resolution into some secondary schools.

Based on the adult model of restorative justice, RAiS has been developed for educational settings and has resulted in some impressive outcomes. The process involves trained staff facilitating 'conferences' between disputing parties; this could be between pupils, pupil and adult or adult and adult. Celebrating the success of RAiS, Sir Charles Pollard described the model as 'a paradigm shift, from "what have you done?" to "what happened?", from "who started it?" to "who has been affected?" and from "what sanction shall I use?" to "what can be done to repair the harm and make things better?"' (Pollard 2009).

Although the primary intention of a conference is to reduce harm, it often results in conflicts being resolved and the self-esteem and well-being of participants being improved (Dowling and Restorative Solutions 2007). The regular use of restorative approaches has been shown to have a positive effect on the atmosphere in a school and the attitudes of pupils towards each other and staff. At Brislington Enterprise College in Bristol, the introduction of restorative approaches has almost completely eliminated the use of detentions and contributed significantly to reducing the number of fixed-term exclusions (Du Rose *et al*. 2009). The head teacher of the college commented: 'the impact of restorative approaches on student behaviour and wellbeing has been dramatic' (Matthews 2009). It is interesting to note that such a dramatic effect has been achieved by using methods that have been successfully practised in early years education for decades.

## Conclusion

When children have effective strategies for coping with the emotional impact of change they can experience a smooth transition between educational settings and their learning journey can be more continuous. As well as the obvious educational benefits of this, there is also a social imperative; as the news headlines constantly remind us, young people who are disaffected in school can cause disruption and damage that extends far beyond their own lives and that of their families. The examples of early years practice provided in this chapter offer a possible way forward for alleviating the negative consequences of discontinuity, and illustrate that the skills and strategies used with younger children can be transferred to Year 6/7 transition. By explicitly addressing children's emotional experiences, providing an emotionally enabling environment and ethos and having skilled adults who are attuned to children's needs and can model and teach coping strategies, transition can be a process that enhances children's emotional well-being and develops their emotional resilience for life.

## Questions to consider

- What do you understand by the 'holistic approach' and what relevance can it have for pedagogy in primary and secondary schools?
- To what extent can the emotional impact of early transitions affect educational progress?

- What would be the implications of introducing the Key Person Approach at Year 6/7 transition?

- How can the 'creative curriculum' be more emotionally enabling than a subject-based curriculum?

- What are the pedagogical imperatives for conflict resolution in schools?

## Note

1.   All names throughout this chapter have been changed to ensure confidentiality.

## Suggested further reading

Dowling, M. (2010) *Young Children's Personal, Social and Emotional Development*, 3rd edn. London: Sage.

This is an invaluable resource for all those studying the social and emotional development of children. It provides practical examples to support theoretical perspectives and uses current research to explain how emotions and cognition are inextricably linked.

Fisher, J. (2010) *Moving on to Key Stage One: Improving transition from the Early Years Foundation Stage*. Maidenhead: Open University Press.

This book challenges the orthodoxy of the primary curriculum and the impact that this has on children moving from a more developmentally appropriate early years pedagogy. It draws on recent evidence on how children learn and promotes a principled, child-orientated approach to transition.

Roberts, R. (2010) *Wellbeing from Birth*. London: Sage.

In this book Rosemary Roberts highlights the essentials of self-esteem and emotional resilience in early years education and care. It provides a comprehensive and accessible discourse on what is meant by 'well-being' and a compelling argument for promoting collective well-being in society for all citizens, whatever their age or stage of life.

## References

Ainscow, M. and Humphrey, N. (2006) 'Transition Club: Facilitating learning, participation and psychological adjustment during the transition to secondary school'. *European Journal of Psychology of Education* XXI (3), 319–331.

Bolton, J., Farrell, P., Humphrey, N., Kalambouka, A., Lendrum, A., Lennie, C. and Wigelsworth, M. (2008) 'Primary Social and Emotional Aspects of Learning (SEAL); Evaluation of small group work'. School of Education, University of Manchester. Online. Available from http://www.pshe-association.org.uk (accessed 28 June 2010).

Bowlby, J. (1969) *Attachment*. London: Pelican.

Bunce, M. and Rickards, A. (2004) *Working with Bereaved Children: A guide* (ed. Harvey, R.). University of Essex: Children's Legal Centre.

Clark, A. and Moss, P. (2001) *Listening to Young Children: The mosaic approach*. London: National Children's Bureau.

Creative Partnerships (2004) *Creative Partnerships. First findings: a review of creative learning*. Available from http://www.creative-partnerships.com.

Dahlberg, G., Moss, P. and Pence, A. (2007) *Beyond Quality in Early Childhood Education and Care: Languages of evaluation*, 2nd edn. Abingdon: Routledge.

Department for Children, Schools and Families (DCSF) (2008a) *Practice Guidance for the Early Years Foundation Stage*. Nottingham: DCSF.

Department for Children, Schools and Families (DCSF) (2008b) *Social and Emotional Aspects of Development*. Nottingham: DCSF.

Department for Children, Schools and Families (DCSF) (2009) 'Independent Review of the Primary Curriculum: Final report'. Nottingham: DCSF.

Department for Education and Skills (DfES) (2005a) *Key Stage 2 to Key Stage 3 Transition Project*. London: Mouchel Parkman.

Department for Education and Skills (DfES) (2005b) *Excellence and Enjoyment: Social and emotional aspects of learning*. Nottingham: DfES.

Dowling, B. and Restorative Solutions (2007) 'Restorative Practice Pack'. Online. Available from http://www.restorativesolutions.org.uk (accessed 28 June 2010).

Dowling, M. (2010) *Young Children's Personal, Social and Emotional Development*, 3rd edn. London: Sage.

Dunlop, A.-W. and Fabian, H. (2007) *Informing Transitions in the Early Years*. Maidenhead: Open University Press.

Du Rose, N., Hough, M. and Skinns, L. (2009) *Key Findings of the Bristol RAiS Evaluation*. Swindon: Restorative Solutions Community Interest Group.

Elfer, P. (2008) 'Children Under Three and their Key Adults: Relationships to support thinking'. Paper at TACTYC conference. Online. Available from http://www.tactyc.org.uk (accessed 28 June 2010).

Elfer, P., Goldschmeid, E. and Selleck, D. (2009) *Key Persons in the Nursery: Building relationships for quality provision*. Oxford: David Fulton.

Evans, B. (2002) *You Can't Come to my Birthday Party: Conflict resolution with young children*. Ypsilanti, MI: High/Scope Press.

Gerhardt, S. (2004) *Why Love Matters: How affection shapes a baby's brain*. Hove: Routledge.

Goleman, D. (1996) *Emotional Intelligence: Why it can matter more than IQ*. London: Bloomsbury.

Hallam, S. (2009) 'An Evaluation of the Social and Emotional Aspects of Learning (SEAL) Programme: Promoting positive behaviour, effective learning and well-being in primary school children'. *Oxford Review of Education* 35 (3): 313–330.

Maines, B. and Robinson, G. (1997) *You Can, You Know You Can! (A Self-Concept Approach)*. Bristol: Lucky Duck.

Matthews, J. (2009) Introductory speech at Restorative Approaches in Schools (RAiS) Conference, Bristol.

National College of School Leadership (2004) *Creativity for Learning in the Primary School*. Nottingham: NCSL.

Niesel, R. and Griebel, W. (2007) 'Enhancing the competence of transition systems through co-construction', in Dunlop, A.-W. and Fabian, H. (eds) *Informing Transitions in the Early Years*. Maidenhead: Open University Press. pp. 21–32.

Pollard, C. (2009) 'Keynote speech', Restorative Approaches conference, Brislington Enterprise College, Bristol, October 2009.

Selleck, D. Y. (2008) 'The Key Persons Approach in Reception Classes', in Department for Children Schools and Families, *Social and Emotional Aspects of Development*. Nottingham: DCSF.

Sharp, P. (2001) *Nurturing Emotional Literacy: A practical guide for teachers, parents and those in the caring professions*. London: David Fulton.

Tyrrell, J. (2002) *Peer Mediation: A process for primary schools*. London: Souvenir Press.

Weare, K. (2004) *Developing the Emotionally Literate School*. London: Paul Chapman.

# Adolescent development

## Physical and biological changes

*Val Richards*

## Chapter summary

This chapter looks at adolescence as a phase of development. It looks particularly at early adolescent development and the physical changes that occur during puberty. These changes often coincide with the transition from primary to secondary school. The chapter concludes, therefore, with a section that explores ideas for how schools can manage and work with these changes effectively to ease the transition.

## Introduction

The main focus of this chapter is to consider the physical changes that take place during adolescence. Those working with pupils going through the transition from primary to secondary school will need to consider the 'whole child' (see Chapter 2). Emotional, educational and cognitive needs form the basis for other chapters, but this chapter considers the physical changes that are experienced by a child 'in transition', and it explores some of the challenges that this presents for the individual, the schools and the teachers. The change from one school to another symbolises an important milestone, which often coincides with rapid changes in development. It could be argued that this is a time of natural developmental progression and therefore the transition from one school to another is appropriate, as it is complementary to the developmental process. Alternatively, it could be viewed as a time when there are already massive, individual changes to cope with, and so is a change of school and environment one change too many, bringing with it a complexity of issues and stresses that, for some, prove too great a challenge?

## Definitions of adolescence

Adolescence is a time of rapid physical, social, emotional and cognitive changes: 'There is virtually no aspect of a child's physical, biological, social and intellectual development that is not subject to change during these years' (Caissy 1994: 2). These changes signify a step towards adulthood and therefore adult responsibilities.

Adolescence is regarded as a phase of development that facilitates a transition from childhood into adulthood. It is usually heralded by the start of puberty, which is a biological and physical transitional period from reproductive immaturity to adult maturity, but it is also a time of psychological development and brings about a change in social roles, with the adolescent being expected to 'assume more responsibility' (Carlson *et al.* 2000: 427).

The age limits and demarcations for this stage of development in western society are not clear-cut. This can cause confusion for the adolescent. At what point are they regarded as adult? There is a broad understanding of the stages of infancy, childhood, adolescence, adulthood and old age but definitions of these stages are socially constructed and therefore subject to change and cultural variation.

In many societies there is a clear-cut demarcation of adulthood, a rite of passage, which is denoted by a specific ceremony and/or ritual. For example, in the Hamar community of southern Ethiopia, adolescent boys are ushered into adulthood by performing a leap over the backs of cattle. Successful completion of this task is witnessed by the whole community and after this they are regarded as 'adult' (*Tribal Wives* 2010). The transition from childhood to adulthood is similarly very clearly defined in other societies. 'In some societies, people are considered to be adults as soon as they are sexually mature, at which time they may assume adult rights and responsibilities, including marriage' (Carlson *et al.* 2000: 427).

For example, a girl's first menstrual period indicates her sexual maturity and denotes a change from child to adult. In many societies this is acknowledged and even celebrated, for example in the Navajo Kinaalda ceremony (Markstrom and Iborra 2003). In western societies it tends to be a cause of embarrassment and can often be a source of stress for the individual. Roberts (2007: 85) observes: 'It would seem that the onset of a child's adolescence is no longer a cause for celebration. Parents, teachers and the media sometimes despair at changes that occur as young people make their journey through adolescence'.

It is apparent that in western societies there is no one single point that allows individuals to become fully fledged adults: 'no single initiation rite signalling the passage into adulthood' (Gross 2001: 532). Is it purely a biological phenomenon when the physical changes in their bodies (menarche for females and spermarche, or semenarche, for males) signal that they are capable of reproduction and therefore in biological terms they have arrived at the adult stage of their species? Or is it denoted by age and age-based legal mechanisms – at 18 years old when they are able to vote? Or 16 when legally they are allowed to marry and live independently?

The legal mechanisms in society can exacerbate the confusion that surrounds the issue and often conflict with the biological stages that an individual reaches. The schooling system compounds this confusion by having a school leaving age that keeps 'young adults' in school for an extended period: 'where formal education . . . continues into the late teens and early twenties, adulthood officially comes several years later' (Carlson *et al.* 2000: 427). For some, this is well beyond their physical 'adult' appearance and 'adult' intellectual capacity. It is hardly surprising that 'frustrations, resentments and confusion arise' (Roberts 2007: 88).

When there are no clear societal demarcations for when a child becomes an adult, it is not so hard to understand why some adolescents find adolescence a time of turmoil, stress, confusion and uncertainty. Adolescence has long been associated with being a period of conflict, turmoil and stress. G. Stanley Hall (1904) viewed adolescence as an inevitable time of 'storm and stress', resulting from the rapid physical changes that were occurring. Unfortunately, this negative view has led to most researchers emphasising the problems and promoting the view of adolescence as being a problematic time, for both the individual concerned and those around them. In fact, more recent research (Richardson *et al.* 1984; Petersen and Ebata 1987; Compas *et al.* 1995; Gross 2000) has shown that, although it is true that many adolescents may have difficulties, this is not the experience of all adolescents. It is also clear that attitudes towards this stage of development vary according to the cultural expectations of particular societies, and so a society in which adolescence is viewed as problematic will readily find endorsement through a negative interpretation of any episodes of non-conformist behaviour, which will consequently be deemed as 'difficult'.

DeHart *et al.* (2004: 454) comment that the adolescent phase of development is extended 'because puberty occurs earlier and because people now need more years of schooling to prepare for most adult occupations . . . These additional years in school have lengthened the transition between childhood and adulthood'.

It is interesting to see that, in societies in which there are no evident 'rites of passage', adolescents create their own rituals and ceremonies. These may take the form of initiation rituals into gangs or specific groups, which can be physical and, at times, brutal. This is discussed further in Chapter 5. Perhaps the physical changes that occur in adolescence are so powerful that, despite the legal mechanisms suppressing adulthood and extending adolescence, some form of overt expression and recognition is needed in order for individuals to establish their new 'adult' self.

The next section looks at puberty and the physical changes that occur during adolescence and explores the reasons for variation in the timing of puberty and why it is occurring at an earlier age in children from western industrialised societies.

## Physical and biological changes during adolescence

In biological terms, an individual reaches sexual maturity during adolescence. This period of sexual maturation from child to adult is known as puberty: 'the processes of biological change that result in an individual's attaining sexual maturity and becoming capable of producing a child' (Sigelman and Rider 2009: 143). The process is triggered by hormones, produced in the pituitary gland of the brain, acting upon, and changing, the sexual and reproductive organs (the ovaries in females and the testes in males). The ovaries and testes secrete hormones (primarily oestrogen in females and testosterone in males) that bring about changes in development. These changes are referred to as primary and secondary sexual characteristics. Figure 3.1 summarises some of the main physical developmental characteristics for both girls and boys.

During puberty there is a significant increase in both height and weight, which is known as the 'growth spurt'. The growth spurt can be quite sudden and can cause significant changes to an individual's appearance, which might require considerable adjustment in terms of how they view themself. For example, they may have been amongst the shortest in the class, but during the growth spurt have overtaken their

| FEMALE DEVELOPMENTAL CHARACTERISTICS | MALE DEVELOPMENTAL CHARACTERISTICS |
|---|---|
| • Sex organs increase in size: vagina, clitoris, labia, uterus<br>• Menstruation (menarche) begins<br>• Pubic and underarm hair appears<br>• Breasts develop: breast buds appear, nipple and areola increase in size<br>• Pelvis enlarges; hips widen<br>• Fat deposited on hips and thighs<br>• Body becomes rounder in shape<br>• Skin changes in texture; produces more oil, possibly causing acne<br>• Sweat glands enlarge; sweat increases; body smell changes | • Sex organs increase in size: testes, scrotum, penis<br>• The first seminal emission occurs (spermarche or semenarche)<br>• Sperm production increases<br>• Pubic, facial and underarm hair appears<br>• Larynx enlarges and voice deepens<br>• Muscle mass increases<br>• Shoulders become broader<br>• Hips appear narrower<br>• Skin changes in texture; produces more oil, possibly causing acne<br>• Sweat glands enlarge; sweat increases; body smell changes |

**FIGURE 3.1** Physical development during adolescence.

peers and found themselves to be one of the tallest. Inevitably, for some, this can be a disconcerting experience. For others the converse experience may be true.

The differences in individuals' development at puberty lead to great differences in the appearance of adolescents who are actually the same age:

There is much individual variability in the age of onset of puberty, and differences in height and weight changes, as well as in the development of secondary sexual characteristics, can lead to striking contrasts in the appearance of adolescents who are the same age.

(Swartwood and Trotter 2004: 128)

Figure 3.2 shows a photo of three individuals, Matthew, Tamsin and Ben, who are aged 11, 12 and 13 years respectively. As can be seen, they vary enormously in height and weight even though there is little difference in their ages.

The average age of the growth spurt for girls is around 10 years, whereas boys tend to have their growth spurt and mature two years later than girls (Rathus 2006) and their sexual maturation starts at about 11 to 11 and a half years (Sigelman and Rider 2009).

Menarche in females (the first menstrual period) usually occurs between age 11 and the late teens, with the average age in western societies being 12 years and 6 months (Shaffer 1999). More recent European statistics support this, indicating that menarche generally commences between 12 and 13 years (Coleman and Coleman 2002). However, some cases of menarche have been reported as young as 8 years and others as late as 17 years (Berger 2001). The age at menarche in the western world has gradually decreased and girls are often experiencing this change to their bodies at the same time as changing from primary to secondary school.

A boy's first ejaculation (spermarche or semenarche) occurs about 2 years after the growth spurt has started (Berger 2001). As DeHart *et al.* (2004: 456) point out, 'this

**FIGURE 3.2** Varying rates of development: left to right, Matthew, Tamsin and Ben, who are 11, 12 and 13 years old respectively. Photograph taken by Geoff Brewer.

event is not so noticeable as menarche' and so 'it is hard to specify an average age for it'. It is also highly unlikely that boys would be willing to disclose and discuss the occurrence, which makes it difficult to obtain reliable statistics. The first seminal fluid does not contain sperm; the amount of sperm gradually increases, and semen with live sperm is in evidence from about 12–16 years.

> By the time menarche and spermarche occurs, an adolescent's body has already been changing for several years. The major noticeable changes of puberty usually occur over a span of about four years, but the total duration of puberty may actually be longer.
>
> (DeHart *et al.* 2004: 456)

This fact is also endorsed by Kroger (2007: 36), who states that, 'Puberty actually begins long before any visible signs of biological change. For young girls, this process can begin as early as age 7, and by 9 and a half for boys'. This is an important point to consider with regards to transition from primary to secondary school: it is highly likely that pupils moving between primary and secondary school will be experiencing massive changes to their bodies.

Their changing body shape is something that adolescents have to come to terms with: 'The classic male growth pattern leads to broadening of the shoulders, narrower hips and longer legs, relative to torso. The classic female growth pattern leads to narrower shoulders, broader hips, and shorter legs relative to torso' (DeHart *et al.* 2004: 460). The difference in female and male development is emphasised because 'boys gain twice as much muscle tissue as girls' (Rathus 2006: 478), whereas female development is characterised by a typical roundness with enlargement of the pelvis and fatty tissue being laid down on the hips, buttocks, thighs and top of the arms, so it is quite natural for girls to put on weight and become more curvy. However, this conflicts with stereotypical media images of slimness being attractive and desirable, and makes 'their bodies less like the Western cultural ideal of the thin, sylph-like supermodel' (Gross 2001: 534). This obviously has implications for girls' views of themselves, which impacts upon their self-confidence and self-esteem.

The adolescent phase is often a time when pupils can appear out of proportion and clumsy or awkward. The adolescent has to learn how to act in their new body. During the growth spurt the legs and arms grow more in relation to the body in both boys and girls and there is likely to be a 'gangly stage'. This is known as 'asynchronous growth', in which 'different parts of the body grow at different rates' (Rathus 2006: 479). This can cause self-consciousness and embarrassment (DeHart *et al.* 2004), when limbs are seemingly out of proportion to the rest of the body. It can also produce a negative response from teachers, parents and friends, particularly if they are intolerant to, and do not understand the reason behind, the apparent clumsiness.

> For a time . . . the everyday movements of early adolescents may be clumsy and awkward, causing them much embarrassment. Examples . . . include tripping over things as their feet grow larger, spilling things at the dinner table, or bumping chairs or tables as they rise to get up.
>
> (Caissy 1994: 29)

There are other physical changes that are also apparent, such as the skin changing in texture and becoming coarser and greasier. This can give rise to acne in some individuals, which provides another potential source of self-consciousness and embarrassment. The sweat glands also change: they increase in size and produce more sweat, which leads to changes in body smell (DeHart *et al.* 2004).

## Factors affecting onset of puberty

There are various factors that influence the onset of puberty and which are responsible for the considerable variation between individuals. Included in these are gender, heredity, nutrition, environment, stress and exercise.

Gender variations are apparent because, as previously discussed, girls generally mature earlier than boys (Rathus 2006). Heredity and genetics can also play a part, with individuals starting puberty at around the same age as their parents did and twins experiencing developmental changes at similar times (Tanner 1990; Kaprio *et al.* 1995).

Sigelman and Rider (2009: 145) comment that 'environment also plays its part in the timing of maturation', with a 'secular trend' towards earlier maturation rates in industrialised societies. It is apparent that girls in such societies tend to reach menarche earlier than those in countries where poverty, malnutrition and disease may be more in evidence (DeHart *et al.* 2004). However, Rathus (2006: 483) states that 'the age threshold for reaching menarche may have been attained because the average age has leveled off in recent years'.

Nutrition and exercise have a significant impact upon the start of puberty. There seems to be a definite correlation between exercise and a delay in puberty. Several studies have found that female athletes, ballet dancers and gymnasts may have late menarche (e.g. Malina 2000; Vadocz *et al.* 2002). There are clear connections between starvation and amenorrhoea (an absence of menstruation): diagnosis of anorexia nervosa in women 'involves the cessation of menstruation' (Conner and Armitage 2002: 92). Rathus (2006) highlights the fact that 'girls must reach a certain body weight to trigger pubertal changes such as menarche' (p. 483) and suggests that the earlier age of puberty might be linked to children today being 'larger than the children of the early 20th century, probably because of improved nutrition and health care' (p. 483). This idea of the link between earlier maturation and 'better' nutrition is echoed in numerous sources (Sigelman and Rider 2009; Shaffer and Kipp 2007). The increase of obesity in western culture certainly appears to coincide with an increase in earlier maturation. However, it cannot pass without comment that the widespread idea of 'improved' or 'better' nutrition is flawed when it is linked to an increase in body fat in societies in which obesity is a significant problem amongst children. What is erroneously referred to as 'improved' or 'better' nutrition leading to larger children is actually more to do with '*malnutrition*' in which high-calorie diets and an imbalance of nutrients lead to greater deposits of body fat.

The effect of stress can either delay or accelerate puberty: 'There is broad agreement that environmental stress affects children's developing hormonal systems' (Cole *et al.* 2005: 587). If the stress response involves a loss of appetite and corresponding loss of weight, then puberty could be delayed or halted. However, evidence from studies on family stress and conflict, cited by DeHart *et al.* (2004), indicates that high levels of stress and conflict within the family can precipitate earlier menarche, 'whereas higher levels of parental warmth have been associated with later menarche' (p. 456). The most plausible reason for this is that it is likely that children living in a family situation where there is frequent conflict are more likely to be assuming adult responsibilities in caring for themselves, their siblings or other members of the family. For example, in cases of family breakdown they may become the confidante of one or both parents and therefore may be in a role reversal situation of comforting and reassuring their parents. This inevitably would shorten their 'childhood' and throw them into an adult role situation.

## Psychological effects of late or early maturation

Being an 'early' or 'late' developer can impact upon an adolescent's social and emotional development, and this differs between boys and girls. For example, Atkinson *et al.* (1993) reported that early or late development in comparison with peers affected adolescents' satisfaction with their appearance and had a considerable psychological effect on self-esteem and self-confidence.

For boys in western society it is regarded as an advantage to be early maturing; it fits with macho images of men in western society. The growth spurt gives increased height and increased muscle development, which gives early-maturing boys an advantage in competitive sports. Sporting prowess and achievement is often a way in which boys construct their sense of masculinity (Connell 1989). Strength and physical ability are qualities that are valued in males in western society. Not surprisingly, against this backdrop of cultural opinion, early-maturing boys are more satisfied with their appearance than late-maturing boys (Atkinson *et al.* 1993: 112).

However, Newman and Newman (2003) suggest that recent studies (e.g. Ge *et al.* 2001) have indicated that there are negative aspects of early maturing amongst boys, such as increased drug and alcohol problems and depression and anxiety. One of their explanations for the change from positive to more negative aspects appearing amongst early-maturing boys is that 'in today's society physical maturation at age 12 and earlier converges with other stressful life events, especially school transitions, disruption of the peer network, more challenging expectations for school performance, and the related risk of failure' (Newman and Newman 2003: 296).

They also consider the explanation that boys are maturing earlier but do not have the necessary adult skills and experience to deal with the changes in expectations of them, such as 'self-control, decision-making, and leadership' (p. 297). If they do not have the resources to deal with this level of expectation, then that could lead to stress and potentially health-impairing activities such as drug and alcohol abuse, which serve as 'coping strategies' to alleviate the stress they are experiencing.

Late-maturing boys may feel more 'dominated by early-maturing males' and 'more dependent and insecure' (Rathus 2006: 486). They might be 'frustrated because others treat them like little boys instead of like young men' (Kail and Cavanaugh 2000: 280). The fact of being early maturing or late maturing seems to make a significant difference to how an individual is treated and the level of expectation upon that individual. Consequently, this affects an individual's self-perception and self-esteem. It is easy to feel inadequate and inferior if those around you are admiring more mature peers.

The difference in the effects upon early- and late-maturing girls tends to be less noticeable than in boys, although it is not uncommon to see a girl who is considerably taller than her peers acting self-consciously and stooping to disguise her height or folding her arms or wearing baggy clothing to hide her developing breasts. The obvious concern for girls is that their early maturity will lead them into premature sexual activity before they are ready to cope with the consequences and emotional impact. For this reason, parents of early-maturing girls are often more strict and restraining and 'may increase their vigilance and restrictiveness' (Rathus 2006: 487). This in fact militates against their increasing maturity and is likely to lead to conflict.

Early-maturing girls are more likely to be anxious and depressed than later-developing girls (Hayward 2003), but in contrast to early-maturing boys they tend to be 'less satisfied with their weight and appearance than their less mature classmates. Early maturing girls tended to be embarrassed by the fact that their bodies were more womanly in shape than their female classmates' (Atkinson *et al.* 1993: 112). This response cannot be viewed in a cultural vacuum and has to be set against the perceived cultural opinion of slimness being the ideal, as indicated earlier in the chapter. The pre-pubescent appearance of many models is inevitably going to exert an influence and lead to early-maturing girls being dissatisfied with their appearance.

Physical appearance is of great concern at this stage for both sexes. Adolescents are bombarded with stereotypical images of perfect appearances from media influences. How individuals look is part of attracting the opposite sex and there is considerable pressure to present a specific image. There is also pressure if an individual is at one of the extremes of development and in some way feels that they are different from others of their age and 'the odd one out'. This can inevitably affect their self-image.

Although there seems to be some variation in findings on the effects of early maturation or late maturation, there is substantial evidence that points to the fact that, in western cultures, maturing earlier is an advantage if you are male, but a disadvantage if you are female. The main interpretation of this seems to be linked to media portrayals of the 'ideal' slender female, and the 'ideal' tall, athletic male. Gross (2000: 23) makes the point that puberty is likely to be a 'more difficult transition for girls than boys' because it 'will bring boys *closer* to their physical ideal . . . while girls move further *away from* theirs'.

## Bridging transitions

This section will consider how schools can cope with, and cater for, the differing levels of development at the age of transition and how they can work with some of the changes that are occurring to gain the best from pupils.

Clifford-Poston (2005: 125) makes the point that 'the changes in tweens' bodies which may have been masked by the security of the primary school become highlighted so that they arrive in this new place feeling clumsy, moody and self-conscious'. Galton *et al.* (1999), in a DfEE study, identified five main areas of activity, or bridges, for schools to consider in their transition programmes:

- bureaucratic;
- social;
- curriculum;
- pedagogic;
- management of learning.

These 'bridges' appear in the Primary Curriculum Review of 2009, known as the Rose Review, and provide a framework for the review's recommendations concerning transfer strategies. There was a slight change in terminology: 'administrative' is used instead of 'bureaucratic'; the 'social' bridge became the 'social and personal' bridge;

and the 'management of learning' bridge became 'autonomy and managing learning'. The bridges will be considered in relation to physical development of the emerging adolescent.

## The administrative bridge

This area concerns the passing on of essential information between the primary and the secondary school. Currently no records of physical development are transferred from primary to secondary school, unless the pupil has special educational needs. Height and weight measurements are taken for the purposes of national statistics during the final term of primary school, but these records are not kept by the school or transferred to the secondary school. The measurements are not compulsory and parents can 'opt out' if they don't wish their children to be measured.

Should there be a transfer of information concerning physical development? Probably not. There seems to be little point in transferring physical development records that, if measurements are taken at the end of Year 6, could be invalid by the following autumn because of the rapid rates of development in some individuals.

In respect of producing national statistics concerning children's health, measures of weight and height might be useful to provide an indication of pupils' state of health, particularly amidst growing concerns of an increase in childhood obesity (Dovey 2010).

The importance of accurate exchange of information is patently obvious for specific pupils for whom there are individual physical and/or cognitive problems and for those who might require special educational needs support. This has implications for the safety of vulnerable children. Information of this nature is conveyed through the special educational needs co-ordinator (SENCO) for the primary school, who would assess the support required for special educational needs pupils on an individual basis, and liaise with the secondary school SENCO to discuss individual needs and ensure continuity of support so that the necessary provision was in place from the time of transition (MacGrain 2010).

## The social and personal bridge

This area will be considered in detail in Chapter 5, but it needs to be mentioned when considering the physical aspects of adolescent development at the age of primary to secondary school transfer. The important point is that anxiety and concern about transferring to a new school can be exacerbated by an individual's view of their own body and concerns as to whether or not they are 'normal' in their development. This view influences their level of self-confidence and their ability to embrace new experiences in a positive way.

Information about the changes happening to their body will help them cope with the changes, as they will know what to expect. At this age they are comparing themselves with others and seeing how they 'measure up' academically and physically. This is known as social comparison (Festinger 1954), which Miell (1990: 66) defines as 'comparing opinions, attitudes and abilities with relevant other people'. To have an understanding that people develop at different rates and that their delayed or early development is nothing to cause concern will help to allay their fears and anxieties in this respect.

## The curriculum bridge

This section will consider the curriculum in terms of explaining the changes that occur during adolescence, for example specifically through personal, social, health and economic education (PSHE) and science.

When there is a reliance on peer information facts can get distorted and this can lead to misconceptions about the biological processes of adolescent development. For example, menstruation has traditionally been viewed in a negative light in western culture. There are three significant aspects to this: first, there is a backdrop of cultural and religious reasons for menstruation being perceived as 'unclean'; second, for some girls and women it is a painful and uncomfortable experience, which understandably elicits negative connotations; third, women themselves have perpetuated the ideas surrounding premenstrual tension, such that 'ill-temper and lack of achievement' are 'not their own fault' (Nicolson 1995: 782).

The role of education is clear. Girls who are better prepared for menstruation and who know what to expect have a more positive attitude towards it: 'Girls who felt positively about menarche were more likely to be educationally prepared to welcome it as a natural event, have a positive body image and reject traditional negative attitudes' (Rathus 2006: 484).

This process of education about their bodies has been subject to much controversy in recent years. The Macdonald Review (2009) recommended that PSHE should be statutory in the National Curriculum at primary and secondary level. This includes sex education. The huge variation in individual maturation rates and the span of biological changes occurring within the transitional age group makes it difficult to take account of everyone's needs and therefore devising appropriate sex education programmes is problematic. The debates surrounding this issue continue.

Some parents have been reluctant to entertain ideas of sex education in primary schools and have opposed moves to introduce it, fuelled by media comments such as 'Sex lessons for 5 year olds' (Macdonald 2009: 21), but, with the onset of earlier maturation, and one of the highest teenage pregnancy rates in Europe, others believe that it is a necessity.

Explanation of the differences between individuals at this stage is important so that pupils have a greater understanding of each other and an awareness that rates of development can vary considerably, so that they do not feel abnormal if they are a late or an early developer. Science deals with the body changes, but in a factual way, focusing on 'the human biology of reproduction. Effective PSHE education contextualises this learning within the framework of relationships' (Macdonald 2009: 21).

The Rose Report (2009: 98) recommends 'improving curricular continuity between Year 6 and Year 7'. A statutory requirement for PSHE throughout primary and secondary school would improve continuity, but it remains to be seen how the ongoing debates will be resolved and how it could be made appropriate to children's development when they develop at such different rates.

## The pedagogic bridge

Delivery of the curriculum relies on the pedagogic bridge. Transition units in which team teaching takes place allow primary and secondary teachers to plan their teaching together so that the gap between the 'two tribes' (Sutherland *et al.* 2010) is lessened.

The Rose Report (2009: 98) recommendation for good pedagogical practice is to improve 'continuity in teaching and classroom practice between Year 6 and Year 7'.

Molony (2005) suggests that "joint 'bridging projects'" are developed. There have been numerous pilot schemes for such projects. Brewer (2007) described how a transitional project between a primary school and its feeder secondary school was piloted. The Year 6 and Year 7 staff met and decided on outcomes. They planned work for team teaching lessons in literacy, numeracy and science. Year 6 pupils were taught by the Year 7 teachers and Year 7 pupils were taught by their previous Year 6 teachers. The pilot was successful: 'staff were able to share planning, ideas and evaluations and most importantly a good relationship was built between the teachers' and they were able to share resources and support one another.

This type of scheme could be implemented for PSHE and science with the aim of looking specifically at developmental issues in adolescence. The theme chosen for the science lessons in this particular example was 'adaptation'. This would be an appropriate area of study for both Year 6 and Year 7, which warrants further exploration and development as it could be related to the pupils' adaptation to new circumstances.

It could also be considered in respect of physical education: awareness of adolescents' diversity in 'adapting physically to the ongoing changes in their bodies' is important. 'This is particularly evident in any type of athletic activity' (Caissy 1994: 27). Caissy makes the point that a child gets used to their own body and the way it acts and feels when, for example, throwing a ball. The growth spurt makes the proportions of the body different and therefore throwing a ball successfully requires a different technique. 'Because early adolescents seldom recognize or attribute their physical co-ordination problems to the fact that their bodies are undergoing rapid change, they become extremely frustrated with themselves and their inability to perform certain tasks and skills' (Caissy 1994: 27). Teacher responses to this apparent lack of co-ordination can exacerbate the situation if based upon their own stereotypes of, for example, clumsy behaviour equating to carelessness. Without consciously being aware of it, those stereotypes can influence their attitudes towards pupils. An understanding and informed teacher will take pains to ensure that pupils are set individual tasks matched to their abilities that allow them to attain their goals. Caissy (1994) recommends that 'competitive sports should be temporarily downplayed or discouraged during the growth spurt'. She advocates that individual goals and targets should be set that 'involve self-competition . . . Early adolescents can then compete with themselves, trying to better their own skills rather than competing with others who have significant advantages over them' (p. 28).

## Autonomy and managing learning bridge

Pupils in Year 6 will be at the top of their primary school. They are likely to be physically larger than the pupils in lower years. A problem for some pupils in transferring to secondary school is that they go from being the big fish in a small pond, where it is likely that younger pupils looked up to them as the oldest in the school, to a dramatically different situation where they are the small fish in a large pond and become the youngest pupils in the institution. They may have had a strong sense of autonomy in their primary school and may have been given responsibilities. Starting again at the bottom of the ladder can knock their self-esteem and confidence. The report 'What Makes a Successful Transition from Primary to Secondary School?' by Evangelou *et al.* (2008) indicates that improved 'self-esteem and confidence' (p. 16) were identified by children as defining a successful transition. Therefore it is crucial that teachers evaluate their teaching, particularly during the transitional process, to identify situations in which pupils' self-esteem may be positively or negatively affected.

Hague (2006) comments on advice from Lynne Ackland, a secondary head teacher, who advocates giving students responsibility and involving them to help them to make a positive contribution. She believes that 'nurturing responsibility gets better results than resorting to punishment'. Encouraging pupils to take responsibility for their own learning and their part in the transition process is an important goal in any transition programme.

## Conclusion

Teachers and pupils need to be aware of the physical changes that occur during puberty. Pupils need to be reassured that the changes are natural and that developing early or late is part of the normal range of development. Effective communication between primary and secondary schools facilitates ease of transfer and helps to reduce some of the anxieties surrounding transfer at this age. It is still an issue whether or not transfer at this age is desirable or necessary. For many pupils the fact that school transfer coincides with the rapid changes that are taking place in their bodies brings another set of problems and issues that have to be dealt with. Pupils who are mature and confident approach the transfer differently from those who crave the security of a smaller school.

The emphasis of many studies of transition from primary to secondary school is on academic and social aspects of the transition, and the way in which physical changes play an important role in these areas can be overlooked. The impact of the physical changes on the intellectual, emotional and social aspects of transfer from primary to secondary school will be considered in the next two chapters.

## Questions to consider

- Is the transition from primary to secondary school a good thing in that it corresponds to the significant developmental stage of puberty, or does it pose one change too many and subsequently cause stress for the individual concerned?
- To what extent is an adolescent's view of their physical development affected by cultural opinion and ideal images presented in the media?
- Adolescence is subject to much negativity. What are some of the positive aspects of this phase of development?

## Suggested further reading

Rathus, S. (2006) *Childhood and Adolescence: Voyages in Development*, 2nd edn. London: Thomson Wadsworth.

This book provides an excellent text for developmental studies of the different stages of childhood to adolescence.

Dehart, G., Sroufe A. and Cooper R. (2004) *Child Development: Its Nature and Course*, 5th edn. London: McGraw Hill. Part 6, 'Adolescence'.

This book gives a good insight into some of the key aspects of adolescent development and draws upon relevant research to support discussion.

## References

Atkinson, R., Atkinson R., Smith, E. and Bem, D. (1993) *Introduction to Psychology*, 11th edn. London: Harcourt Brace.

Berger, K. (2001) *The Developing Person Through the Lifespan*, 5th edn. New York: Worth.

Brewer, T. (2007) 'Review of pilot transition project'. Unpublished.

Caissy, G. (1994) *Early Adolescence: Understanding the 10 to 15 Year Old*. London: Plenum Press.

Carlson, N., Buskist, W. and Martin, G. (2000) *Psychology: The Science of Behaviour (European Adaptation)*. Harlow: Allyn & Bacon.

Clifford-Poston, A. (2005) *Tweens – What to Expect From and How to Survive – Your Child's Pre-teen Years*. Oxford: One World.

Cole, M., Cole, S. and Lightfoot, C. (2005) *The Development of Children*, 5th edn. New York: Worth.

Coleman, L. and Coleman, J. (2002) 'The measurement of puberty: A review'. *Journal of Adolescence*, 25, 535–550.

Compas, B. E., Hinden, B. R. and Gerdhart, C. E. (1995) 'Adolescent development: Pathways and processes of risks and resilience'. *Annual Review of Psychology*, 46, 265–293.

Connell, R. (1989) 'Cool guys, swots and wimps: The interplay of masculinity and education'. *Oxford Review of Education*, 15 (3), 291–303.

Conner, M. and Armitage, C. (2002) *The Social Psychology of Food*. Buckingham: Open University Press.

DeHart, G., Sroufe, A. and Cooper, R. (2004). *Child Development: Its Nature and Course*, 5th edn. London: McGraw Hill.

Dovey, T. M. (2010) *Eating Behaviour*. Maidenhead: McGraw Hill/Open University Press.

Evangelou, M., Taggart, B., Sylva, K., Melhuish, E., Sammons, P. and Siraj-Blatchford, I. (2008) 'What makes a successful transition from primary to secondary school?' London: DCSF.

Festinger, L. (1954) 'A theory of social comparison processes'. *Human Relations*, 7, 117–140.

Galton, M., Gray, J. and Ruddock, J. (1999). 'The impact of school transitions and transfers on pupils' progress and attainment'. Research Report RR131. Nottingham: DfEE.

Ge, X., Conger, R. and Elder, G. Jr. (2001) 'The relation between puberty and stress in adolescent boys'. *Journal of Research on Adolescence*, 11, 49–70.

Gross, R. (2000) 'Adolescence: Time of crisis or crisis of timing?' *Psychology Review*, 6 (3), 23–25.

Gross, R. (2001) *Psychology: The Science of Mind and Behaviour*, 4th edn. London: Hodder & Stoughton.

Hague, H. (2006) 'Responsibility works better than punishment'. Online. Available from http://www.guardian.co.uk/news/2006/oct/11/guardianextra3.guardianspecial61 (accessed 12 June 2006).

Hall, G. Stanley (1904) *Adolescence*. London: Appleton.

Hayward, C. (ed.) (2003) *Gender Differences at Puberty*. New York: Cambridge University Press.

Kail, R. and Cavanaugh, J. (2000) *Human Development: A Lifespan View*, 2nd edn. London: Wadsworth Thomson Learning.

Kaprio, J., Rimpela, A., Winter, T., Viken, R. J., Rimpela, M. and Rose, R. (1995) 'Common genetic influences on BMI and age at menarche'. *Human Biology*, 67, 739–753.

Kroger, J. (2007) *Identity Development: Adolescence through Adulthood*. London: Sage.

Macdonald, Sir A. (2009) *Independent Review of the Proposal to make Personal, Social, Health and Economic (PSHE) Education Statutory*. London: DCSF.

MacGrain, S. (2010) 'Transitional procedures in a primary school'. Interview.

Malina, R. (2000) 'Growth, maturation and performance'. In Garrett, W. and Kendall, D. (eds) *Exercise and Sport Science*. Philadelphia: Lippincott, Williams and Wilkins.

Markstrom, C. and Iborra, A. (2003). 'Adolescent identity formation and rites of passage: The Navajo Kinaalda ceremony for girls'. *Journal of Research on Adolescence*, 13, 339–425.

Miell, D. (1990) 'The self and the social world'. In Roth, I. (ed.) *Introduction to Psychology*, Vol. 1. Hove: Lawrence Erlbaum Associates in association with the Open University.

Moloney, S. (2005) 'Five bridges for successful transition management'. Available from http://wsgfl. westsussex.gov.uk/ccm/cms-service (accessed 1 November 2009).

Newman, B. and Newman, P. (2003) *Development through Life*. Belmont: Thomson Learning.

Nicolson, P. (1995) 'The menstrual cycle, science and femininity: Assumptions underlying menstrual cycle research'. *Social Science and Medicine*, 41 (6), 779–784.

Petersen, A. and Ebata, A. (1987) 'Developmental transitions and adolescent problem behaviour: Implications for prevention and intervention'. In Herrelmann, K. (ed.) *Social Prevention and Intervention*. New York: de Gruyter.

Rathus, S. (2006) *Childhood and Adolescence: Voyages in Development*, 2nd edn. London: Thomson Wadsworth.

Richardson, R., Galambos, N., Schulenberg, J. and Petersen, A. (1984) 'Young adolescents' perceptions of the family environment'. *Journal of Early Adolescence*, 4 (2), 131–153.

Roberts, I. (2007) 'Adolescence'. In Zwozdiak-Myers, P. (ed.) *Childhood and Youth Studies*. Exeter: Learning Matters.

Rose, J. (ed.) (2009) 'Independent review of the primary Curriculum'. Nottingham: DCFS.

Roth, I. (ed.) (1990) *Introduction to Psychology, Volume 1*. Hove: Lawrence Erlbaum Associates with OUP.

Santrock, J. (2010) *Adolescence*, 13th international edn. New York: McGraw-Hill.

Shaffer, D. (1999) *Developmental Psychology: Childhood and Adolescence*, 5th edn. London: Brookes/Cole.

Shaffer, D. and Kipp, K. (2007) *Developmental Psychology: Childhood and Adolescence*, 7th edn. Belmont: Thomson Wadsworth.

Sigelman, C. and Rider, E. (2009) *Life-Span Human Development*, 6th edn. Belmont: Wadsworth Cengage Learning.

Sutherland, R., Yee, W., McNess, E. & Harris, R. (2010) *Supporting Learning in the Transition from Primary to Secondary Schools*. Bristol: University of Bristol.

Swarthood, M. and Trotter, K. (2004) *Observing Children and Adolescents*. London: Thomson Wadsworth.

Tanner, J. M. (1990) *Foetus into Man: Physical Growth from Conception to Maturity*. Cambridge, MA: Harvard University Press.

*Tribal Wives* (2010) Channel 4, 29 July 2010.

Vadocz, E., Siegal, S. and Malina, R. (2002) 'Age at menarche in competitive figure skaters: Variation by competency and discipline'. *Journal of Sports Sciences*, 20, 93–100.

# Adolescent development

## Intellectual and emotional changes

*Val Richards*

## Chapter summary

This chapter looks at the emotional and intellectual changes that occur during adolescence, and the way in which these changes affect how adolescents think and feel. The interplay between the developing cognitive structures and control of the emotions is discussed. The final section looks at the transition between primary and secondary school in respect of intellectual and emotional development. The intellectual changes that occur during adolescence allow for greater cognitive capacity, so the way in which transition can provide opportunities for pupils to develop intellectually is explored. For some pupils transfer to a new situation is fraught with anxiety, apprehension and fear. The reasons why transition for some pupils is stressful, and yet for others it is a positive experience, are also considered.

## Introduction

The previous chapter focused on the physical development of adolescents. This chapter looks at the impact of those developmental changes on the intellectual and emotional development of adolescents. Although puberty may be defined as a purely biological phenomenon (see Chapter 3), it also has psychological and social dimensions because of the associated changes in the way adolescents think and feel. This chapter explores how schools can work with the changes in thinking that occur at this transitional phase and considers how this relates to the emotional changes that are likely to be taking place. Is the adolescent capable of applying reasoning and logic to control the sometimes overpowering feelings and emotions that can emerge at this time? Problems associated with adolescents at this stage can be manifested through 'bad' behaviour and disengagement from school. Can these problems be attributed to a mismatch between the development of intellectual capacity and emotional development?

## Intellectual changes in adolescence

During the adolescent phase of development there are physical changes in the brain that influence the way individuals think and behave. 'As the body undergoes significant changes during puberty, so too does mental activity' (Newman and Newman 2003: 297).

There are three sections of the brain that appear to develop significantly during adolescence. These are the *frontal lobes* in the prefrontal cortex, which are involved in problem-solving and logical reasoning, selecting the best options and making decisions and exerting control over feelings and reactions; the *amygdala*, which is involved with emotional responses; and the *corpus callosum*, which affects information processing and is responsible for connections between the two hemispheres of the brain (Santrock 2010; Feinstein 2004).

The key change in the way adolescents think is that they can think in abstract terms. This idea comes from Piaget's (1952) work on cognitive processes. He identified four key stages in intellectual development:

- *Sensorimotor* (from birth to 18 months), in which a child receives information via the senses and then physically reacts, that is, uses their motor skills.

- *Preoperational* (from 2 to 7 years), in which the child starts to represent things symbolically. Language develops rapidly and words are used to represent the world around them during this stage. This is the time of pretend play in which objects are used to represent, or symbolise, other things, for example a crayon 'becomes' a helicopter in their imagination and is played with by 'flying' it around the room.

- *Concrete operations* (from 7 to 11 years), in which children need to relate to concrete referents, or experiences, in order to solve problems.

- *Formal operations* (from 11–12 years onwards), in which individuals apply logic and more abstract thinking to problems. At this stage they can propose a hypothesis and deduce from the information they collect and the tests they carry out whether or not the hypothesis is proved true: they are able to apply hypothetico-deductive reasoning.

At the age of transition from primary to secondary school it is likely that there is also a transition in the mode of thinking, that is, from concrete operations to formal operations. However, it cannot be assumed that age, or physical maturation, equates to corresponding maturation in terms of intellectual development. Caissy (1994: 102) makes the point that 'early adolescents are in a transitional intellectual state between child-like (concrete) thinking and adult-like (formal) thinking . . . Because individual growth rates are variable, we cannot predict exactly when a child actually begins developing formal thinking processes'.

Santrock cites the work of Broughton (1983), who distinguished two stages in formal operations: *early* and *late* formal operational thought. In the early stages, the freedoms of being able to think in a less restrained way may lead adolescents into 'flights of fantasy' in which 'the world is perceived too subjectively and idealistically'.

In later formal operational thought the adolescents are able to 'test their reasoning against experience and intellectual balance is restored' (Santrock 2010: 97).

The danger is that, as an individual is channelled into more formal operational thought, the initial liberation of being able to think in an unrestrained and creative manner becomes stifled. The current education system is all too steeped in traditional views of arriving at one single correct answer or solution to a problem, known as convergent thinking, whereas in fact there are distinct advantages to generating multiple potential solutions, as this opens up possibilities and encourages more divergent thinking and creativity.

Piaget's view of cognitive development was 'constructivist', that is, individuals make sense of their environment as a result of engaging with, and understanding, new experiences and adapting accordingly: 'the learner him- or herself actively builds up or construes his or her learning as mental structures. These structures exist in the central nervous system as dispositions that can be described as *schemes* or *mental patterns*' (Illeris 2003: 401).

Piaget's theories have been criticised for not including 'social, emotional, and cultural contributions to cognitive development in any central way' (Parke and Gauvain 2009: 297). This contrasts with the work of Vygotsky (1978), who proposed a socio-cultural perspective on learning and intellectual development in which the socio-cultural context and interaction with other people were emphasised as fundamental in an individual's development: 'whereas Piaget tended to see children as independent explorers, Vygotsky saw them as social beings who develop their minds through their interactions with parents, teachers, and other knowledgeable members of their culture' (Sigelman and Rider 2009: 48).

Vygotsky's theory is also constructivist but it is 'a social constructivist approach, which emphasizes the social contexts of learning and the construction of knowledge through social interaction' (Santrock 2010: 101). Vygotsky demonstrated the importance of social interaction in facilitating learning by proposing a zone of proximal development (ZPD), which Berger (2001: 56) describes as 'the magic middle. Somewhere between the boring and the impossible . . . the place where interaction between the teacher and learner results in knowledge never before grasped or skills not already mastered'.

Figure 4.1 demonstrates different levels of attainment, learning and teaching and how they can affect motivation. Level 2 corresponds to Vygotsky's ZPD, in which teachers, or more competent others, provide assistance to take the learner from the knowledge they already have to the next level of skills and learning. This guidance is known as 'scaffolding', a term proposed by Wood *et al.* (1976). Tasks at this level would be stimulating, challenging and attainable with assistance. Level 3 would be at too high a level, which could cause pupils to become demotivated and consequently 'switch off' or disengage. Level 1 could also produce the same response, with the pupils' lack of motivation stemming from the fact that they have already learnt the information and skills at this level and so it would be unstimulating and boring for them to repeat work they have already covered.

Vygotsky's theories are more usually applied to early learning, but the concept of the ZPD is relevant to any learning that is undertaken throughout life and is especially befitting to adolescence, in which motivation can be an issue. From a pedagogical

| ATTAINMENT LEVEL | LEARNER STATUS | TEACHING STRATEGY |
|---|---|---|
| 1 Already attained skills or knowledge at this level | Learner bored: knows this already | Avoid teaching: it will be boring and unchallenging |
| 2 Appropriate level: ZPD attainable with guidance and support | Learner motivated: enjoys the challenge and the goal is within reach | Teach at this level, providing guidance (scaffolding) to support learning |
| 3 Too high: unattainable; learner not yet ready to accomplish skills or understand work at this level | Learner demotivated: goals are unattainable; learner faced with failure if they attempt work at this level | Avoid teaching: too challenging; learner not able to understand work, or accomplish skills, at this level |

**FIGURE 4.1** Different levels of attainment, learning and teaching [based on Berger (2001: 56)].

point of view, teaching to the appropriate level is of paramount importance in order to enable pupils to achieve their maximum potential. It is one of the huge challenges of teaching, especially when faced with a class of pupils who are at different levels.

A third model for intellectual development, which provided a different view from either Piaget's or Vygotsky's theories, emerged with the advent of the computer: the information-processing approach. This approach 'emphasizes the basic mental processes involved in attention, perception, memory and decision-making' (Sigelman and Rider 2009: 217). Essentially this model was based on the fact that an individual takes in information into the mind's 'hard drive', that is, the brain and nervous system. This is then subject to interpretation and analysis and becomes stored in the 'files' of the brain ready to be retrieved as memory.

An adolescent's 'metamemory skills also improve and contribute to increased memory performance and problem-solving ability' (Sigelman and Rider 2009: 232), but this is hardly surprising when they are immersed in a cultural context which places them in an educational system that expects development of, and affords opportunities to practise, such skills. Memory is part of metacognition. As adolescents develop they become more aware of how they learn and think, that is, their metacognition develops. This enables them to develop strategies for their learning. Cole *et al.* (2005: 473) describe metacognition as 'the ability to think about one's own thoughts . . . Metacognition allows one to assess how difficult a problem is likely to be and to choose strategies to solve it in a flexible way'. Metacognition enables adolescents to think about their thinking, and as such it enables a degree of reflexivity in their thoughts. They can reflect upon their own thoughts about themselves. This is connected with the development of their self-identity, which will be discussed in Chapter 5.

This reflection and inward view of themselves and their identity can lead to self-absorption and adolescent 'egocentrism' as proposed by Elkind (1967), in which adolescents exaggerate their social significance. This can be an almost retrograde step in cognitive terms, as they seem to disregard, or be unaware of, the needs of others around them, as their needs are perceived as being of prime importance and they are centre stage. 'Focused on their own needs and wants, at times, early adolescents develop a complete disregard for inconveniencing parents and other adults to get what they need or want' (Caissy 1994: 71).

Santrock (2010: 18) makes the point that 'adolescents begin to think in more egocentric ways, often sensing they are onstage, unique and invulnerable'. Berger (2001: 413) commented on the potential problem that 'younger adolescents tend to hypothesize about what others might be thinking (especially about them) and then egocentrically take their hypotheses to be fact – a kind of deductive reasoning that can lead to very false conclusions'. The 'imaginary audience' is one of these 'false conclusions', leading them to feel that 'all eyes are on them'. This can cause them to curl up with embarrassment and be highly self-conscious and uncomfortable in social situations or, conversely, they might enjoy being, and indeed expect to be, the centre of attention.

A second misperception is the belief that they are invincible. This way of thinking is dangerous as it can play a part in leading adolescents into risk-taking behaviour simply because they think that they are not going to get caught, or suffer from the consequences of their actions, for example smoking, drinking or drug taking.

The 'personal fable' idea is also a misconception in which 'they perceive themselves as different from others, distinguished by unusual experiences, perspectives and values' (Berger 2001: 413). For example, their state of being 'in love' is far more intense than anyone else has ever experienced previously.

Part of adolescent intellectual development is to develop moral reasoning. Kohlberg (1976) proposed three stages of moral reasoning; these are summarised by Cole *et al.* (2005):

- *The preconventional stage*, based on an individual's own needs.
- *The conventional stage*, characterised by adhering to rule-based morals and a sense of law and order, but showing an awareness of 'social conventions' and 'the shared standards of right and wrong' (p. 629).
- *The postconventional or principled stage*, which 'requires people to go beyond existing social conventions to consider more abstract principles of right and wrong' (p. 631). Global issues such as human rights, fair trade issues and the environment would be included in this category of 'universal ethical principles' (p. 630).

The final stage typically starts in adolescence but may not actually occur at all (Rathus 2006). Early adolescents are regarded as being at the conventional stage, which can be divided into two substages: that of 'the good-child morality', in which 'being moral' means 'living up to the expectations of one's family, teachers and other significant people in one's life'; and the 'law-and-order morality', in which laws are upheld and individuals will make positive contributions to their schools, society and other groups to which they belong (Cole *et al.* 2005: 630).

Roberts (2007: 93) states that: 'These stages are not the product of maturation . . . The stages are also not entirely a product of socialisation. The stages emerge instead, from experience. Social experiences promote development, by stimulation of cognitive processes'. There is a change from a child's view of the world in which things are either straightforwardly right or wrong, and in which adult rules are accepted without question, to an understanding that, at times, the boundaries can be blurred and that something may be considered wrong in one case, but acceptable in another. This recognition that there are different ways of viewing a situation involves application of logic and reasoning to take account of all aspects of the situation. Moral judgements tend to be more autonomous at this stage, as an individual evaluates the circumstances and makes a decision.

Woolfolk *et al.* (2008: 116) state that:

> abstract thinking becomes increasingly important in the higher stages of moral development, as children move from decisions based on absolute rules to those based on abstract principles such as justice and mercy. The ability to see another's perspective, to judge intentions and to imagine alternative bases for laws and rules also enters into judgements.

Moral development is also connected to emotional development, as emotional responses play a significant part in moral decisions. This can cause conflict for the adolescent when there are discrepancies between what they feel they 'would like to do' and 'what they ought to do' in accordance with social convention and expectations.

The next section considers how emotions are affected by adolescent development.

## Emotional changes in adolescence

Development of emotions and feelings is part and parcel of the adolescent period. In the same way as adolescents have to learn about, and adjust to, their changing bodies, they also have to learn about their emotions. Fluctuations of mood are part of the stereotypical view of adolescence, but it is important to acknowledge that not all adolescents will be moody. Santrock, however, adheres to the stereotype, but offers reassurance: 'It is important for adults to recognize that moodiness is a normal aspect of early adolescence, and that most adolescents eventually emerge from moody times and become competent adults' (Santrock 2010: 154).

At one time an adolescent may be the 'happiest person alive' and then the next they may be depressed and sullen. Hormonal changes are often blamed for the extreme emotions and behaviour of some adolescents. However, we are living in an age when hormonal changes are part of the stereotyped response to explain anti-social or poor behaviour. For example, premenstrual syndrome can be regarded as an excuse for adolescent girls and women to be 'stroppy' and 'moody' and behave irrationally, when in fact the evidence points to the premenstrual phase being 'accompanied by heightened activity, intellectual clarity, feelings of well-being [and] happiness' (Nicolson 1995: 780). However, this is not to diminish the fact that hormonal change can cause havoc with an individual's emotions, resulting in a whole gamut of emotional responses ranging from excessive anger to tearfulness; from positive feelings to anxiety and depression.

Hormones precipitate puberty and bring about massive changes in the adolescent (see Chapter 3), and this includes changes in feelings as well as in physical appearance. The socio-emotional aspect of adolescent development is part of the socialisation process and rooted in the cultural context. It should be recognised that adolescents are learning 'how they should feel' and 'how they should respond' as part of the socialisation process specific to the cultural context in which they are living, so their mood fluctuations could in part be explained as testing people's reactions to their behaviour and testing the boundaries of acceptability. For example, if they become angry and react with aggression, how do people respond to this? Behaviourist principles (see Skinner 1938) underpin such situations, as people's responses will determine how the adolescent reacts in the future. For example, if anger enables the adolescent to get what they want, then they are likely to repeat this behaviour if faced with a similar situation. Similarly, if they sulk and as a result get their own way, this reinforces, and in fact rewards, the sulkiness as an effective manipulative tool and therefore the behaviour is likely to be repeated.

This type of emotional display can also be connected with expectations of adolescent behaviour. It could be viewed that the behaviour is exhibited to live up to perceived expectations of stereotypical adolescent behaviour. This demonstrates and confirms their role as an 'adolescent'. This is an interesting aspect and one that is difficult to determine. Which comes first? Do adolescents live up to the stereotyped expectations of moody and 'bad' behaviour or is it the behaviour itself that initially gave rise to the stereotype in the first instance?

In the same way that it cannot be assumed that an adolescent's physical and intellectual development will occur simultaneously, then it also cannot be assumed that a person's emotional development will be at the same stage as their intellectual or physical development. If the emotional development is not matched by the intellectual processes then this could explain some of the out of control behaviour presented by some adolescents who have not yet developed the cognitive capacity to rationalise and deal with their emotions.

Feinstein (2004) suggests that, rather than hormones being to blame for adolescent stereotypical behaviour, the reason that adolescents 'can't act like adults' is 'because they don't think like adults' and 'the adolescent brain is still under construction' (p. 1). She states that an adolescent's 'lack of mature thought processes to regulate their emotions, provides an insight into an adolescent's emotional state' (p. 86). As stated previously, the amygdala in the brain is central to emotional responses in the adolescent. Feinstein highlights the differences between the functioning of the amygdala in an adult and an adolescent:

Adults depend less on the amygdala than the frontal lobes of their brain, so they respond rationally to information . . . they are ready to take on the . . . responsibilities of reacting logically and reasonably. The adolescent, on the other hand, tends to rely more on the amygdala, which helps to explain their emotional and impulsive behavior.

(Feinstein 2004: 84)

How the brain functions in response to emotions is connected to ideas of emotional intelligence, described by Davies and Banyard (2010: 15) as 'an ability to identify, assess and manage the emotions of yourself, other individuals and groups'. Goleman (1995) popularised the idea of emotional intelligence. Siegler and colleagues draw on the research in this area and conclude that emotional intelligence includes such abilities as

> being able to motivate oneself and persist in the face of frustration, control impulses and delay gratification, identify and understand one's own and others' feelings, regulate one's moods, regulate the expression of emotion in social interactions, and empathize with others' emotions.
>
> (Siegler *et al.* 2006: 375)

Through emotional intelligence the emotional responses are regulated and interpreted by the cognitive structures. In Chapter 2 the SEAL (Social and Emotional Aspects of Learning) programme (DfES 2005) was considered as a way of developing strategies that encourage children to cope with, and manage, their feelings. Parke and Gauvain (2009: 180) state that 'being able to express and interpret emotions is just as important as being able to solve a cognitive problem'. There is evidence (Feinstein 2004) to suggest that adolescents misinterpret emotions and facial expressions because their interpretive skills are not developed and this can lead to hostile responses when they misunderstand a situation. Feinstein gives the example that:

> Teenagers have not yet mastered the art of body language . . . A look of surprise is interpreted as a glare of anger. A teacher cracks a joke and a teen takes it seriously and finds offense. These misunderstandings and misinterpretations are common occurrences behind much moodiness and temperamental behavior.
>
> (Feinstein 2004: 85)

Newman and Newman (2003) discuss the effects of problems and feelings being internalised or externalised. They cite the work of Achenbach (1991) and distinguish between internalised problems – directed 'inward on the self', for example 'feelings of hopelessness or worthlessness' – and externalised problems – such as aggression or delinquency in which 'the adolescent's conflicts are directed outward toward property or other people' (p. 303). Externalisation of emotions can also be referred to as displacement, stemming from Freudian psychoanalytical theory on 'defence mechanisms' employed to resolve conflict and reduce anxiety (Eysenck 2000: 16). However, displacement in Freudian terms is an unconscious action. Freud identified defence mechanisms that come into play when the feelings of the individual conflict with their moral standards and thus throw them into confusion. This relates to Kohlberg's theory of moral development in early adolescence, discussed earlier, and the 'good-child' morality in which children try to live up to the expectations of significant others (Cole *et al.* 2005). This tussle between right and wrong is a dilemma between their cognitive development, in which they apply reasoning, and their emotional development, in which their feelings come to the fore. This can cause anxiety or aggression and gives credence to the stress and turmoil stereotype of adolescence discussed in Chapter 3.

# Bridging the transition

## Stress and anxiety

In Chapter 3 the idea was put forward that the transition from primary to secondary school might be one challenge too far for the adolescent, by creating an additional change at a time when massive physical, social, emotional and intellectual changes are already occurring. The stress response, that is, an individual's reaction to stressors, is an emotional and psychological response that can produce physical symptoms such as sweating, palpitations and anxiety. For some, the transition to a larger, new school will act as a stressor and be the cause of considerable stress.

When a person is under stress the body reacts with an adaptive response to prepare for fight or flight (Cannon 1932). There are two aspects of stress: good stress, which can be responding to change with excitement, and bad stress, in which the response is negative and the result of feeling threatened. Good stress, also known as eustress, can be beneficial and can be harnessed so that people work or perform to their optimum capacity; it enables the body to respond and be motivated, healthy and stimulated. Bad stress, known as distress, is the more usual perception of stress. Too much or prolonged stress of this nature is harmful. An individual's ability to cope becomes depleted and, in cases of prolonged stress, the body does not have an opportunity to recover and replenish its store of coping resources. Effectively the body is in a constant state of preparation for flight or fight capacity and this is harmful, so stress is a risk factor for ill health. Parke and Gauvain (2009: 180) make the point that 'physical health suffers . . . when emotional development goes wrong'; the physiological responses can be influenced by an individual's psychological and emotional responses.

It is important to recognise that stress for one person might be excitement for another. Different people react very differently to the same types of stressors. For example, performing a part in a play might give one person a buzz of excitement and actually enable them to perform better, whereas another person may become crippled with nerves and not be able to cope with the demands of the situation at all. This can be applied to transition. Some pupils will be excited about moving to a new, and often bigger, school, whereas others will dread the prospect and find it stressful. Essentially a person will feel stressed if they perceive that they are unable to cope with the demands and pressures of a given situation. It is their *perception* of their ability to cope that is the critical point.

Seligman (1975) identified 'perceived lack of control' as a key characteristic of stressful situations. The idea of control is apparent in many models to explain stress. Lazarus and Folkman (1987) considered 'self-efficacy': a person's belief in themselves to meet the challenge presented to them. Kobasa *et al.* (1982, in Ogden 2007) discussed the idea of 'hardiness', which Ogden (2007: 228) describes as 'reflecting personal feelings of control; a desire to accept challenges; and commitment'. A similar idea to hardiness has more recently been described by Claxton (1999) as 'resilience'. Claxton uses the term in the context of tenacity in terms of learning and not giving up if the 'first whiff of frustration makes you want to withdraw' (p. 15). However, underlying both terms is their relationship to the emotions and how an individual perceives a challenge, and both are applicable within the context of adapting to change. It is important that teachers, parents and schools recognise this aspect of the stress response and empower pupils so that they perceive and believe that they are able to cope with the transition and that moving schools will be a positive change and something to be embraced and enjoyed. This links to the autonomy and managing learning bridge.

## The autonomy and managing learning bridge

The Rose Report (2009: 98) focuses on 'ensuring that pupils are seen as active participants in the transition process and in their own learning'. This statement supports the conclusions of Phelan *et al.* (1994: 443), who recommend that pedagogical programmes should take account of pupils' opinions and concerns and the importance of their role in mediating their personal experiences. This is also echoed in the Cambridge Review (Alexander 2010: 19), in which securing children's 'active and enthusiastic engagement in their learning' is highlighted as one of the key aims.

To reduce the potential stress surrounding transitions it is necessary to empower pupils and put them in control of their own transition process. The Cambridge Review comments that 'Children who feel empowered are more likely to be better and happier learners'. The review also identified the need to 'respect children's experience, voices and rights [and] engage them actively and directly in decisions that affect their learning' (Alexander 2010: 12).

Roberts (2007: 88) states that 'one of the principal issues facing young people concerns the establishment of autonomy'. He explains further that 'rather than severing relationships autonomy really means becoming an independent and self-governing person'. His conclusion is that 'Autonomous people should have the ability to make meaningful choices and the conviction to follow through with their own decisions. They are principled with regard to right and wrong, and have become less emotionally dependent on their significant others' (Roberts 2007: 88).

## The social and personal bridge

Pupils of transitional age are likely to be in Kohlberg's conventional stage, as discussed previously, where they want to make a contribution and be part of an institution or group. Teachers can work with this idea to give pupils a strong sense of being part of the school community at the new school. Visits from head teachers, Year 7 teachers and other members of staff, during the summer term before they move to their new school, provide the opportunity to introduce them to ideas of belonging to a new school community. Half- or whole-day visits to the new school for Year 6 pupils are also popular. The aim of such visits is to introduce pupils to the new premises so that they can familiarise themselves with the buildings and meet new staff. The idea is that this dispels anxieties, but unfortunately for some pupils, if the experience is negative, they will spend a fretful summer worrying about the new school and how they will cope.

Some of the strategies discussed here and throughout the book have been designed to allay fears and reduce anxiety for pupils. However, it could be argued that a degree of stress enhances pupils' personal development as it allows them to explore their own resourcefulness and overcome their fears. As explained earlier in the chapter, for some pupils the stress response manifests itself in excitement and heightened anticipation of a new experience, therefore the role of the school is to make the transition exciting and enjoyable rather than something to be feared.

A degree of apprehension is to be expected as most pupils will inevitably be facing new challenges and experiences, such as a larger school; many teachers instead of a 'single teacher with whom they spend most of their time'; and 'student populations . . . from a variety of socioeconomic and ethnic communities' (Sullivan *et al*. 2004: 45–46).

The issue for teachers and schools is maintaining the balance between allowing pupils the opportunity to use their own initiative and resources and easing the difficulties of transition for them. It is worth exploring the continuity–discontinuity issue further. This 'focuses on the extent to which development involves gradual cumulative change (continuity) or distinct stages (discontinuity)' (Santrock 2010: 23). The examples that Santrock employs are those of a 'seedling gradually growing into a giant oak' tree to represent continuity, or a 'caterpillar suddenly becoming a butterfly' to explain discontinuity. In Santrock's analogy, the chrysalis stage is omitted, but caterpillars don't suddenly change into butterflies: there is an interim stage of chrysalis, which is the butterfly pupa. Inclusion of this stage would actually emphasise the point further, that is, in situations of discontinuity there are distinct differences at each stage. The chrysalis stage corresponds to the adolescent stage, the interim stage between childhood and adulthood. However, the analogy appears to end there because, although beneath the surface there are complex changes that take place before the butterfly emerges, the chrysalis has the external appearance of being dormant, whereas adolescence is far from dormant.

The view of development as either being continuous and gradual or, alternatively, going through distinct stages can be related to the transition process as a whole. If it is the former then this suggests that adolescents will cope best with changes that are gradual. If it is the latter then attempting to ensure a smooth transition, which emphasises continuity, would be a wasted effort as adolescents would be going through abrupt changes and would have different needs before and after transition. The problem with applying this view to transition is that individuals will not all be at the same developmental level at the age of transition. The opportunity to make a completely fresh start and embark on a new phase of their lives may suit some but not others, who may not be ready for such an abrupt change. Current policy emphasises continuity to minimise and dovetail the transition.

## The pedagogy bridge

The Rose Report (2009: 98) recommendation for good pedagogical practice was to improve 'continuity in teaching and classroom practice between Year 6 and Year 7'. Brewer (2007) discusses the implementation of bridging units and comments that the joint 'lessons were planned to be progressive to give teachers, and pupils, an understanding of the skills progression in the subject areas' (p. 1). This type of collaborative work enables teachers to gain an 'understanding of how students learn and what constitutes effective teaching practice. Greater alignment of teaching practices in late primary and early secondary school reduces the possibility of decline in student achievement in Years 7 and 8' (NSW 2007: 1).

The levels of attainment, learning and teaching (see Figure 4.1) need to be considered in terms of setting work at the appropriate level for pupils. If work they have already covered is repeated they will be bored and demotivated; if it is too hard they will become disengaged and demotivated and feel that the goals are unattainable. This relates to levels of learning and goal setting so that targets are achievable and therefore learning will be motivating and enjoyable. Joint planning and communication between primary and secondary teachers will ensure that this can be addressed and a greater understanding of the levels of work will be attained and repetition of work will be avoided.

The Cambridge Review draws upon comments from children who have identified good teachers as those who 'make sure it's not in too big steps (graduated instruction)' (Alexander 2010: 29). Scaffolding the learning experience for pupils will ensure that they move to the next level of attainment when they are ready, and this will enable them to achieve their goals.

A pertinent issue is the need to ensure that all pupils are able to read at transition level. Without the ability to read, their chances of achieving their full potential and any degree of academic success are severely limited. This obviously impacts upon their emotional response to school and their self-esteem. Clifford-Poston (2005: 131) stresses the importance of this:

> Learning to read seals the fate of a child's academic future. All further study depends upon it. Becoming self-reliant, finding our own way in the world, is also dependent upon it . . . the tween who cannot read is seriously handicapped – and not only in their ability to learn. Their self-esteem and general curiosity may suffer . . . many non-readers, not surprisingly, are disruptive.

This point is exemplified in a damning report by Harriet Sergeant, who identified that white working-class boys and black Caribbean boys who 'were not taught to read and write properly by seven' and who were 'unable to understand what was going on . . . began to misbehave in the last two years of primary school. At secondary school their behaviour deteriorated' (Sergeant 2009: 15).

A pupil who cannot read and who is unable to understand the work that they are supposed to be doing will inevitably experience stress and frustration and be demotivated. Disruptive behaviour may be part of the coping strategy that they employ to precipitate a disrupted lesson so that their failure to complete the work is not exposed.

Clearly, if levels of illiteracy are not being picked up at transition level and the consequence is disruptive behaviour then this is problematic for both the pupils and teachers. In such cases there is a clear case for favouring continuity as a transitional strategy and the transfer of records highlighting the special educational needs of such pupils is of paramount importance.

## Conclusion

In cognitive terms we have seen how the ZPD can come into play in that pupils have to be ready to make the next transitional step in their learning. Might this not be applied to the whole process of transition to a new school? Are there some pupils who are simply not ready for this massive change and who do not have the skills and abilities to cope with it? If this is indeed their perception then it would explain the 'dip in results' in Year 7 (Sutherland *et al.* 2010) because they lose confidence in their own abilities, that is, they lack self-efficacy, and are held back by beliefs that this process is too hard for them. Without belief that they can control and cope with the changes they face, the whole process elicits a negative emotional response and becomes stressful.

We have considered issues of continuity and discontinuity and whether or not there is an overemphasis on bridging the transitional gap, which would mean that pupils are not having the opportunity to rise to the challenges presented by transition. Phelan *et al.*'s (1994) research into junior to senior school transitions acknowledged that exposure to different social contexts can provide the opportunity for adolescents to develop and grow on both a personal and a social level. However, they concluded that, if the challenges pupils faced outweighed their ability to cope and, as a result, they could not adapt successfully to the new circumstances, they would be under pressure and would experience stress. This is the danger in the transition from primary to secondary school when some of the pupils do not have either the social skills or the confidence to cope with the transition. This needs to be addressed not only from the school perspective, but also from the perspective of family and friends, who provide support structures for the individual.

The next chapter (Chapter 5) looks at how self-confidence stems from a strong sense of identity and explores the way in which support structures provided by the school, peers and the family can encourage the development of a confident individual and can assist in providing a smooth transition and a positive adaptive response to transition.

## Questions to consider

- Suggest ways in which teachers can develop lessons that will take account of, and provide opportunities for, the adolescent's new way of thinking.

- How can teachers cater for the different levels of learning as depicted in Figure 4.1? Can you think of examples in which the ZPD was in evidence in your own learning experience?

- To what extent do you feel that emotional problems experienced by adolescents are a result of a mismatch between cognitive and emotional development?

- What was your personal experience of the transition between primary and secondary school? Was it stressful? If so, what were your symptoms? What could have been done to help reduce the stress? If it was positive, what made it positive?

## Suggested further reading

Berger, K. (2001) *The Developing Person through the Lifespan*, 5th edn. New York: Worth. This book covers all aspects of development from birth through to death and dying.

The sections on the school years and adolescence cover biosocial, cognitive and psychosocial development and provide good examples of specific issues.

Santrock, J. (2010) *Adolescence*, 13th international edn. New York: McGraw-Hill.
This book provides an excellent overview of adolescence and explores some of the key theories and debates that are pertinent to this phase of development.

## References

Achenbach, T. (1991) *Manual for the Youth Self-Report and 1991 Profile*. Burlington: University of Vermont, Department of Psychiatry.

Alexander, R. (ed.) (2010) *Children, their World, their Education: Final Report and Recommendations of the Cambridge Review*. London: Routledge.

Banyard, P., Davies, M., Norman, C. and Winder, B. (eds) (2010) *Essential Psychology: A Concise Introduction*. London: Sage.

Berger, K. (2001) *The Developing Person through the Lifespan*, 5th edn. New York: Worth.

Brewer T. (2007) 'Review of Pilot Transition Project'. Unpublished.

Broughton, J. (1983) 'The Cognitive Developmental Theory of Adolescent Self and Identity'. In Lee, B. and Noam, G. (eds) *Developmental Approaches to Self*. New York: Plenum Press.

Caissy, G. (1994) *Early Adolescence: Understanding the 10 to 15 Year Old*. London: Plenum Press.

Cannon, W. (1932). *The Wisdom of the Body*. New York: Norton.

Claxton, G. (1999) *Wise Up. The Challenge of Lifelong Learning*. London: Bloomsbury.

Clifford-Poston, A. (2005). *Tweens: What To Expect From – and How to Survive – your Child's Pre-teen Years*. Oxford: One World.

Cole, M., Cole, S. and Lightfoot, C. (2005) *The Development of Children*, 5th edn. New York: Worth.

Davies, M. and Banyard, P. (2010) 'Sex, Lies and Digital Horizons'. In Banyard, P., Davies, M., Norman, C. and Winder, B. (eds) *Essential Psychology: A Concise Introduction*. London: Sage, Chapter 1.

DfES (2005) 'Excellence and Enjoyment: Social and Emotional Aspects of Learning'. London: DfES.

Elkind, D. (1967) 'Egocentrism in Adolescence'. *Child Development*, 38, 1025–1034.

Evangelou, M., Taggart, B., Sylva, K., Melhuish, E., Sammons, P. and Siraj-Blatchford, I. (2008) 'What Makes a Successful Transition from Primary to Secondary School?'. London: DCSF.

Eysenck, M. (2000) *Psychology: A Student's Handbook*. Hove: Psychology Press.

Feinstein (2004) *Secrets of the Teenage Brain: Research-based Strategies for Reaching and Teaching Today's Adolescents*. San Diego: The Brain Store.

Galton, M., Gray, J. and Ruddock, J. (1999) 'The Impact of School Transitions and Transfers on Pupils Progress and Attainment'. Research Report RR131. Nottingham: DfEE.

Goleman, D. (1995) *Emotional Intelligence*. New York: Bantum Books.

Illeris, K. (2003) 'Towards a Contemporary and Comprehensive Theory of Learning'. *International Journal of Lifelong Education*, 22 (4), 396–406.

Kobasa, S., Maddi, S. and Pucetti, M. (1982) 'Personality and Exercise as Buffers in the Stress–Illness Relationship'. *Journal of Behavioral Medicine*, 5, 391–404.

Kohlberg, L. (1976) 'Moral Stages and Moralization: The Cognitive-Developmental Approach'. In Lickona, T. (ed.) *Moral Development and Behavior: Theory, Research and Social Issues*. New York: Holt, Rinehart and Winston.

Lazarus, R. and Folkman, S. (1987) 'Transactional Theory and Research on Emotions and Coping'. *European Journal of Personality*, 1, 141–170.

Newman, B. and Newman, P. (2003) *Development through Life*, 8th edn. Belmont: Thomson Learning.

Nicolson P. (1995) 'The Menstrual Cycle, Science and Femininity: Assumptions Underlying Menstrual Cycle Research'. *Social Science and Medicine*, 41 (6), 779–784.

NSW (New South Wales) Department of Education and Training (2007) Online. Available from http://www.schools.nsw.edu.au/gotoschool/highschool/transition (accessed 26 October 2009)

Ogden, J. (2007) *Health Psychology: A Textbook*, 4th edn. Maidenhead: McGraw-Hill/Oxford University Press.

Parke, R. and Gauvain, M. (2009) *Child Psychology: A Contemporary Viewpoint*, 7th edn. London: McGraw-Hill.

Phelan, P., Yu, H. and Locke Davidson, A. (1994). 'Navigating the Psychosocial Pressures of Adolescence: The Voices and Experiences of High School Youth'. *American Educational Research Journal*, 31 (2), 415–447.

Piaget, J. (1952) *The Origins of Intelligence in Children*. New York: International Universities Press.

Rathus, S. (2006) *Childhood and Adolescence: Voyages in Development*, 2nd edn. London: Thomson Wadsworth.

Roberts, I. (2007) 'Adolescence'. In Zwozdiak-Myers, P. (ed.) *Childhood and Youth Studies*. Exeter: Learning Matters.

Rose, J. (ed.) (2009) 'Independent Review of the Primary Curriculum'. Nottingham: DCFS.

Santrock, J. (2010) *Adolescence*, 13th international edn. New York: McGraw-Hill.

Seligman, M. E. (1975) *Helplessness*. San Francisco: W. H. Freeman.

Sergeant, H. (2009) *Wasted. The Betrayal of White Working Class and Black Caribbean Boys*. London: Centre for Policy Studies.

Siegler, R., DeLoache, J. and Eisenberg, N. (2006) *How Children Develop*, 2nd edn. New York: Worth.

Sigelman, C. and Rider, E. (2009) *Life-Span Human Development*, 6th edn. Belmont: Wadsworth Cengage Learning.

Skinner, B. F. (1938) *The Behavior of Organisms: An Experimental Analysis*. New York: Appleton-Century-Crofts.

Sullivan, K., Cleary, M. and Sullivan, G. (2004) *Bullying in Secondary Schools: What it Looks Like and How to Manage it*. London: PCP.

Sutherland, R., Yee, W., McNess, E. and Harris, R. (2010) 'Supporting Learning in The Transition from Primary to Secondary Schools'. Bristol: University of Bristol.

Vygotsky, L. S. (1978) *Mind in Society: The Development of Higher Mental Processes*. Cambridge, MA: Harvard University Press.

Wood, D., Bruner, J. and Ross, G. (1976) 'The Role of Tutoring in Problem-Solving'. *Journal of Child Psychology and Psychiatry*, 17, 89–100.

Woolfolk, A., Hughes, M. and Walkrup, V. (2008) *Psychology in Education*. Harlow: Pearson Education.

# Adolescent development

## Personal and social changes

*Val Richards*

## Chapter summary

This chapter focuses on personal and social development during adolescence. It builds upon the information in Chapters 3 and 4 and demonstrates how the intellectual, physical and emotional development of the adolescent can have an effect upon their development as social beings. Relationships with peers will be considered, as will the issues of identity, peer pressure and risk-taking behaviour and self-esteem. This chapter looks specifically at the social and personal changes that arise at the age of the transition, particularly those that lead to a positive adaptive response or a negative maladaptive response to the changes brought about by transition from primary to secondary school.

## Introduction

The changes in physical, emotional and intellectual development during adolescence impact upon the social and personal aspects of an individual's life. Whether they like it or not, their physical features will change and they will experience new emotions and feel different in social contexts. These changes inevitably alter their relationships with peers, family and members of the wider community, including teachers. The tendency of research to focus on the negative aspects of these changes leads to an overemphasis on the problems experienced during transition, but for many adolescents this period can be an exciting time when they establish a strong sense of self-identity, make close and long-lasting friendships and revel in the opportunities that are afforded them as a result of greater independence and autonomy.

This chapter explores the concept of developing a self-identity and how this is embedded in social roles, social groups and friendships. The social networks surrounding the adolescent, provided by relationships with family, friends and teachers, are central to identity formation and the development of a person's self-esteem and confidence. These support networks, coupled with an individual's developing sense of identity, are fundamental in the process of transition and will be underlying factors that determine whether or not the individual will adapt successfully to the changes brought about by transition. The social and personal bridge is regarded as a distinct and important area to be considered in transitional programmes (Galton *et al.* 1999). The final section of this chapter will consider the support structures involved in managing this bridge to ensure a positive adaptive response to change.

## Self-identity

Adolescence is a stage when development of a 'self-identity' is a central issue. The changes that occur in an adolescent's physical, intellectual and emotional development inevitably mean that they have to reassess themselves and adjust their view of themselves according to the changes that they are experiencing. For example, the intellectual development of the adolescent enables them to consider and reflect upon themselves in a different way. It also enables them to consider, and reflect upon, the opinions of others.

Muuss discusses the idea of social cognition in which 'adolescents . . . learn how to understand others: their thoughts, their intentions, their emotions, their social behavior, and their general point of view. Social cognition involves role-taking, perspective taking, empathy, moral reasoning, interpersonal problem solving, and self-knowledge' (Muuss 1982: 504).

Arriving at self-knowledge and identifying who and what you are is very complex and yet almost everyone does seem to have a distinct sense of their own individual identity. An adjustment to, or crisis of, one's identity often occurs because of a change of life and having to adapt to new circumstances. Erikson (1968) talked about crises or psychosocial conflicts occurring at different developmental stages from early infancy through to late adulthood. In respect of adolescent development, he believed that puberty brought about changes in social role and social expectations which led to the individual reassessing themself in the development of a secure sense of 'self-identity'. He referred to the occurrence of an identity crisis, with the 'crisis' being the tension between achieving a sense of identity or remaining in a state of role confusion. Kroger discusses role confusion as 'the counterpoint of identity' and makes the point that

> it is necessary for adolescents to experience some kind of role confusion in undergoing the identity formation process. Letting go of early childhood identifications to forge one's own commitments in life is a sobering task, often resulting in feelings of loss and confusion.
>
> (Kroger 2007: 9)

This view is echoed by Stevens (2008: 68): 'Adolescence is inevitably and normally a time of crisis for identity. How far this is disruptive will vary depending on individuals and their contexts'.

Erikson's work was elaborated upon by James Marcia (1966, 1980), who believed that individuals had to engage with, and explore, ideas and alternative views (the crisis phase) and then make a decision as to which beliefs and values became integral to their sense of 'self' (the commitment phase). Marcia identified four identity statuses; Figure 5.1 summarizes the ideas.

| CRISIS | COMMITMENT | IDENTITY STATUS |
|---|---|---|
| Yes; has had a crisis | Yes | Identity achievement |
| Yes; is having a crisis | No | Moratorium |
| No; no crisis or examination of values | Yes | Foreclosure |
| No; no crisis or examination of values | No | Identity diffusion |

**FIGURE 5.1** Summary of Marcia's identity statuses.

It is important to recognise that these may not be permanent statuses, but may change according to life experiences and circumstances. For example, *identity achievement* in the area of religion may be transformed by encountering a different belief system when travelling during a 'gap year', or by meeting someone who exerts a considerable influence over one's views, such as a charismatic and persuasive spiritual leader. This could precipitate an entirely new crisis, which would entail re-evaluation of an individual's beliefs.

A person can be said to have attained *identity achievement* when they have explored their views and the options available to them, and they have made a definite commitment to a particular way of life, or way of thinking. The idea of 'identity crisis' was used to demonstrate the conflict that such an examination of one's beliefs could induce. An example of this might be committing to a specific religion, perhaps converting to Catholicism or becoming a 'born-again' evangelical Christian. Other examples might be committing to vegetarianism – being a vegetarian becomes part of their identity and who they are as an individual; or deciding on a particular career path, which entails them working hard at school so that they obtain a place at university to gain qualifications in order to pursue their career. This therefore involves their future identity.

For the state of *moratorium* to exist this involves the adolescent being 'in crisis'. This could be about life in general or it could relate to one specific area of their life. A person in moratorium would challenge the views of their parents and significant others. They would typically oscillate between viewpoints, appearing fiercely passionate about, for example, a particular political stance or religious belief, only to reject it after further evaluation.

*Identity diffusion* (Marcia used 'diffusion' rather than Erikson's idea of identity 'confusion') is experienced when young people have not really examined their own feelings and views beyond experiencing a vague interest in, for example, a career. Comments such as 'yeah, I might be a vet' might be made, perhaps to gauge a reaction, but without having investigated the details of what the job might entail, or what qualifications and training would be needed. Another example might be that they regard themselves as 'apolitical' and consequently they are apathetic about political ideologies and do not engage with political ideas and debates, decrying them as 'boring'. In this state they might have had a past crisis but they have no true sense of themselves in terms of their beliefs and opinions.

*Foreclosure* would apply to someone who has made a commitment to a particular way of thinking but who has not examined or questioned the beliefs that lie behind that commitment. In other words, they have foreclosed on any debate or discussion. An example of this would be when someone adopts their parents' religion or political views without questioning the underlying beliefs.

Bee and Boyd (2010) cite research by Waterman (1985) which indicates that identity achievement occurs later than Erikson first proposed. This could be connected with the lengthening of 'childhood' and the extended period in education, which effectively means that the expectation of adolescents becoming more responsible and more independent cannot be achieved in today's western society (see Chapter 3), and it is difficult for them to carve out an identity when they are in limbo between being a child and an adult. Bee and Boyd (2010: 264) point out that

> young people do not normally or necessarily adopt the same roles or occupations as their parents. Indeed they are encouraged to choose for themselves. In such a cultural system, adolescents are faced with . . . a bewildering array of options, a pattern that might well foster the sort of identity crisis Erikson described.

Bee and Boyd's suggestion of a 'bewildering array of options' does suggest that identity is a matter of choice, but in fact many aspects of an individual's identity result from birth, so there is a nature versus nurture element to identity. In many societies, who you are is conferred by your age, your gender and your relationships with other individuals, for example being someone's son or daughter. These are *ascribed* roles, which result from birth. There are also *achieved* roles, which are gained through an individual's own actions, such as career roles. How much of an individual's identity is determined through their birth and characterised by inherent aspects of their being and their personality, and how much is developed during their life and the result of social circumstances and influences, or personal choice?

There are many different facets of an individual's identity, and people will emphasise certain aspects that they regard as central to their identity. For example, they might identify themselves according to their nationality or ethnic roots, for example Cornish or Japanese. An individual's identity depends on the cultural context of their birth and their development: how people live, dress and speak all constitute their identity. These are all elements that are presented to the world and represent expressions or symbols of a person's identity, but they can be changed by exercising personal choice. For example, an adolescent with a broad regional accent may move to a different area and may modify their accent to become more neutral in order to fit into their new school situation. In this example the individual adjusts their behaviour according to social interactions that they experience. The neutral accent then becomes part of their identity. This fits with Mead's (1934) view that our sense of self results from our social experiences and interactions and that individuals reflect upon what other people think about them, and reflect upon themselves in the same way, that is, they make an objective appraisal of their actions or behaviour.

Without doubt individuals are able to select components of their identity and the cultural context determines the choices people have in defining their identity. This raises issues of whether there is a central core identity or whether an individual's identity comprises many identities and is subject to variation in different social contexts. Miell (1990) discusses the idea of an individual having 'many selves' and cites the ideas of James (1890, 1892), who explored the interaction between individuals and society and considered that the self was 'multi-faceted' and that what makes us into the people we are are the social roles we adopt in life. James suggested that there were two components of self – the 'I' and the 'me' – where the 'I' is the central hardcore 'you', the person for oneself and what you know you are really like, and the 'me' refers to what others know about you, the person for others, for example your physical appearance, how you dress and your views (those you have openly expressed). Goffman (1959) proposed a third facet of the 'self' as the 'character performed', that is the face or 'mask' that is presented to others in accordance with an individual's perception of how they are *expected* to act in a particular role.

One's role is powerful in determining how other people see us: for example, the uniform of a particular school immediately conveys a person's role as a pupil from that school and produces a set of responses that carries with it a host of perceptions and expectations about how people will, and should, behave in their particular role. Perhaps schools seek to control a person's identity by imposing a uniform on its pupils. This could be viewed negatively and be perceived as an obstacle to achieving self-identity. Alternatively, perhaps they are fostering a sense of 'belonging', which could be perceived as a positive element to be absorbed into a pupil's identity.

People's reactions to individuals in particular roles confirm their identity in that role. This can impact upon and affect people's self-concept. Unfortunately, this can give rise to the formation of stereotypes, and adolescents are frequently on the receiving end of negative stereotypes. Hague (2006) commenting on ASBO (anti-social behaviour orders) stereotypes wrote that

> young people are fed up with 'asbo' stereotypes: most want society to recognise their potential . . . it emerges that they are fed up with being seen as a problem and would rather be celebrated for the positive contribution they can make to society.

When surrounded by negative images and expectations of poor behaviour there is a danger that young people will live up to the expectations according to the role in which they have been cast. They will act in expected ways to conform to the role and gradually they will take on that role and start to think of themselves in that way. People adjust themselves to fit their perception of the role and their new self-concept. This self-fulfilling prophecy can be damaging to self-esteem amongst adolescents. It also becomes a vicious circle as the perceived attitudes and perspectives of others become internalised so that they become part of the self.

If a person has a strong sense of 'I' it frees them from relying on the views of others for their sense of who they are (Miell 1990). They are self-aware and their sense of self does not depend on others confirming it. However, we are social beings and generally have a desire to conform and fit in. At the age of transition self-absorption and egocentrism are likely to be making the adolescent feel self-conscious and will make them acutely aware of what other people think about them (see Chapter 4). Emotions play an important role in the way that adolescents construct their identity. How an individual *feels* about who they are is integral to the development of their identity. During adolescence individuals experiment with different roles and different identities. Part of this experimentation is to determine how they feel in those roles and to gauge other people's responses to them in those roles.

Caissy (1994: 70) states that 'During the process of identity formation, the early adolescent constantly tests out new identities, seeking confirmation of the characteristics of his or her new self'.

> Adolescence is a time for trying out new identities and for asking 'Who am I?'. This period of life is marked by the central question of who we are in terms of an individual identity, place and role in life. Puberty forces all of us to ask and answer this question. To the degree to which we address this question, we can develop a sure sense of identity. Otherwise we may be confused about our roles.
>
> (Matsumoto 2000: 202)

In answering that question it is likely that the early adolescent will include comparative statements about their physical appearance, for example whether they are tall or thin. They are also likely to include abstract ideas, such as they are 'kind' or 'good', and they will also include comments about how others view them, for example whether they are popular or well liked. Younger children do not include such descriptors in defining themselves: 'as the child moves through the . . . concrete operations period . . . self-definition becomes more complex, more comparative, less tied to external features, and more focused on feelings and ideas' (Bee and Boyd 2010: 261).

Perceptions of self are often formed in comparison with other people. People constantly compare themselves with others. This is called social comparison (Festinger 1954). For example, someone can be tall only if they are tall in comparison with others around them. It is significant that people tend to compare themselves with others like themselves. This is known as a *reference group* and can include people from their class, people of the same gender, other adolescents who are popular, others who do well at sports in school; the list is extensive. It is often, but not necessarily, a peer group or a friendship group.

Santrock (2010: 135) suggests that making social comparisons 'can be confusing to adolescents because of the large number of reference groups available to them' and that 'considering all of these social comparison groups simultaneously can be perplexing for adolescents'.

Comparisons with others can impact upon an individual's self-esteem. This can be directly because of other people's views of the individual or it could be the result of what an individual thinks that other people are thinking of them. This, as explained in the previous chapter, is something that concerns adolescents but it is also something that they can wrongly interpret and, if they feel that they do not compare favourably with someone, this can impact negatively upon their self-esteem.

Adolescents might ask themselves, 'How do I know who I am?'. If they have achieved an identity then they will have a strong sense of who they are and will not need to rely on the opinions of others to confirm their identity. However, in early adolescence confirmation of who they are is likely to be from the social groups they are in and the people around them, that is, their family, friends, social groups, school and the wider community.

## Peer pressure

The peer group is important as the primary source of feedback for adolescents and it confirms their identity. It often provides a reference group and a source of social feedback so that they can evaluate how they compare with others (Miell 1990): 'feedback from friendships and the peer group provides not only support but also a mirror for the self as different behaviors are tried and different possibilities for self-definition are tested' (Kroger 2007: 78).

Peer pressure tends to have negative connotations but, as Caissy (1994: 88) states, 'peer pressure does not always result in negative consequences'. Studies have consistently shown 'that adolescents who are uncertain about their social identity' and who have 'low self-esteem and high social anxiety are more likely to conform to peers. This uncertainty often increases during times of transition' (Santrock 2010: 316).

Selman *et al.* (1997) recognised the need for a balance between autonomy and intimacy in adolescent relationships. If this balance was not maintained then it could account for peer pressure leading to risk-taking behaviour. Either the individual would be dominated and would not be able to withstand peer pressure, or, in cases in which the imbalance was reversed, they would be dominant and likely to be a bully or lead others into risk-taking behaviours. Caissy (1994: 87) comments that

> Early adolescents with a good self-concept and positive self-esteem are less prone to peer pressure because they have the confidence to walk away from a situation with which they are not comfortable. They are not afraid of disagreeing with others. Conversely, children who have a negative self-image and poor self-esteem are more easily influenced by peers because they desperately want to be liked and accepted.

Wolfe *et al.* (2006: 17) examined adolescent risk behaviours and stressed the importance of an adolescent's relationships with family and peers and how the relationships 'protect against, or increase, risk behaviors'. The relationships are fundamental in determining whether or not adolescents engage in risk-taking behaviour. Risk behaviours that were considered were substance use and abuse, violence, educational failure, truancy, delinquent behaviour, crimes and unsafe sexual practices. They considered the physical, social and cognitive changes that are part of adolescent development and the 'choices and pressures' that exist for adolescents. 'Part of adolescent development is learning how to establish one's own principles and boundaries' (p. 74). It was suggested earlier (see Chapter 4) that an adolescent's physical, emotional and intellectual development could be at various stages and that cognitive structures might not have been developed sufficiently to regulate behaviour. Wolfe *et al.* (2006: 75) suggest that there is a

> gap between physiological changes . . . and cognitive and emotional maturity . . . [which] may account for some of the risk-taking behaviour characteristic of adolescents. The pubertal changes increase novelty and sensation seeking, but the self-regulatory competence that offsets sensation seeking does not fully mature until adulthood.

Kail and Cavanaugh (2000: 257) comment that 'peer pressure is most powerful when the standards for appropriate behavior are not clear-cut'. This could be related to a lack of identity. In adolescence, who you are is of fundamental importance in establishing yourself as an independent, autonomous individual with a strong sense of identity. The frustrations of not being able to reach an identity, or settle on a future identity, for example in terms of a career, may well lead to a crisis and result in stress and turmoil for the adolescent.

Erikson highlighted the problem of negative identity, in which 'Some adolescents will consciously choose an identity which is based on a rejection of the values of others, rather than on a positive choice of their own . . . purely to assert their independence' (Hayes 2000: 680). This connects to ideas that in western culture demarcations between childhood and adulthood are not clear-cut and this causes confusion for the adolescent (see Chapter 3). Segall *et al.* (1990: 281) suggested a 'compensatory machoism' in which, in the absence of clear-cut ceremonies to prove their masculinity and manhood, adolescent males resort to aggressive behaviour to 'assert their masculinity'. In the United States, initiation ceremonies, termed 'hazing', involving 'harassment, abuse or humiliation [are] most "celebrated" in the context of fraternities, as young people seek acceptance in schools and universities' (Roberts 2007: 89). Scheer and Blumenkrantz (2007: 10) state that 'rites of passage are powerful social events that help guide and affirm a transition from one status in life to another'.

It is apparent that where there are no distinct rites of passage, peer groups will construct their own initiation ceremonies to act as rites of passage into their group. Successful completion of these rites of passage enables individuals to belong to that group and adopt their identity.

## Friendships

Ask Year 6 pupils what is their biggest concern about moving to secondary school and their answer will be that they are worried that they will be separated from their friends (MacGrain 2010). Friendships for this age group are extremely important: potential disruption of friendships is a cause for concern (Galton 2010).

Peer interaction increases considerably in adolescence so that often adolescents are spending much more time with their friends than they do with their parents and family. 'Although relationships with parents generally remain positive, the role of peers as a source of activities, influence and support increases markedly during the teen years . . . Friendships occupy an increasingly important place in the lives of adolescents' (Rathus 2006: 556).

Close friendships increase in intensity. Friends during adolescence become confidantes and secrets are disclosed and expected to be kept as secrets. There is a high level of trust and intimacy. 'The emergence of intimacy in adolescent friendships means that friends also come to be seen as sources of social and emotional support' (Kail and Cavanaugh 2000: 254).

Romantic attachments appear in adolescence. Sullivan *et al.* (2004: 38) comment that 'Dating in young teenagers has little to do with intimacy, communication and caring, and more to do with attractiveness, belonging, and acceptability. It tends to be experimental, superficial, and short-lived in early adolescence'. However, Parke and Gauvain (2009: 464) dispel the myths of adolescent relationships being transitory, trivial or leading to problem behaviour and state that 'romantic relationships . . . represent an important developmental milestone in adolescence'. Attraction and being attractive to others is part of adolescent development and linked to an individual's identity. Romantic attachments provide the opportunity to take on the roles of boyfriend or girlfriend and to experience emotional responses and feelings.

Gender differences in same-sex friendships are apparent. There is less intimacy in boys' relationships than in girls' in that they are less likely to discuss their problems or 'co-ruminate' (Rose 2002). Boys are more likely to have a group of friends rather than an intense relationship with one, or a few, others. Perhaps this is because they trust one another less, or perhaps it is set against a cultural backdrop in which constructions of masculinity involve not being 'gay', so a degree of aloofness is maintained. Girls' relationships are often characterised by having an intense dyadic friendship with a 'best friend'. The intense nature of girls' friendships, for example dressing the same, having the same hairstyles, maintaining almost constant contact by phone, or via social network sites, if not in person, diminishes by late adolescence.

Selman (1980) proposed stages of friendship development. Pupils at transitional age could be in the pre-adolescent stage in which there is a high degree of mutual support and understanding and an awareness of other people's perspectives, or they could be at the adolescent stage in which their friendship with close friends provides a sense of personal identity. Recognition of each other's needs is apparent.

## The social and personal bridges

For some pupils the change from a primary setting to a secondary school setting allows them to adopt a new, and more adult, role. It enables them to leave behind a set of friends and seek new relationships and friends who are more in tune with their self-concept. This is where increased numbers in the 'big pond' can provide the opportunity for diversity and choice. The emerging adolescent will select friends who confirm their identity and enable them to grow into their new roles.

To enable young adolescents to arrive at a strong sense of identity, schools need to provide the forum to facilitate exploration of different viewpoints. To some extent drawing pupils from different feeder schools will introduce a diversity of intake from different backgrounds, which will inevitably enable pupils to meet others and discuss and explore different attitudes, values and beliefs. Unfortunately, one of the aspects of human nature is that 'like will attract like' and pupils will migrate to those who have similar ideas and backgrounds as themselves and who will confirm their sense of identity. 'Friends often have similar attitudes toward school, similar educational aspirations, and closely aligned achievement orientations' (Santrock 2010: 322). If pupils are feeling insecure, this migration towards similar people is even more apparent.

Many schools have taken on board the concerns of pupils moving between primary and secondary school and have recognised the support offered by friends and the boost to self-confidence if pupils move with friends. Hartup (1996) found that pupils who had friends coped more effectively with transition between schools than those who didn't. Some schools, as part of their transitional programme, allow pupils to choose a friend who will then be placed in the same tutor group as them in Year 7 when they move to secondary school (MacGrain 2010). Obviously there are problems in implementing this type of scheme when there are several feeder schools involved. Other schools focus on developing a group identity. It depends whether discontinuity or continuity in transition is encouraged, but, as in early years education in which a parent or carer acts as a 'secure base' (Bowlby 1988) to give the child confidence to explore their environment, the familiar friend can often act in a similar supportive role as a parent, so that 'the adolescent can make sorties into the outside world' (p. 11) and has the confidence to embrace new experiences.

## The importance of self-esteem

It has already been considered how an adolescent's self-esteem helps them to resist peer pressure. High self-esteem also gives them the confidence to overcome the potential problems that can occur during early adolescence as a result of the rapid physical, intellectual and emotional changes that take place. It is apparent that an individual's self-esteem is crucial in determining whether or not they can cope with the changes of transition. Santrock (2010: 139) comments that self-esteem decreases 'during and just after many life transitions'.

The use of social comparison with the peer group as a means of self-evaluation has consequences for the development of an individual's self-esteem:

> How well children think they 'stack up' against their peers plays a major role in the development of their self-esteem. If you think you are as good as your peers, your self-esteem is high, but if you see yourself as falling short, your self-esteem suffers.
>
> (Parke and Gauvain 2009: 443)

However, the downside of this is that, for someone to look good and compare favourably, someone else is going to 'stack up' less well against their peers and this is going to dent their self-esteem. This poses a problem for teachers and schools: How can they reconcile an increase in self-esteem for one pupil at the expense of the self-esteem of another? Is it something in which they can intervene? Will pupils make the comparisons themselves regardless of attempts to discourage this? The answer is that they will, because it is part of their natural development to make social comparisons. The important thing is to give every pupil a chance to excel in something so that they have the opportunity to develop self-esteem.

Self-esteem is closely related to the support from significant others such as family and friends (Caissy 1994; Harter 2006). The support structures provided by friends, family and the schools are fundamental in easing the transition. Figures 5.2 and 5.3 propose models of transition for a positive adaptive response or a negative maladaptive response respectively.

In Figure 5.2 the individual has support from schools, home and friends, which increases self-esteem and leads to a positive adaptive response in which the individual embraces new experiences, makes new friends, has a positive attitude to challenges

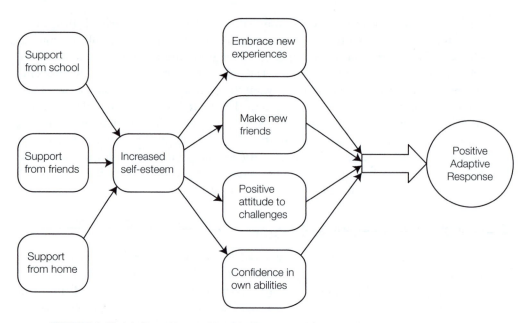

**FIGURE 5.2** Model of transition: positive adaptive response.

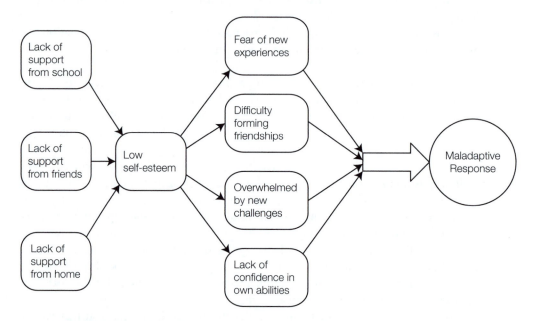

**FIGURE 5.3** Model of transition: negative maladaptive response.

and exudes confidence, all of which contribute to a further increase in self-esteem (see Figure 5.4). All of these factors would enable them to see transition as exciting and stimulating.

In Figure 5.3 there is a lack of support from schools, home and friends, which leads to a decrease in self-esteem and confidence; a dread of new experiences; difficulty in forming friendships; and a feeling of being overwhelmed at the prospect of any new challenges and changes. For this person transition is likely to result in a negative maladaptive response. The outcome of this is that the pupil is likely to become isolated, and possibly school-phobic, because they do not enjoy school (see Figure 5.5). This leads them into non-conformist, problem behaviour and they start to disengage from school.

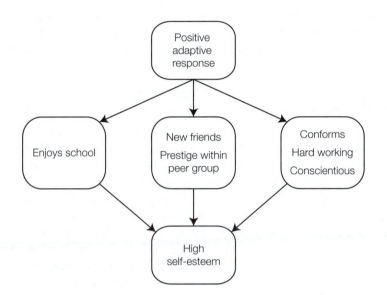

**FIGURE 5.4** Potential consequences of a positive adaptive response to transition.

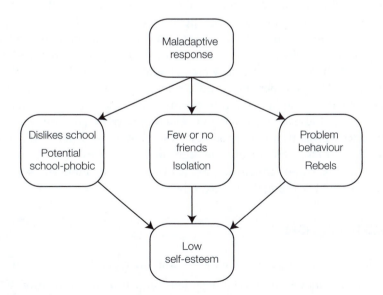

**FIGURE 5.5** Potential consequences of a maladaptive response to transition.

The situation can be exacerbated by bullying: pupils who lack self-esteem and who are not confident are often 'victims'. 'Students who are potential victims of bullying are often unsure of themselves and do not know how and whether they fit into the peer group' (Sullivan *et al.* 2004; 50). These factors all contribute to a further decline in self-esteem and a spiralling down in terms of social relationships and achievement.

The need for a strong support structure from all those involved in transition between schools is evident. Caissy remarks on how those pupils with a high self-concept do better academically and socially than those with a low self-concept. She comments that 'Early adolescents who have the best chance of developing positive self-esteem are those who have the love and support of their parents and the support of their peers, their teachers, and other significant people in their lives' (Caissy 1994: 214).

## Conclusion

Wolfe *et al.* (2006) focus on the importance of family and peer relationships in influencing beliefs and attitudes and ultimately the choices of behaviour that are made by adolescents. The influence of the cultural context, the wider community and the ethos of the school are also considered. They advocate the importance of multi-faceted, integrated programmes to encourage and promote healthy adolescent development. They also stress the need to understand adolescent development and to work with adolescents and the changes that they are undergoing, rather than imposing regimes upon them. Although their recommendations are applied specifically to reducing risk-taking behaviour in adolescents, there are significant parallels between this and measures to ease the transition from primary to secondary school.

Without doubt the support structures provided by family, friends and schools help to develop an individual's self-esteem and self-confidence. This enables them to embrace change and adapt positively to new circumstances. However, there is a tension between providing sufficient support to allow individuals the opportunity to develop their self-esteem and confidence and become autonomous, and smothering them, which maintains their dependence and curtails development. Whenever they are 'out of their comfort zone' they are going to be 'learning' because they will have to engage with new experiences and challenges. This often entails them drawing upon resources, social skills and resilience they never knew they had, and this can be exhilarating and liberating. Adaptation occurs only when an organism is exposed to threat. If we constantly wrap our adolescents in cotton wool and don't allow them to gain new experiences that involve them using their initiative and personal resources, then we will be stunting their development in both cognitive and social terms and therefore we will be doing them a great disservice.

## Questions to consider

- Why is development of an identity an important part of adolescent development?
- Are there times when social integration conflicts with self-identity? Which aspect do you think should be given priority?

- Do you agree with the idea that people are cast in different roles throughout life? Does anything about you change when you are in a different role or different social grouping, for example the way in which you behave or your clothes and appearance? To what extent do you become a different person?

- What are your views on providing support for pupils at the time of transition? Do you think we do too much for pupils and that they are more resourceful than we give them credit for, or do you think that more should be done to ease the transition between schools?

## Suggested further reading

Bee, H. and Boyd, D. (2010) *The Developing Child*, 12th edn. London: Allyn & Bacon. This book provides an excellent overall view of childhood and adolescence with extensive coverage of some of the key theories in developmental psychology.

Kroger, J. (2007) *Identity Development: Adolescence Through Adulthood*. London: Sage. This book discusses identity development in detail from adolescence through adulthood. It looks at various aspects of identity development and considers the different social contexts influencing development.

Wolfe, D., Jaffe, P. and Crooks, C. (2006) *Adolescent Risk Behaviors: Why Teens Experiment and Strategies to Keep Them Safe*. London: Yale University Press. This book is essential reading for anyone concerned about adolescent risk-taking behaviour. It includes theoretical underpinning, which provides an understanding of the physical, social, emotional and cognitive changes that take place during adolescence, and it effectively illustrates the reasons why adolescents might be drawn into risk-taking behaviour. It then provides solutions by suggesting health promotion programmes that empower adolescents by involving them in the process.

## References

Bee, H. and Boyd, D. (2010) *The Developing Child*, 12th edn. London: Allyn & Bacon.

Bowlby, J. (1988) *A Secure Base: Clinical Applications of Attachment Theory*. London: Tavistock/Routledge.

Caissy, G. (1994) *Early Adolescence: Understanding the 10 to 15 Year Old*. London: Plenum Press.

Erikson, E. (1968) *Identity: Youth and Crisis*. London: Faber.

Festinger, L. (1954) 'A Theory of Social Comparison Processes'. *Human Relations*, 7, 117–140.

Galton, M. (2010) 'Moving to Secondary School: What Do Pupils in England Say about the Experience?'. In Jindal-Snape, D. (ed.) *Educational Transitions*. London: Routledge.

Galton, M., Gray, J. and Ruddock, J. (1999) 'The Impact of School Transitions and Transfers on Pupils Progress and Attainment'. Research Report RR131. Nottingham: DfEE.

Goffman, E. (1959) *The Presentation of Self in Everyday Life*. Harmondsworth: Penguin.

Hague, H. (2006) 'Their Time Has Come'. Available from http://www.guardian.co.uk/news/2006/oct11/guardianextra3.guardianspecial62.

Harter, S. (2006) 'The Development of Self-representations in Childhood and Adolescence'. In Damon, W. and Lerner, R. (eds) *Handbook of Child Psychology*, 6th edn. New York: John Wiley & Sons.

Hartup, W. (1996) 'The Company They Keep: Friendships and their Developmental Significance'. *Child Development*, 67: 1–13.

Hayes, N. (2000) *Foundation of Psychology*, 3rd edn. London: Thomson Learning.

James, W. (1890) *The Principles of Psychology*. New York: Henry Holt.

James, W. (1892 [1961]) *Psychology: The Briefer Course*. New York: Harper Torch Books.

Kail, R. and Cavanaugh, J. (2000) *Human Development: A Lifespan View*. Belmont: Wadsworth.

Kroger, J. (2007) *Identity Development: Adolescence Through Adulthood*. London: Sage.

MacGrain, S. (2010) 'Transitional Procedures in a Primary School'. Interview.

Marcia, J. (1966) 'Development and Validation of Ego Identity Status'. *Journal of Personality and Social Psychology*, 3: 551–558.

Marcia, J. (1980) 'Identity in Adolescence'. In Adelson, J. (ed.) *Handbook of Adolescent Psychology*. New York: Wiley.

Matsumoto, D. (2000) *Culture and Psychology: People Around the World*, 2nd edn. London: Wadsworth.

Mead, G. (1934) *Mind, Self and Society*. Chicago: University of Chicago Press.

Miell, D. (1990) 'The Self and the Social World'. In Roth, I. (ed.) *Introduction to Psychology*, Vol. 1. Hove: Lawrence Erlbaum Associates in association with the Open University.

Muuss, R. (1982) 'Social Cognition: Robert Selman's Theory of Role Taking'. *Adolescence*, 17 (67): 499–525.

Parke, R. and Gauvain, M. (2009). *Child Psychology: A Contemporary View Point*, 7th edn. London: McGraw-Hill.

Rathus, S. (2006) *Childhood and Adolescence: Voyages in Development*, 2nd edn. London: Thomson Wadsworth.

Roberts, I. (2007) 'Adolescence'. In Zwozdiak-Myers, P. (ed.) *Childhood and Youth Studies*. Exeter: Learning Matters.

Rose, A. (2002) 'Co-numeration in the Friendship of Girls and Boys'. *Child Development*, 73: 1830–1843.

Roth, I. (ed.) (1990) *Introduction to Psychology, Volume 1*. Hove: Lawrence Erlbaum Associates in association with the Open University.

Santrock, J. (2010) *Adolescence*, 13th international edn. New York: McGraw-Hill.

Scheer, S. and Blumenkrantz, D. (2007) 'Rites of Passage During Adolescence'. Forum for Family and Consumer Issues. Online. Available from http://ncsu.edu/ffci/publications/2007/v12-n2–2007 (accessed 20 August 2010).

Segall, M., Dasen, P., Berry, J. and Poortinga, Y. (1990) *Human Behavior in Global Perspective: An Introduction to Cross-Cultural Psychology*. Oxford: Pergamon.

Selman, R. (1980). *The Growth of Interpersonal Understandings*. New York: Academic Press.

Selman, R., Levitt, M. and Schultz, L. (1997) 'The Friendship Framework: Tools for the Assessment of Psychosocial Development'. In Selman, R., Watts, C. and Schultz, L. (eds) *Fostering Friendships: Pair Therapy for Treatment and Prevention*. New York: Aldine de Gruyter.

Stevens, R. (2008) *Erik Erikson, Explorer of Identity and the Life Cycle*, revised edn. Basingstoke: Palgrave Macmillan.

Sullivan, K., Cleary, M. and Sullivan, G. (2004) *Bullying in Secondary Schools: What it Looks Like and How to Manage it*. London: Paul Chapman.

Waterman, A. (1985) 'Identity in the Context of Adolescent Psychology'. *New Directions for Child Development*, 30: 5–24.

Wolfe, D., Jaffe, P. and Crooks, C. (2006) *Adolescent Risk Behaviors: Why Teens Experiment and Strategies to Keep Them Safe*. London: Yale University Press.

# Smoothing the trajectory

## Primary–secondary transfer issues in science education

*Dan Davies and Kendra McMahon*

## Chapter summary

This chapter examines the particular problems that children encounter in adjusting to science lessons in their secondary schools. We argue that these difficulties stem largely from discontinuities between the kinds of science that children do in primary and secondary classrooms; the teaching styles adopted by primary and secondary science teachers; and the lack of useful assessment information transferred between the two. The chapter goes on to evaluate specific strategies for smoothing children's learning trajectory in science, including 'bridging units' jointly planned and taught across the transfer period, involving teachers observing each other's practice and agreeing on useful forms of assessment of children's scientific learning that can accompany them across the divide.

## Introduction

Although children in upper primary often look forward to doing 'proper science' at secondary school, their expectations based on images of explosions and test tubes of exotic liquids – sometimes reinforced by pre-transfer visits to secondary science departments – are often disappointed. Many experience a post-transfer 'dip' in enthusiasm and attainment in science (Schagen and Kerr 1999; Galton 2002), possibly contributing to the well-documented decline in young people going on to study physics or chemistry at post-16 level (JCQ 2010). Several studies have noted apparent *regression* following transfer (e.g. Jones and Jones 1993), sometimes attributed to the low expectations of secondary teachers (e.g. Weston *et al.* 1992), leading to repetition. Braund (2008: 29) identifies three other factors leading to post-transfer regression:

1    Teaching environments, teaching styles and teachers' language are often very different (pedagogical discontinuity).
2    Teachers in secondary schools often fail to make use of, or refer to, pupils' previous science learning experiences (curriculum discontinuity).

3    Teachers in secondary schools distrust the assessed levels of performance gained by pupils in national tests in science (assessment discontinuity).

In this chapter we will focus upon the gaps between primary and secondary practice in three important aspects of science education – curriculum, pedagogy and assessment – together with some of the initiatives aimed at bridging these gaps to ensure a smoother learning trajectory for pupils. It should be noted, however, that primary–secondary transfer necessarily involves a 'status passage' (Measor and Woods 1984) involving a change from childhood to adolescence (see also Chapter 3). Pupils expect, arguably, to experience a degree of discontinuity as a result of the move to secondary school. It is perhaps not surprising that in science, as in other areas of the curriculum, pupils may become temporarily disengaged. So, although we might be concerned about the majority who eventually get back on track with their scientific learning – particularly as their attitudes towards science may have received more lasting damage – it is the minority reported by Galton *et al.* (1999) who begin to become more seriously disaffected who should spur us to action to bridge the gaps between primary and secondary science education.

## The curriculum gap

The introduction of the National Curriculum (DES 1988) for science in primary and secondary schools in England and Wales had the effect of aligning the subject content for the two phases and, through various versions of the curriculum, key concepts have persisted: understanding the relationship between ideas and evidence; being able to undertake practical scientific enquiry; and understanding about materials, about living things and about different physical processes. All versions of the National Curriculum have also included in some form the notion that teaching should bring scientific *processes* and *concepts* together (see, for example, DfEE/QCA 1999: 83). However, the cultural/historical differences between primary and secondary meant that in practice this apparently common message has different roots.

The introduction to this book explains that the roots of primary education are in the 'elementary' tradition and are dominated by concerns with reading and mastery of number. Science, as such, is a relative newcomer in primary education. Although nature study had long been part of young children's schooling, primary science education gradually evolved through the 1900s within the context of a broader movement away from didactic approaches to teaching in the primary school (de Boo 2001). After the First World War, primary education in general was influenced by a number of 'thinkers', such as Dewey, Montessori, Froebel and Isaacs, who advocated a more 'child-centred' approach, focused less on the knowledge to be gained and more on arousing curiosity and interest and developing a broad range of skills. The primary curriculum was seen as being about activity and experience (de Boo 2001) and Piaget's emerging work on children learning about the world 'as scientists' was a further important development of these principles. These constructivist views of learning underpinned the influential Nuffield Junior Science Project (NJSP) in the mid-1960s (Wastnedge 2001).

The book *Primary Science: Taking the Plunge,* edited by Wynne Harlen (1985), provides a good overview of a primary perspective on science pre-National Curriculum. The notion of a child-centred approach is evident in many chapters, for example: 'From all around comes the invitation, from all around comes the challenge. The question is there, the answer lies hidden and the child has the key' (Elstgeest 1985: 10).

There is a common view that scientific knowledge is a discovery of the natural world, that the knowledge comes simply by observing what is there; this 'naïve empirical' view of science can lead to teaching that overemphasises children discovering ideas for themselves. Driver *et al.* (1994) challenge this, arguing that scientific knowledge is not there to be seen in the natural world; it is created by people, who construct concepts such as 'gravity' or 'habitat' to explain what they see. Science at the end of primary schooling is increasingly concerned with children understanding these constructed scientific explanations, although first-hand experience and enquiry continue to be vital. The considerable challenge for teachers is to continue to value children's own ideas and experience and work with those while also ensuring that they come to understand the scientific view. In more recent years, science at the end of the primary phase of education has also been affected by external testing of children's attainment at this point. This, taken together with the challenge of introducing children to more abstract scientific ideas, has had a significant impact on how science is taught. In England in particular, the impact of the end of Key Stage 2 Standard Assessment Tests ('SATs') has been to shift the focus away from children's own enquiries and towards drilling them to be able to reproduce a body of knowledge, largely conceptual knowledge in a pencil and paper test situation (Harlen 2006).

Although secondary science has also been strongly influenced by those recommending an enquiry-led approach, such as the Nuffield Secondary Science Education Programme, 1965–1974, and the Children's Learning in Science Project (CLiSP) (Needham 1987), secondary science education has focused on the aim of generating a small body of highly qualified specialists to serve the needs of industry, medicine and university-based research. The discourse of science education in secondary schools has been dominated by a view of science education as the transmission of an authoritative body of conceptual knowledge from one generation to the next (Osborne and Chin 2010). There is more emphasis on using a technical vocabulary and specialist equipment such as glass flasks on stands, voltmeters and oscilloscopes. The justification for funding secondary education more generously than primary is often about providing this equipment as well as retaining specialist teachers with subject expertise (Noden and West 2008).

This exclusive model of secondary science has been challenged (Millar and Osborne 1998) as being irrelevant to the needs and interests of the majority of the children in school, and the curriculum shifted in recent times in England with the introduction of the central theme 'How Science Works' in 2006:

Developing ideas and theories to explain the world is at the heart of science. *How science works* focuses on the critical analysis and linking of evidence to support or refute ideas and theories. Effective enquiry work involves exploring questions and finding answers through the gathering and evaluation of evidence. Pupils need to understand how evidence comes from the collection and critical interpretation of both primary and secondary data and how evidence may be influenced by contexts such as culture, politics or ethics.

(DCSF 2010)

Perhaps there is evidence here that the curriculum gap is reducing and that similar issues and concerns are common to both primary and secondary science teaching. However, one effect of the implementation of a national curriculum has been an 'upward drift' in the level of science coverage at primary level (Peacock 1999), which has further exacerbated the perceived 'dip' in achievement over the first few years of secondary school science (Ofsted 1998; Braund and Driver 2005).

## The pedagogy gap

Both primary and secondary science education have been much influenced by constructivist principles (see, for example, Scott 1987). However, the ways in which primary and secondary teachers have interpreted constructivist pedagogy have varied. Broadly speaking, primary educators have taken a more Piagetian approach, with a focus on concepts that can be derived from first-hand experience, whereas secondary pedagogy makes more use of discussion to define and explain abstract concepts using experiments to illustrate them. The constructivist models argued that the role of teachers was to provide experiences and support children in developing the process skills that would enable them to make generalisations from concrete experiences. Discussion was seen as having an important role in the development of process skills, such as in focusing attention on relevant variables, and in comparing results and drawing conclusions. Concepts that could not be attained in this way were seen by most authors as inappropriate aims for learning in the primary school. In common with the Piagetian constructivist models, the centrality of individual children's ideas as the starting point for conceptual change is the dominant feature of social constructivist concept-led models. Influenced by Bruner and Vygotsky, the Piagetian idea that children could not grasp more abstract constructs until the age of 11, which underpinned the constructivist models, had been challenged, and the role of the teacher in helping children to understand these ideas shifted accordingly.

As a result of this development in views of children's learning, in the last 10 years discussion of science pedagogy has increasingly focused on the role of talk in learning. Exploring this provides an example of how the two cultures of primary and secondary continue to lead to different pedagogical emphases. The influential primary science author Wynne Harlen acknowledges that:

It is possible that by following the ideas of Piaget, mediated by educators who have translated his views of learning into classroom experiences, there has been an overemphasis in primary classrooms on activity at the expense of discussion . . . Children need not only to have direct experience but to develop their understanding of it through negotiation – exchanging views with others. It is important, therefore, to plan time for discussion into practical work.

(Harlen 2006: 163)

However, there remains a strong sense of the child as an individual and of the importance of hands-on experiences: '. . . we may still think of the individual as taking from this shared understanding what helps them make sense of their own experience. Thus we consider learning being developed through interaction with objects as well as people' (Harlen 2006: 8).

A number of recent primary science projects funded by the AstraZeneca Science Teaching Trust (AZSTT), such as 'Pupil Questions' (Porter and Harwood 2010), 'Bright Ideas' (AZSTT 2010) and 'Discussions in Primary Science' (DIPS) (Braund 2009), have focused on encouraging children to engage in open-ended discussions without fear of getting the answer wrong. For example, the 'Bright Ideas' project includes a discussion activity in which children are asked to justify their ideas on 'the odd one out', for example out of chocolate, water and paper. The projects emphasise the value of talk in stimulating creativity and imagination and in engaging the children's interest in science. They also discuss cross-curricular learning, and explain the value of science as a context in which to develop language skills. Primary teachers are particularly concerned with protecting children's self-esteem, and this can lead to discussions that do not challenge children's ideas or ask them to justify them (Alexander 2001). This can be particularly true in science, when primary teachers may also be concerned about weaknesses in their own understanding of the subject matter and so limit the talk to 'safe ground'. Naylor *et al.* (2007) found that the use of puppets could overcome some of these barriers so that children and teachers could engage more freely in talk, and that it led to a far greater proportion of talk that involved reasoning.

In general, talk in secondary science pedagogy has focused on conceptual development and reasoning skills. Supporting children to reason and debate through argumentation (Osborne and Chin 2010) involves children using the structures of argument such as claims, warrants and rebuttals. As well as aiming to develop conceptual understanding, the rationale for argumentation is that it is fundamental to gaining an understanding of the nature of science, how science works: as rational logical debate with claims supported by evidence. It aims to motivate children by situating them as citizens making decisions about science-related issues in the wider world. Mortimer and Scott (2003) focus on the development of conceptual understanding through talk in secondary classrooms – they identify different 'communicative approaches' that have different pedagogical roles. In non-interactive–authoritative talk the teacher presents or summarises scientific ideas. In interactive–dialogic talk the attention is on the children's ideas. Interactive–authoritative talk involves the children, but it is the scientific version of knowledge that is the only accepted one. In this model the teacher will need to make some form of authoritative intervention in order to make the scientific ideas available, but it should be preceded or followed by children's dialogic talk so that children can make sense of it in relation to their own ideas (Scott and Ametller 2007). Their research was extended into the later primary years (Mercer 2007) focusing on topics such as forces, which have a high learning demand.

In their professional text for teachers, Howe *et al.* (2009) have applied the notion of 'dialogic' talk (Alexander 2008), which refers to primary education in general, to the particular context of science. As well as advocating a repertoire of different talk for different teaching and learning purposes they discuss how dialogic teaching helps build a classroom culture of mutual trust and respect, forming a community of learners building on each other's ideas.

Although discussion of children's ideas has been valued by both secondary and primary pedagogy, secondary pedagogy places more emphasis in science on reasoning and evidence, and less on the emotional and social dimension of learning, whereas primary science pedagogy has more emphasis on the creative, imaginative dimensions of science, perhaps overestimating what knowledge can be gained from first-hand experience.

However, the above are perhaps idealised descriptions of what actually happens in primary and secondary classrooms. There are differences in how the academic literature and practitioners see the relationship between scientific processes and conceptual learning. In her review of teachers' and educationalists' views of the aims of science education, Eady (2008: 17) concluded that:

> while science educationalists perceive this [the role of processes] in terms of capitalising on the interrelationship between skills and concepts, by eliciting and developing pupils' preconceived ideas and turning them into a form that can be tested, schools are more likely to focus mainly on developing process skills . . . and teaching scientific knowledge as a separate entity and specifically for tests.

The effect of national testing in science at the end of primary schooling since 1996 has been to emphasise 'transmission' pedagogy in the final year of primary school for revision purposes, leading to 'remarkable similarity in the way in which science teaching is organised in the primary and lower secondary classroom' (Galton 2002: 251). The ORACLE (Observational Research and Classroom Learning Evaluation) project (1975–1980) and its replication study (1996) found low levels of expectation by secondary teachers of pupils' enquiry skills and correspondingly high percentages of whole-class teaching in Year 7 (first year secondary) (Galton *et al.* 1999). Schagen and Kerr (1999) noted that the more formal and specialised environments in secondary schools tended to elicit higher expectations yet less independence in pupils' learning.

## The assessment gap

Providing pupils with accurate feedback on their achievements and ways in which they can improve is widely acknowledged to be the single most important factor in promoting learning (Black and William 1998; Hattie 2008). Yet the transfer of primary school assessment data on children's scientific learning to enable informed planning by secondary teachers appears to be one of the chief stumbling blocks in the way of smooth progression. The key issues are as follows:

1   The amount and quality of assessment information transferred and reaching science departments is inconsistent. This is partly because, particularly in urban areas, the traditional clusters and pyramids of primary 'feeder schools' have largely broken down in England after decades of increased parental choice. Therefore, secondary departments may be receiving small numbers of children from dozens of primary schools, and so ensuring that assessment data reaches the

right people – let alone that it is in a consistent, usable format – is a considerable logistical challenge. In many cases all that is transferred is a single number, the national curriculum level for science, derived from either teacher assessment or (up to 2009) standardised testing (Davies and McMahon 2004). The credence given to this number then leads to the second problem outlined below. Portfolios or examples of pupils' work are infrequently made available to secondary schools (Braund 2008), but, even when they are, secondary teachers may not have time to read them thoroughly or the information is not presented in a form that can easily be translated into curriculum planning.

2    Primary and secondary teachers tend to interpret assessment standards differently. These differences in interpretation have been amplified in England over recent years by the high-stakes testing and reporting regime. For primary schools, there has been a pressure to meet central government targets for the percentage of pupils reaching the 'benchmark' of level 4 at the end of Year 6, and for higher-attaining schools this pressure has been transferred to the level 5 threshold. Primary schools have therefore invested considerable time in preparing pupils for science tests, learning the 'right answers' to meet the criteria for higher-level assessments. The pressures on secondary science departments are quite different. Yes, they are required to move as many pupils as possible to the 'benchmark' level 6 at the end of Year 9, but there is also the notion of 'value added' that has been introduced into school league tables, attempting to measure the difference between the entry levels of pupils and their achievements at the end of the Key Stage. A pupil entering secondary school with a level 5 in science represents a problem for secondary departments as there is comparatively little room for adding value. So, although primary teachers have a vested interest in high levels of pupil attainment at transfer, teachers in secondary schools – understandably – claim that these levels have been artificially inflated by intensive revision or generous marking (Bunyan 1998; Braund 2008). Another reason for this scepticism may be that secondary science teachers do not see much evidence for high levels of pupil attainment in the early weeks of Year 7, as some material has been forgotten over the summer holiday or pupils may simply be shy and lacking in confidence to show what they can do in their new, unfamiliar environment.

So, in summary, partly because of the failure to consult records that are passed over from primary schools, and partly through distrust of the levels awarded by primary teachers, secondary teachers often set out to establish a new baseline (Barber 1999), often re-testing pupils within a few weeks of entering Year 7. In the rest of this chapter we now turn to attempts to bridge the three gaps we have identified above.

## Bridging the curriculum gap

Of the five 'bridges' identified in Chapter 1, one of the most significant affecting the quality of progression in children's scientific learning is the curriculum bridge. For example, Schagen and Kerr (1999) champion a 'curriculum-focused' model of cross-phase liaison, as distinct from a more commonly successful 'transfer-focused' approach addressing pastoral and bureaucratic concerns. In some respects, the curriculum bridge cannot be considered without reference to its sister, the pedagogic bridge, as what we teach is intrinsically bound up with how we teach it and the two are often used alongside each other: 'The range of strategies used by schools to address curricular and pedagogical discontinuities . . . include [sic] co-observations of teaching, improving teachers' knowledge of content taught each side of transfer, shared assessment of pupils' work and jointly planned teaching' (Braund 2008: 79).

However, as well as being arguably easier to implement, the curriculum bridge is considerably more common than its pedagogical equivalent, recorded by Galton *et al.* (1999, 2003) as being 'more or less in place' in about one-third of schools. This meant that the schools exchanged information about the curriculum and how they organised it, and sometimes schools co-ordinated what they taught. It therefore merits being considered separately before we move on to look at pedagogy.

One common strategy for bridging the curriculum gap is the introduction of 'bridging units' undertaken by pupils in the final term of primary school and first term of secondary school. For example, in the Improving Science Together (IST) project (Davies and McMahon 2004), units on the theme of 'travelling through air and liquids' were planned jointly by participating primary and secondary teachers, with support from local authority science advisers, primary science tutors from Bath Spa University and BAE Systems engineers. Projects could be interpreted flexibly by the schools involved, but there was sufficient commonality so that Year 7 teachers could easily interpret information from many different feeder schools. One unit on 'projectiles' involved 13 primary schools and three secondary schools, and had a important focus on modelling a 'real-life situation' in order to make it more accessible to investigation in the classroom. Pupils were to investigate how projectiles move through the air, considering the forces involved. The project was designed to form part of an introduction to science at the beginning of Year 7, either as a follow-on from investigative work carried out in Year 6 or as a stand-alone investigation for pupils from non-project schools. In Year 6 the assessment focus for teachers was 'planning and obtaining evidence'; in Year 7 it shifted to the higher-order skills of 'interpreting and evaluating data' in an attempt to build in progression through increased expectations.

The starting point for 'projectiles' in Year 6 was an exploration and observation of how different balls move through the air, considering the factors affecting the distance they travel. This situation was then modelled by rolling a marble over a sloping board, with the marble being 'launched' at pre-determined angles and velocities using a grooved ramp. In Year 6 pupils were to investigate the effect of changing the angle of launch, whereas in Year 7 they were to investigate launch speed. The understandings they gained from the main activity using the model were then to be applied in another real-life context, using 'stomp rockets' (toys propelled by compressing air in a foot pump). Additional activities were planned for both age groups, including in Year 7 the calculation of launch angles and velocities to 'hit' prespecified targets. There was evidence from teacher and pupil questionnaire and interview data in the IST project that the projectiles bridging unit had a reassuring effect on the Year 6 children prior to their transition and that they found the project engaging and interesting. There was also evidence of progression between primary and secondary attainment in the work of half of the pupils sampled. There was more use of line graphs in samples from Year 7 than in samples from Year 6, and more attempts at explanation rather than description of results in the secondary samples than in the primary.

Another example of bridging units in science is provided by the Science Transition AstraZeneca York (STAY) project (Braund 2002: 28). Rather than inviting teachers to write the units themselves, the STAY team produced two bridging units, one called 'Fizzy Drinks' and the other called 'Bread', each representing about 6 hours of teaching in Year 6 and 4 hours in Year 7. Investigations in each unit were framed in industrial and commercial contexts judged likely to appeal to pupils of this age. At the start of both primary and secondary sections of each project the teacher provided or read out a letter from a (fictitious) company inviting pupils to carry out investigations to solve a particular 'problem', for example whether or not the warmth of a 'proving oven' would be needed to raise bread dough. In the Year 7 part of the unit, a second letter from the bakery invited pupils to extend their investigations to discover the most suitable range of temperatures and minimum amounts of time that dough would need in the oven. Each bridging unit had inbuilt progression in both conceptual and procedural understanding. For example, in the 'Fizzy Drinks' unit Year 6 pupils learnt that the 'fizziness' of a drink is due to the amount of carbon dioxide gas dissolved in it at different temperatures, whereas Year 7 pupils considered what effect the colour of a can has on the warming of drink that it contains, thus shifting the conceptual focus to heat transfer (Braund 2008: 84). Progression in procedural understanding in the 'Bread' unit was achieved by asking Year 6 pupils to chose a place (cold, warm, hot and therefore a categoric variable) to store lumps of dough and then measure the increase in their size, whereas in Year 7 they were introduced to the concept of an experimental model – a convenient and controllable test-tube version of reality. They investigated the effect of a range of temperatures (a continuous variable) on the quantity (volume or number of bubbles) of gas escaping from a tube containing a mixture of yeast, sugar and water (Braund 2008: 84). Pupils in the STAY project were even more enthusiastic about the work than those in the IST project, stating that bridging work gave them a sense of comfort and familiarity at the start of the secondary course; improved their confidence in Year 7 as a result of experience of practical techniques or previous knowledge gained; and avoided repetition of primary experience as the Year 7 elements were complementary and covered new ground. Assessment of pupil work demonstrated less regression between Year 6 and Year 7 in pupils who had participated in one of the bridging units than in those from primary schools that had not been part of the project.

Despite the apparent benefits of projects such as IST and STAY, together with considerable government endorsement of such approaches (SCAA 1996; QCA 1998; DfES 2002) the use of jointly planned projects to smooth the transfer between primary and secondary education is relatively uncommon. The Council for Science and Technology study (CST 1999) found that only 10 per cent of 215 schools surveyed were making use of this approach in any curriculum area. There could be several reasons for this. For example, criticisms of bridging units include the perception by primary teachers that they represent an inroad of 'sterile' secondary practice into the final half-term of Year 6 normally dedicated to 'fun' or 'creative' activities, as well as a reluctance by primary teachers to assess the work in a way that could be useful to secondary colleagues (Galton 2002). Experiences in Australia (Scharf and Schibeci

1990) showed that lengthy bridging projects have a negative impact on pupils' attitudes at transfer, particularly low-achieving girls. Braund (2008) has identified a number of other potential barriers to this approach, including the breakdown of school 'pyramids' referred to above, so that not all pupils will have covered the primary part of the bridging unit; the stress of national tests at Year 6, leaving teachers and pupils exhausted, so that they may be unwilling or lack time to carry out and mark the work at the depth required; and the widespread expectation of primary pupils, noted previously, that they want to do 'new' things at secondary school whilst leaving their primary education behind. The evidence from the IST project would suggest that implementing a published bridging unit is unlikely in itself to influence attitudes and practice; rather, the process of collaboration provides the context for developing greater continuity in pedagogy between the phases. Bridging work needs to be integrated with other efforts to improve transfer in science, such as co-observation of each other's teaching, meetings to compare standards of work, and pupil induction visits (Braund 2008: 97). The biggest danger of implementing this approach in isolation is that it can easily become an exercise in papering over the deeper divisions between primary and secondary practice, providing the surface appearance of continuity in a science topic whilst underneath the discontinuity in pedagogy may persist. It is for this reason that we now need to consider the pedagogic bridge.

## Bridging the pedagogy gap

The differences between teaching styles of the 'two tribes' of primary and secondary teachers (Sutherland *et al*. 2010) can run much deeper than any apparent discontinuity in content coverage, so it is hardly surprising that schools operating the pedagogic bridge are much rarer than those seeking to close the curriculum gap. Galton *et al*. (2003) found that only 9 per cent of transfer initiatives focused on helping Year 7 teachers build on effective primary practice, in comparison with 46 per cent addressing curriculum continuity. They recommended:

> exploring specific pedagogic strategies that are known from research to improve pupil attainment and motivation. These include amongst other things,
> * helping pupils to work together *cooperatively*,
> * the effective use of appropriate *questioning techniques* and
> * the capacity of pupils to *evaluate* their own learning.
>
> (Galton *et al*. 2003: 72)

Simultaneously, the Council for Science and Technology concluded that 'effective teaching is likely to be more influential on pupils' attitudes and interests than curriculum materials or novel instructional techniques designed to affect them' (CST 1999: Appendix A). What appears to be needed are opportunities for primary and secondary teachers of science to arrive at a consensus of what constitutes effective teaching in their phase, and to build on the commonalities of practice around the point of transfer to minimise the dislocation for pupils.

Both of the bridging unit projects described in the previous section paid attention to the pedagogic as well as curriculum bridges. In the IST project, a feature of the collaborative planning process for the 'projectiles' bridging unit was a series of visits by primary and secondary teachers to each other's schools to observe science lessons. This was undertaken both before and during the implementation of the unit in order to promote greater mutual understanding of each other's practice, to enhance continuity and progression in planning and to enable secondary teachers to adjust the content of the Year 7 component in response to their observations of the primary phase 'in action'. As with all classroom observations – but particularly important given the potential for different interpretations of pedagogical intentions by primary and secondary teachers – such co-observation needs to be undertaken with clear ground rules:

1    Observations require a focus, for example on teachers' questioning, the organization of practical work, pupils' group discussion skills, etc.;
2    What is recorded should be factual or framed as questions to discuss rather than being judgemental;
3    The lesson observed must be discussed afterwards to clarify interpretations;
4    Records and notes should be left with the teacher observed, with nothing taken away.

(Braund 2008: 130)

The IST project overall focused strongly on effective strategies for teaching the procedural skills of scientific enquiry, drawing upon the work of the Association for Science Education and King's College London Science Investigations in Schools (AKSIS) project (Goldsworthy *et al.* 2000), the effects of which could be observed in common approaches to questioning and use of the language of enquiry.

In the STAY project, the teaching and learning approaches prescribed by the bridging unit materials were carefully designed to promote continuity in approach. For example:

- Lessons were planned around a three-part structure – starter activity, main activity and concluding (plenary) phase – and were presented in common formats;
- Common teaching strategies were used in each phase. These included the use of posters to help pupils plan investigations . . . concept cartoons to stimulate discussion of key ideas . . . and the letters referred to above.
- Common frameworks were provided for pupils to report findings of investigations and select and use appropriate graphing strategies.
- Emphasis was placed in lesson plans and teacher guidance notes on questioning and learning actions to guide pupils towards considering the status (for example, reliability) of the evidence they obtained from investigations.

(Braund 2008: 82)

The STAY project went on to extend the concept of bridging units to develop generic Scientific Enquiry Progression Tasks (SEPTs), which adopted a common approach whilst allowing clusters of primary and secondary teachers to drop their own content into the framework. Based on integrated progression of procedural and conceptual knowledge and understanding, each SEPT was designed to make progression lines in both areas and teaching approaches highly visible, encouraging teachers in both Key Stages to make explicit links both forwards and backwards to help pupils recognise this as progression rather than repetition. One further strategy used by STAY was co-teaching by primary and secondary teachers working together in the classroom on an element of the bridging units or SEPTs. Braund (2008: 134) found that this prompted reflections on subtle yet important differences in pedagogical approaches, and noted the surprise of one secondary teacher at the autonomy given to pupils by their primary colleague.

Another potential building brick in the pedagogic bridge is the use of information and communication technology (ICT). Cox and Webb (2004: 19) claim that 'the most extensive uses of ICT in education have been in science at both primary and secondary levels', whilst Cox and Abbott (2004: 25) maintain that it 'has had a positive effect on many areas of pupil attainment in science'. In a study of pupils' perceptions of using ICT in science during transfer to secondary schools, Beauchamp and Parkinson (2008) found that they actually used ICT in science more often in the primary school, but that this tended to be rather passive, involving information seeking, simulations and text-based activities. Although they enjoyed the practical nature of science in their secondary schools, pupils found the lack of ICT integration frustrating. Clearly there is potential here for active ICT tools such as data loggers to enhance pupils' experience of science in both phases. One approach that has been trialled in both secondary and primary schools but not yet used at transfer is the 'e-scape' e-portfolio assessment approach (Davies 2009). This includes an online assessment 'task authoring tool' that teachers can use to write sets of instructions to guide children through an enquiry activity, together with questions they can respond to using one of the tools on a hand-held mini-laptop such as a 'Fizzbook Spin'. For example, they could use the stylus on the touch screen to draw a diagram or have their handwriting turned into text using the 'transcribe' function; they could access the inbuilt webcam to take video or still photographs of their investigation as it progressed; or they could use the device's microphone to record short voice files reflecting on the decisions they'd taken in setting up their experiment. The structuring of the tasks into 'boxes' appearing in sequence on pupils' screens tends to drive the pedagogy in a particular direction, which may help primary and secondary teachers adopt a similar approach if used across transfer.

## Bridging the assessment gap

As a potential replacement for existing testing and teacher assessment schemes at the end of Key Stage 2, the e-scape project described in the previous section could assist in making children's primary science learning available to secondary teachers in the form of online e-portfolios. However, before dealing with the delivery mechanisms for assessment data at transfer, primary and secondary teachers need to arrive at shared understandings of attainment in science. For example, from initial discussions between primary and secondary teachers during the IST project above, some mismatches emerged in their understanding of progression, particularly in procedural aspects. The STAY project (Braund 2002: 124) included joint assessment by primary and secondary teachers of samples of work, specifying the process skills they would focus on for development, stating what year group they thought it was from, and providing one comment giving diagnostic and formative feedback. Some secondary teachers in this project refused to accept that the high standard of some primary work was actually undertaken unaided by children in Year 6!

With regards to the passing over of assessment data, at the beginning of the IST project, 60 per cent of primary participants perceived the use made by secondary science teachers of transfer information to be weak, a point agreed by the four participating secondary schools. To try and address this issue, pupils' work from the Year 6 elements, together with self-assessment and teacher assessment of their attainment in scientific enquiry, was passed from primary to secondary teachers before the end of the school year. This information was later combined with Year 7 assessment in order to obtain a fuller picture of each pupil's attainment; this was important in encouraging secondary teachers to use and value assessment carried out by their primary colleagues. The comments of teachers and observations of Year 7 lessons point towards some improvement in this aspect as a result of the material passed on as part of the bridging unit. Because secondary teachers knew about the context and focus of the work they were in a better position to interpret the judgements of Year 6 teachers, which arrived considerably earlier than in previous years. They had also developed personal relationships with many of the primary teachers, which led them to value their judgements and trust their understanding of scientific enquiry.

In the STAY project, teachers used a pupil self-review sheet focusing on science enquiry skills, revisited twice during Year 6 and again in Year 7, annotated by both teachers with 'up to three aspects that you think each pupil should concentrate on' plus one concise diagnostic statement for each aspect highlighted (Braund 2008: 38). This was accompanied by a short sample of pupil work from the bridging unit. The local authority arranged a collection scheme whereby each primary school's records were collected before the end of the summer term in envelopes coded with the names of secondary schools to which pupils would transfer. These were sorted and delivered into the hands of the heads of science at each of the receiving secondary schools. Nine secondary schools confirmed that they had received assessment transfer sheets from primary schools, yet only two said they continued the pupils' self-review scheme into Year 7, citing lack of time to read all of the information. A simplified version the following year was used less by primary schools as there was less opportunity to provide evidence of progression, leading Braund (2008: 121) to conclude that 'too much information is unusable and too little is not useful.' Assuming that secondary science teachers do actually want to make use of assessment data to inform their teaching in Year 7, getting the balance right in the transfer of material that can be acted on is a problem that has yet to be solved.

## Summary and conclusion

In this chapter we have argued that achieving a smooth trajectory in pupils' scientific learning across the primary–secondary transfer point requires bridging three important discontinuities: the gaps in curriculum, pedagogy and interpretation of assessment evidence. We have reviewed two significant projects that have endeavoured to bridge these gaps in various ways: by devising bridging units started by children in Year 6 and continued into Year 7; by bringing primary and secondary teachers of science together to discuss and observe each other's practice, plan together and co-teach; and by passing across meaningful assessment data whilst trying to arrive at shared interpretations. Ultimately the success of projects such as Improving Science Together lies in adopting a socio-cultural perspective on the issue of transfer; this involves breaking down historical cultural divides between primary and secondary science education by establishing shared understandings between teachers. Ultimately it is the joint planning of such projects and the arguments about issues that seem to be the key to success.

## Questions to consider

- What in your experience are the main curriculum and pedagogical differences between science education in primary and secondary schools?

- Does the new Key Stage 3 curriculum, which seeks to bring secondary practice closer to primary, remove the need for bridging units in science?

- Could primary schools bringing in science 'experts' from secondary departments be part of the solution or make the problem worse?

## Suggested further reading

Braund, M. (2008) *Starting Science – Again? Making Progress in Science Learning*. London: Sage.
This book summarises the York University STAY project and other research undertaken by Martin Braund into the issues of primary–secondary transfer in science.

Davies, D. and McMahon, K. (2004) 'A smooth trajectory: Developing continuity and progression between primary and secondary science education through a jointly-planned projectiles project'. *International Journal of Science Education*, 26 (8): 1009–1021.
This article reports on the findings from the Improving Science Together project, run in 24 schools in the West of England from 2000 to 2002 and involving primary and secondary colleagues developing greater understanding of each other's practice in science education through jointly planning and implementing a bridging unit.

Galton, M. (2002) 'Continuity and progression in science teaching at Key Stages 2 and 3'. *Cambridge Journal of Education*, 32 (2): 249–265.
This article reports on the findings of the large-scale ORACLE project concerning the pedagogy adopted by primary and secondary teachers of science. It defines some of the major discontinuities that this chapter has sought to address.

# References

Alexander, R. (2001) *Culture and Pedagogy: International Comparisons in Primary Education*. Oxford: Blackwell.

Alexander, R. J. (2008) *Towards Dialogic Teaching: Rethinking Classroom Talk*, 4th edn. Cambridge: Dialogos.

AstraZeneca Science Teaching Trust (AZSTT) (2010) 'Bright Ideas'. Online. Available from http://www.azteachscience.co.uk/resources/cpd/bright-ideas-in-primary-science/view-online.aspx (accessed 31 August 2010).

Barber, M. (1999) 'Taking the Tide at the Flood: Transforming Education in the Middle Years'. The Middle Years of Schooling Conference, Melbourne, Australia, 28 March 1999.

Beauchamp, G. and Parkinson, J. (2008) 'Pupils' attitudes towards school science as they transfer from an ICT-rich primary school to a secondary school with fewer ICT resources: Does ICT matter?' *Education and Information Technologies*, 13: 103–118.

Black, P. and William, D. (1998) *Inside the Black Box*. London: King's College, Department of Educational Studies.

Braund, M. (2002) 'STAYing the course: Smoothing the transfer from Key Stage 2 to Key Stage 3'. *Education in Science*, 197: 28–29.

Braund, M. (2008) *Starting Science – Again? Making Progress in Science Learning*. London: Sage.

Braund, M. (2009) 'Talk in primary science: A method to promote productive and contextualized group discourse'. *Education 3–13,* 37: 385–399.

Braund, M. and Driver, M. (2005) 'Pupils' perceptions of practical science in primary and secondary school: Implications for improving progression and continuity of learning'. *Educational Research*, 47 (1): 77–91.

Brown, J. M., Taggart, B., McCallam, B. and Gipps, C. (1996) 'The impact of Key Stage 2 tests'. *Education 3–13*, 24 (3): 3–7.

Bunyan, P. (1998) 'Comparing pupil performance in Key Stages 2 and 3 science SATS'. *School Science Review*, 79 (289): 85–87.

Council for Science and Technology (CST) (1999) 'School Science: Fit for the Future? A Preliminary Report of the Council for Science and Technology Education Sub-Group'. London: CSTE.

Cox, M. and Abbott, C. (2004) *ICT and Attainment – A Review of the Research Literature*. London: DfES/BECTA.

Cox, M. and Webb, M. (2004) *ICT and Pedagogy – A Review of the Research Literature*. London: DfES/BECTA.

Davies, D. (2009) 'Digital Portfolio Assessment of Secondary Students' Scientific Enquiry Skills: The E-scape Project'. European Science Education Research Association (ESERA), Istanbul, 31 August–4 September 2009.

Davies, D. and McMahon, K. (2004) 'A smooth trajectory: Developing continuity and progression between primary and secondary science education through a jointly-planned projectiles project'. *International Journal of Science Education*, 26 (8): 1009–1021.

de Boo, M. (2001) 'Setting the scene'. In de Boo, M. and Randall, A. (eds) *Celebrating a Century of Primary Science*. Hatfield: ASE.

Department for Children, Families and Schools (DCSF) (2010) 'The National Strategies: Science Framework'. Online. Available from http://nationalstrategies.standards.dcsf.gov.uk/node/102668 (accessed 26 July 2010).

Department for Education and Employment (DfEE) (1998) 'Teaching: High Status, High Standards'. Circular 4/98. London: DfEE.

Department for Education and Employment (DfEE) (1999) *The National Curriculum: Handbook for Primary Schools*. London: DfEE.

Department for Education and Employment/Qualifications And Curriculum Authority (DfEE/QCA) (1999) *Science in the National Curriculum*. London: DfEE/QCA.

Department for Education and Skills (DfES) (2002) *Key Stage 3 National Strategy: Framework for Teaching Science: Years 7, 8 and 9*. London: DfES.

Department of Education and Science (DES) (1988) *The National Curriculum: Science for Ages 5 to 16*. London: DES and Welsh Office.

Donaldson, M. (1978) *Children's Minds*. Glasgow: Fontana.

Driver, R., Asoko, H., Leach, J., Mortimer, E. and Scott, P. (1994) 'Constructing scientific knowledge in the classroom'. *Educational Researcher*, 23 (7): 5–12.

Eady, S. (2008) 'What is the purpose of learning science? An analysis of policy and practice in the primary school'. *British Journal of Educational Studies*, 56 (1): 4–19.

Elstgeest. J. (1985) 'Encounter, interaction, dialogue'. In Harlen, W. (ed.) *Primary Science: Taking the Plunge*. London: Heinemann Educational.

Galton, M. (2002) 'Continuity and progression in science teaching at Key Stages 2 and 3'. *Cambridge Journal of Education*, 32 (2): 249–265.

Galton, M., Gray, J. and Ruddock, J. (1999) 'The Impact of School Transitions and Transfers on Pupil Progress and Attainment'. Research Report RR131. Nottingham: DfEE.

Galton, M., Gray, J. and Ruddock, J. (eds) (2003) 'Transfer and Transitions in the Middle Years of Schooling (7–14): Continuities and Discontinuities in Learning'. Nottingham: DES.

Goldsworthy, A., Watson, R. and Wood Robinson, V. (2000) *Science Investigations: Developing Understanding*. Hatfield: ASE.

Harlen, W. (ed.) (1985) *Primary Science: Taking the Plunge*. London: Heinemann.

Harlen, W. (2006) *Teaching, Learning and Assessing Science 5–12*. London: Sage.

Harlen, W. and Jelly, S. (1989) *Developing Science in the Primary Classroom*. Edinburgh: Oliver and Boyd.

Hattie, J. (2008) *Visible Learning*. London: Routledge.

Howe, A, Davies, D., McMahon, K., Collier, C., Towler, L. and Scott, T. (2009) *Science 5–11: A Guide for Teachers*, 2nd edn. London: Routledge.

Joint Council for Qualifications (JCQ) (2010) 'National Trends in AS and A Level Entries 1995 to 2010'. London: JCQ.

Jones, L. and Jones, L. P. (1993) 'Keeping up the momentum: improving continuity'. *Education 3–13*, 21 (3): 46–50.

Leach, J. and Scott, P. (2002) 'Designing and evaluating science teaching sequences: An approach for drawing on the concept of learning demand and a social constructivist perspective on learning'. *Studies in Science Education*, 38: 115–142.

Measor, L. and Woods, P. (1984) *Changing Schools: Pupil Perspectives on Transfer to a Comprehensive*. Buckingham: Open University Press.

Mercer, N. (2007) 'Dialogic Teaching in Science Classrooms: Full Research Report'. ESRC End of Award Report, RES-000-23-0939-a. Swindon: ESRC.

Millar, R. and Osborne, J. (eds) (1998) *Beyond 2000. Science Education for the Future*. London: School of Education, King's College London.

Moore, C. (2008) 'Bridging the divide – Part 1'. In Braund, M. (2008) *Starting Science – Again? Making Progress in Science Learning*. London: Sage.

Mortimer, E. F. and Scott, P. (2003) *Making Meaning in Secondary Science Lessons*. Maidenhead: Open University Press.

Naylor S., Keogh B., Downing, B., Maloney, J. and Simon, S. (2007) 'The Puppets Project: Using puppets to promote engagement and talk in science'. In Pinto, R. and Couso, D. (eds) *Contributions from Science Education Research*. Dordrecht: Springer.

Needham, R. (1987) *Children's Learning in Science Project: Teaching Strategies for Developing Understanding in Science*. Leeds: Leeds University.

Noden, P. and West, A. (2008) 'The Funding of English Primary Education'. Primary Review Research Survey 10/1. Cambridge: University of Cambridge Faculty of Education.

Ofsted (1998) 'Science: A Review of Inspection Findings 1997/8'. London: HMSO.

Osborne, J. and Chin. C. (2010) 'The role of discourse in learning science'. In Littleton, K. and Howe, C. (eds). *Educational Dialogues: Understanding and Promoting Productive Interaction*. Abingdon: Routledge.

Peacock, G. (1999) 'Continuity and Progression between Key Stages in Science'. Paper presented at the British Educational Research Association Annual Conference.

Piaget, J. and Inhelder, B. (1969) *The Psychology of the Child*. London: Routledge & Kegan Paul.

Porter, J. and Harwood, P. (2010) 'Pupil Questions'. Online. Available from http://www.azteachscience.co.uk/resources/cpd/pupil-questions.aspx (accessed 31 August 2010).

Qualifications and Curriculum Authority (QCA) (1998) *Building Bridges – Pupil Transfer from Key Stage 2 to Key Stage 3*. London: QCA.

Qualifications and Curriculum Authority (QCA) (2002) *Transition Units (English and Mathematics)*. London: QCA.

Schagen, S. and Kerr, D. (1999) *Bridging the Gap? The National Curriculum and Progression from Primary to Secondary School*. Slough: NFER.

Scharf, P. and Schibeci, R. (1990) 'The influence of a "transition science" unit on student attitudes'. *Research in Science and Technological Education*, 8: 79–88.

School Curriculum and Assessment Authority (SCAA) (1996) *Promoting Continuity between KS2 and KS3*. Middlesex: SCAA.

Scott, P. (1987) *A Constructivist View of Teaching and Learning in Science*. Leeds: Centre for the Study of Science and Mathematics Education, University of Leeds.

Scott, P. And Ametller, J. (2007) 'Teaching science in a meaningful way: Striking a balance between "opening up" and "closing down" classroom talk'. *School Science Review*, 88 (324): 77–83.

Sutherland, R., Yee, W., McNess, E. and Harris, R. (2010) 'Supporting learning in the transition from primary to secondary schools.' Bristol: University of Bristol. Online. Available from http://www.bris.ac.uk/education/news/2010/transition-bristoluniversity.pdf (accessed 1 March 2011).

Vygotsky, L. S. (1987) *The Collected Works of L. S. Vygotsky, Volume 1*, ed. R. W. Rieber and A. S. Carton, trans. N. Minick. New York: Plenum Press.

Wastnedge (2001) 'A revolutionary project'. In de Boo, M. and Randall, A. (eds) *Celebrating a Century of Primary Science*. Hatfield: ASE.

Weston, P., Barrett, E. and Jamison, J. (1992) *The Quest for Coherence: Managing the Whole Curriculum 5–16*. Slough: NFER.

# Mathematics and transition

*Marcus Witt*

## Chapter summary

This chapter seeks to explore the following:

- some of the issues peculiar to mathematics in the transition from Key Stage 2 to Key Stage 3;
- the concept of curriculum discontinuity and why mathematics might be susceptible to it;
- attempts to make transition smoother, particularly 'bridging units' that are available as part of the Primary Framework for Literacy and Maths and other bridging projects.

## Introduction

There is considerable evidence of problems with the transition between primary and secondary school, with several authors (e.g. Coad and Jones 1999) suggesting that later problems of disaffection might have their roots in the transition period. This chapter seeks to examine the situation in mathematics and to ask what is peculiar to mathematics that might make the process of transition difficult. The transition in mathematics will be considered from a number of different perspectives with reference to the bridges metaphor introduced in Chapter 1. The social, personal and emotional bridge is considered in the context of mathematics anxiety. The chapter will examine why pupils in their final term at primary school rate mathematics as the thing they are least looking forward to in secondary school and whether the reality of learning mathematics in Key Stage 3 is as bad as this seems to suggest. The chapter also looks at the curriculum and pedagogy bridges and explores curriculum continuity and the reasons why mathematics might be particularly vulnerable to problems of discontinuity. There will be a brief examination of the 'bridging units' and other interventions that have been introduced to ease the mathematical transition between

Key Stages. Some general principles will be drawn from them that may point towards ways of improving transition in mathematics.

## Pupil anxiety prior to transfer

Research by Galton *et al.* (2003) has suggested that pupils in their final term of primary school are not relishing the prospect of doing mathematics at secondary school. In a survey of 609 Year 6 pupils preparing to transfer to secondary school, mathematics was the aspect of secondary school life (not just school subjects; pupils included things such as 'bullying', 'school dinners' and 'detention' in their lists of potential likes and dislikes) that was cited most often as the thing they were not looking forward to (151 of the 609 pupils ranked mathematics top). Of 304 boys in the survey, 66 cited mathematics as the thing they were least looking forward to (making mathematics ranked second behind English, which was cited by 70 boys). Among the 305 girls in the survey, mathematics was cited by 85, putting it clearly at the top of the list.

So what is it that makes mathematics so feared by pupils making the transition between Key Stage 2 and Key Stage 3? For some subjects such as science and design technology, the prospect of access to 'exciting' equipment and resources might induce more enthusiasm about the prospect of transition. There is some evidence (see Chapter 6) that initial visits to secondary school science laboratories do nothing to dampen expectation. Mathematics does not benefit from this anticipated boost in excitement, as it is a subject that Year 6 pupils will have been studying for 7 years and in which there is little in the way of new equipment to look forward to. There are a number of possible reasons why mathematics is seen as a particularly anxiety-producing subject. Its abstract nature makes it appear mysterious and therefore produces anxiety in some children. The widely held perception of mathematics as a set of rules and procedures that must be carried out in order to arrive at a 'right' answer, often in a very visible way in a classroom, can also contribute to its producing anxiety in children (Jackson 2008).

Although there is not a lot of research about mathematics anxiety among children in primary school, there is clear evidence that children this young are developing anxious reactions to mathematics and are able to articulate this (Newstead 1998). Mathematics is a subject in which pupil performance is very visible; in many cases, answers are either right or wrong. Some of the elements of secondary school that primary school pupils perceive, such as teachers being stricter, lessons being more regimented and formal and expectations being higher, might be particularly anxiety-producing in a subject such as mathematics and would exacerbate existing anxieties. For many children who are developing anxious feelings about the subject in primary school, overly demanding teachers and the very obvious nature of their mistakes in mathematics lessons are often triggers for deeper-rooted and more extreme anxious reactions (Fiore 1999).

Midgley *et al.* (1989), in a study conducted in the United States, found that teachers in secondary schools have less of a personal connection with the pupils they teach and are generally seen as less supportive of pupils than are primary school teachers. This is largely because of the inherent differences between primary and secondary education such as class size, the frequency of contact with teachers and the number of pupils with whom each teacher is involved. Given the structure of primary and secondary education in the UK, it seems reasonable to expect that this is also the case here. Children who are anxious about mathematics therefore need to be dealt with very carefully by their teachers and not put in high-pressure, highly visible, performative situations that could heighten their anxiety. Teachers in secondary schools are less likely to know about the specific anxieties of individual pupils and are therefore less likely to deal with them in an appropriate way (see Fiore 1999 for case studies of pupils whose relationship with mathematics was significantly damaged as a result of inappropriate demands made by secondary school teachers).

The study reported by Galton *et al.* (2003) also broke down the children's responses by the attainment level of the children involved. Among the 'low-attaining' children, both boys and girls, mathematics was most frequently cited as the thing that they were least looking forward to. Among the high-attaining girls, mathematics was still cited most often as the least looked forward to thing (cited by 13 of the 57 girls, placing it second behind the school's size). Among high-attaining boys, mathematics did not feature in the list of least looked forward to aspects of transition. This would seem to corroborate the idea that the performative nature of many mathematics lessons may be at the root of its unpopularity on transfer; higher-attaining pupils (particularly boys) appear to be less daunted by the prospect of secondary school mathematics than their lower-attaining peers are. Among the low-attaining boys there seemed to be a focus on academic subjects, with English and science ranked second and third, respectively, behind mathematics in the list of things least looked forward to. Among the low-attaining girls mathematics appears to have a particular status as a producer of anxiety, as the other things in the list were not academic subjects (with being bullied, detention and homework coming in behind mathematics in their list). West *et al.* (2010) found that children with lower attainment in mathematics had less successful transitions in terms of their academic progress than their higher-attaining peers.

What are the causes of these differences in gender? Studies looking at mathematics anxiety might shed some light here. Ma and Xu (2004) looked at mathematics anxiety among children in the United States and found interesting gender differences. They found that levels of mathematics anxiety varied much less among girls than among boys, with previous mathematical achievement a significant predictor of future anxiety. Interestingly, they found no such correlation in the opposite direction, suggesting that anxiety about mathematics is not a cause of poor mathematical performance. However, there are several studies that suggest that there is a causal link (albeit indirect) between levels of anxiety and mathematical performance.

Ma and Xu also found that girls were particularly vulnerable to the development of anxiety about mathematics just before and during transition between schools. Their study found that previous mathematical performance was a strong predictor of future anxiety about mathematics amongst boys, but that this prediction was much less reliable for girls. However, this causal relationship between mathematical performance and future anxiety levels was strong for girls at certain key times, particularly during the transition from primary to secondary education. Although the research was carried out in the United States, there is no reason to suppose that a similar phenomenon is not at work in the UK. The link may be exacerbated by the high-pressure end of Key

Stage tests that all children take towards the end of Year 6. Poor performance in these tests, or perceived poor performance, could have a strongly negative effect on girls' anxious feelings about mathematics. Such a hypothesis is consistent with the findings of the Galton *et al.* (2003) study in which low-attaining girls cited mathematics as the thing they were least looking forward to in secondary school.

There is evidence (Sutherland *et al.* 2010) that transfer to secondary school causes anxiety among children, and the Galton *et al.* (2003) study suggests very strongly that mathematics is one of the chief causes of this anxiety. There is considerable evidence to suggest that mathematics anxiety has a highly detrimental effect on the cognitive processes that are crucial to efficient mathematical performance (e.g. Ashcraft and Kirk 2001; Ashcraft 2002). Anxiety is thought to disrupt the cognitive system that enables people to store and process information concurrently, something that is highly important in mathematical functioning.

The connection between mathematical performance and mathematics anxiety was more stable for boys. However, there is considerable evidence (Galton and Hargreaves 2002) that mathematical performance for both boys and girls does stagnate or even dip on transfer to secondary school. The next section of the chapter will explore possible reasons for this dip in mathematical performance and will suggest things that schools might do to prevent the dip.

## Curriculum continuity

It is worth stating at the outset that the introduction of Standard Assessment Tests (SATs) into English schools has altered the nature of teaching in Year 6 (the final year of primary school). The position of schools in widely published performance or league tables is determined by their SAT results and therefore teachers of children in Year 6 are under great pressure for their children to perform well. Given this pressure, it is not surprising that the majority of schools run some form of 'booster' lessons to prepare children for SATs and give the children practice papers. Indeed, the National Strategies website provides materials for this purpose. These tests are the main indicator of academic performance in Year 6 (although many schools still report teacher assessments of the children). Given the importance of the SAT results, and the high profile that they are given, it is less surprising that there is a dip in performance when children enter Year 7 (the first year of secondary school) after a 5- to 6-week break from school.

Alexander (2009) is among many who lament the fact that, for many children, Year 6 mathematics is dominated by preparation for SATs. The introduction of SATs has, according to Alexander, led to a significant narrowing of the curriculum, in terms of both an increased focus on the core subjects and within the mathematics curriculum an increased focus on number. The emphasis on preparation for the tests may well colour the views of mathematics of pupils in Year 6. It is unclear whether this leads pupils to look forward to mathematics in Year 7, or whether such experiences put them off learning mathematics. The results from the survey cited above (Galton *et al.* 2003) suggest the latter.

A further reason for the dip in performance is a discontinuity in the curriculum between Year 6 and Year 7. The DfES (2004) highlights that ensuring curriculum continuity is multi-faceted and involves continuity in both content and the process of teaching. It emphasises the importance of secondary school teachers being aware of what their Year 7 pupils have covered in primary school and being able to adapt their teaching to accommodate this. The National Strategies and latterly the Primary Framework have sought to standardise curriculum coverage, but primary schools are not all using the Primary Framework.

Although curriculum continuity is not a problem that is peculiar to mathematics, there is some suggestion (Nicholls and Gardner 1999) that there are features of mathematics that make it particularly difficult to achieve. Secondary teachers report a particularly wide variation in mathematical attainment among children entering Year 7. The nature of mathematics is such that there are some activities and ideas that cannot be tackled until earlier, prerequisite concepts have been mastered (e.g. without a good understanding of place value, later work on written algorithms is no more than the application of a set of mysterious procedures). For secondary teachers who are dealing with children with widely varying levels of attainment and who need to get the lower-attaining children to a point at which they can access the Key Stage 3 curriculum, concentrating efforts on those children may be the most pragmatic way forward.

Sutherland *et al.* (2010) have characterised primary and secondary school teachers as 'two tribes' and highlight the fact that there is sometimes a gulf of understanding between them. Some secondary school teachers are sceptical about the information that their colleagues in primary schools pass on about the mathematical capabilities of the children. There are several reasons why the information may not be as accurate as secondary schools would want. Primary teachers may be unwilling to prejudice the attitudes of their secondary colleagues and may want some children to have the benefit of a 'fresh start' in mathematics. There is also the possibility (East Riding Council 2001) that some mathematical knowledge can be forgotten during the summer break. This can only heighten the 'two tribes' divisions and undermine secondary school teachers' trust in the validity of mathematics assessments made in primary school (Sutherland *et al.* 2010).

Although the notion of a 'fresh start' may be helpful to pupils who have experienced problems socially or with behaviour, it is potentially disastrous in the context of learning. The idea that primary schools have not taught the children well enough and that they therefore now need a 'fresh start' so that they can be taught properly can only exacerbate existing discontinuities in lesson content and style.

Other reasons for curricular discontinuity may include the following:

- Children from the different feeder schools may have followed different mathematical pathways, that is, some will have used published schemes of work, others will have followed the National Numeracy Strategy, etc. With the recent lowering of the status of the National Strategies and a number of schools opting not to use the new Primary Framework for Literacy and Mathematics, this problem seems set to be exacerbated in the future.

- Children from some feeder schools may have followed a more cross-curricular approach to mathematics in which at least parts of the mathematics curriculum were approached through other subjects (e.g. data handling through science), or in a more holistic way (e.g. enterprise games). The change in pedagogical approach may cause a dip in performance for some pupils; this may get worse if curriculum reform is implemented and a more holistic approach to education with subject-specific boundaries becoming more blurred becomes the norm in primary schools.

- Children in Year 6 take their SATs in May and then have 2 months before the school term ends. There is considerable evidence (Alexander 2009) that children's mathematical experiences before the tests are narrow. Year 6 teachers may be taking the opportunity in the period after the tests to engage their children in mathematical activities that are not explicitly tested such as more open-ended investigative and/or more practical, problem-solving, cross-curricular mathematical activities. If pupils then move to more regimented, subject-specific lessons in secondary school, the pedagogical discontinuity could be heightened.

The lack of communication between the 'two tribes' identified by Sutherland *et al.* (2010) means that secondary teachers are less likely to trust the evaluations of pupils from SATs and are therefore more likely to impose their own assessments as the pupils enter Year 7. This can lead to some pupils 'treading water' (DfES 2004) while their attainment is measured. This could account for a particular dip in motivation and performance among higher-attaining children.

## Bridging the gap

Many local authorities and the government through the National Strategies have tried to alleviate the problem of curriculum discontinuity by using 'bridging units' designed to ease the transition between Year 6 and Year 7. These units take the form of a series of mathematics lessons that are carried out at the end of Year 6 and are picked up again at the beginning of Year 7.

The Department for Children, Schools and Families' bridging unit 'Calculations and Problem Solving', which is available through the Primary Framework, outlines a number of potential benefits to such units. The fact that the units straddle the transition period means that the children move into Year 7 mathematics using material with which they are already familiar and in the context of an existing and familiar lesson structure. The guidance provided with the bridging unit materials is clear about the need to continue the lesson structure familiar to primary school children. The units also give the pupils an opportunity to demonstrate their ability in mathematics to their future mathematics teachers. Projects carried out specifically to ease transition in mathematics (e.g. those funded by the National Centre for Excellence in Teaching Mathematics, NCETM) suggest that children on the brink of transition are eager to impress their new teachers, but are also somewhat anxious about the potential demands made by specialist mathematics teachers. The guidance from the DCSF is also clear about the importance of collaborative mathematical work during the Year 7 lessons, to ensure that the participating children have the opportunity to work on familiar mathematical material with their new peers.

Although the 'bridging units' are intended to ensure some continuity for the pupils involved, they can also provide a further source of useful assessment information for secondary teachers. Examples of children's work are possibly seen as a more reliable source of evidence. The work completed during the Year 6 lessons provides secondary school teachers with evidence of the children's strengths and weaknesses, enabling more informed planning. Given that the children entering Year 7 will come from a range of feeder schools, there are clear benefits to secondary teachers of having examples of children's mathematical work done on a common theme.

A small-scale research project on the transition of pupils from Year 6 to Year 7 in Plymouth (Centre for Teaching Mathematics 2004) elicited responses from secondary mathematics teachers about the efficacy of the bridging units. Overall the responses were not particularly favourable, with only one-third of schools feeling that the bridging units had been successful. The reasons given for the lack of success centred on a lack of cross-phase visiting between staff and the fact that the units had not been completed by all the pupils. More concerning was the fact that half of the schools questioned reported that the activities were not sufficiently engaging for the children.

Given that the professional teachers who spend their lives working with children of transition age are effectively given the bridging units and appear to have little discretion as to the content, it is interesting that they reported the activities to be insufficiently engaging. This could be doubly problematic in that the bridging units are the first experience that these Year 6 children have of secondary school mathematics. If this experience is disappointing, then the anxieties, or disengagement, reported earlier in the chapter are more likely to come to the fore.

There has been a plethora of local authority and smaller-scale projects to try and improve pupils' mathematical transition experience. Many seek to remedy some of the problems highlighted by the Plymouth study (Centre for Teaching Mathematics 2004). The provision of bridging units through the National Strategies does not ensure that teachers from feeder primary schools and secondary schools meet; the work that the children complete during the Year 6 lessons either is sent to the secondary school or goes with the child on transition.

The NCETM has funded a number of projects. The Coventry project (NCETM 2009) involved teachers from feeder primary schools and from the secondary school planning a unit of work jointly. The lessons used mathematics to investigate waste and packaging. In contrast to the pupil responses about bridging units (Centre for Teaching Mathematics 2004), the children in the Coventry project were motivated and engaged by the practical and 'real-life' context of the mathematics. The report of the project identified this co-operation and informal sharing of the ways of working in the different Key Stages as highly important in the project's success. The teachers then used a 'portal' to communicate once the children had made the transition to secondary school. However, the members of the project team identified that communication from the secondary school back to feeder primaries was limited. This echoes findings of Sutherland et al. (2010), who reported that primary teachers would like to have been kept better informed about the progress of their pupils after transfer (and might have been able to offer useful insights to secondary colleagues). The joint planning in the Coventry project was time-consuming at a particularly busy period in the school year. However, the participants in the project acknowledged that, once the lessons were planned, they could be used again the following year. This raises the interesting question of whether it is the lessons themselves that were significant in the project's success, or the process of planning them jointly.

The NCETM also funded a transition project in Cornwall (NCETM 2008) that focused on the development of thinking skills in mathematics. Like many 'bridging units', the project included a number of lessons taught in primary school that would then be picked up after transition. The pupils involved in the project identified mathematics as being one of the things that was causing most anxiety prior to transition, but stated that encountering familiar lessons in secondary school had served to reduce anxiety levels. This particular project was instigated by the participating secondary schools, which produced the materials. Many of the teachers involved lamented the 'missed opportunity' for collaborative planning of the units.

Taken together, these different initiatives suggest some common principles for successful mathematical 'bridging units':

- The theme of the mathematics should be locally decided and based on something rooted in the 'real world', to be as motivating as possible to pupils.

- The initiatives are much more likely to be successful if a majority of the eligible pupils complete the work before transition.

- Most importantly, both primary and secondary teachers should be involved in planning the work through face-to-face meetings.

- Channels of communication should be established and information should flow both ways.

The findings from these NCETM-funded projects suggest that the provision of ready-made units through the Primary Framework or the local authority will miss the opportunity for collaborative planning, which is important in bridging the 'two tribes' divide.

## The reality of mathematics in Year 7

We began the chapter with some research evidence (Galton *et al.* 2003) that children's expectations of mathematics at secondary school were low at best and full of anxiety at worst. There is not much research investigateing children's experiences of mathematics at secondary school, but that which does exist suggests that the pessimistic outlook of those Year 6 pupils cited at the start of the chapter may by unfounded.

The study of Plymouth secondary schools cited earlier questioned the pupils about their mathematics lessons both before and after transition. The findings support the research of Galton *et al.* (2003) that mathematics is something that causes anxiety among pupils about to undergo transition. Whereas only 5 per cent of pupils 'strongly agreed' with the statement 'I worry about the mathematics I do at primary school' and 14 per cent 'agreed', these figures rose rapidly in response to the statements 'I worried about the mathematics I would do in Year 7', to 22 per cent and 30 per cent respectively. This suggests that, despite relatively low levels of overt anxiety about mathematics in primary school, more than half the children questioned were concerned about mathematics in Year 7. However, when responding to the statement 'I worry about maths now that I am in Year 7' the percentages who strongly agreed or agreed were 5 per cent and 10 per cent, respectively, suggesting that children in Year 7 are less anxious about mathematics than they were in Year 6.

Although this is a small sample, it does suggest that the pessimistic view of secondary mathematics is not borne out by the reality: fewer of the pupils questioned were concerned with mathematics in secondary school. There may be things underlying these numbers that are not wholly positive. For some children, a lack of worry may be caused by the mathematics being simple and well within their ability. If this is the case, they may worry about it less, but may still be experiencing a lack of motivation.

These findings are broadly in line with a more comprehensive study conducted by the National Audit Office during 2008 with more than 1,000 pupils in Years 7 and 8. The study found that the majority of pupils questioned were positive about their experiences of primary school mathematics (52 per cent agreed that mathematics lessons were interesting whereas only 24 per cent disagreed) and did not struggle overly (only 19 per cent agreed that maths in primary school was difficult whereas 52 per cent disagreed). Sixty-three per cent of those surveyed agreed that primary mathematics lessons had been enjoyable. This survey did not ask pupils specifically about their expectations of mathematics before transition.

When asked about their experiences of mathematics after transition from primary school, almost 50 per cent of the Year 7 pupils asked agreed that they were enjoying mathematics more than they had done at primary school whereas less than 30 per cent disagreed. This was despite the fact that almost 75 per cent agreed that the mathematics they were doing at secondary school was more difficult. Interestingly, almost 60 per cent of the Year 7 pupils questioned agreed that they were learning new things in secondary school mathematics as opposed to only 17 per cent who disagreed.

Interestingly, there was a significant difference in the responses of the Year 7 and Year 8 pupils who took part in the survey. The Year 8 pupils were unsurprisingly more likely to say that they were learning new things and that the maths they were doing was more difficult than it had been at primary school, whereas the number agreeing that they were enjoying mathematics more than they had done at primary school was significantly lower than among the Year 7 children. This suggests not only that there is a significant step up in the cognitive demands made by mathematics between Year 7 and Year 8, but also that this could be a time when pupils are beginning to lose their enjoyment of mathematics. Although there has been a lot of focus on the transition between primary and secondary school, the findings of this survey suggest that, at least where mathematics is concerned, there are 'transition' issues to be confronted within as well as between schools.

## Questions to consider

- Why might children be particularly anxious about mathematics in the transition from primary to secondary school?
- What factors peculiar to mathematics might cause a curricular discontinuity between Year 6 and Year 7?

- How might schools make bridging units more successful?
- What does research evidence tell us about pupils' feelings about mathematics both before and after transition?

## Suggested further reading

Galton, M. and Hargreaves, E. (2002) *Transfer from the Primary Classroom: 20 Years On.* London: Routledge.

This is an excellent book that examines changes in several transition issues.

Sutherland, R., Yee, W. C., McNess, E. and Harris, R. (2010) 'Supporting Learning in the Transition from Primary to Secondary School'. Bristol: University of Bristol.

This is a very recent report that looks at a number of issues relating to transfer.

National Audit Office (2008) 'Young People's Attitudes to Mathematics: A Research Study among 11–13 Year Olds'. London: National Audit Office.

This provides statistical analysis of the change in attitudes to mathematics between Years 6, 7 and 8.

Coad, J. and Jones, K. (1999) 'Curriculum Continuity in Mathematics: A Case Study of the Transition from Primary to Secondary School'. University of Southampton Centre for Research in Mathematics Education Working Paper. Southampton: University of Southampton Centre for Research in Mathematics Education.

This paper looks at how differences in pedagogical approach might contribute to a lack of continuity between primary and secondary school.

## References

Alexander, R. (ed.) (2009) *Children, their World, their Education: Final Report and Recommendations of the Cambridge Primary Review.* London: Routledge.

Ashcraft, M. H. (2002) 'Math Anxiety: Personal, Educational and Cognitive Consequences'. *Current Directions in Psychological Science*, 11 (5): 181–185.

Ashcraft, M. H. and Kirk, E. P. (2001) 'The Relationships Among Working Memory, Math Anxiety and Performance'. *Journal of Experimental Psychology: General*, 130 (2): 224–237.

Centre for Teaching Mathematics (2004) *Centre for Teaching Mathematics News*, Issue 12. Plymouth: CTM.

Coad, J. and Jones, K. (1999) 'Curriculum Continuity in Mathematics: A Case Study of the Transition from Primary to Secondary School'. University of Southampton Centre for Research in Mathematics Education Working Paper. Southampton: University of Southampton Centre for Research in Mathematics Education.

DfES (2002) 'The Literacy, Numeracy and Key Stage 3 National Strategies: Transition from Year 6 to Year 7 Mathematics'. Nottingham: DfES.

DfES (2004) 'Curriculum Continuity. Effective Transfer between Primary and Secondary Schools'. Nottingham: DfES.

East Riding Council (2001) 'Ensuring Effective Transition from Primary to Secondary School'. Online. Available at http://www.eriding.net/resources/assessment/030313_assess_ks23_tranguide.doc (accessed 28 March 2011).

Fiore, G. (1999) 'Math-Abused Students: Are We Prepared to Teach Them?' *The Mathematics Teacher*, 92 (5): 403–406.

Galton, M. and Hargreaves, E. (2002) *Transfer from the Primary Classroom: 20 Years On*. London: Routledge.

Galton, M., Gray, J. and Ruddock, J. (eds) (1999) 'The Impact of School Transitions and Transfers on Pupil Progress and Attainment'. Research Report RR131. Nottingham: DfEE.

Galton, M., Hargreaves, E. and Pell, T. (2003) 'Progress in the Middle Years of Schooling: Continuities and Discontinuities at Transfer'. *Education 3–13*, 31 (2): 9–18.

Jackson, E. (2008) 'Mathematics Anxiety in Student Teachers'. *Practitioner Research in Higher Education*, 2 (1): 36–42.

Ma, X. and Xu, J. (2004) 'The Causal Ordering of Mathematics Anxiety and Mathematics Achievement: A Longitudinal Panel Analysis'. *Journal of Adolescence*, 27: 165–179.

Midgley, C., Feldlaufer, H. and Eccles, J. S. (1989) 'Student/Teacher Relations and Attitudes toward Mathematics Before and After the Transition to Junior High School'. *Child Development*, 60: 981–992.

National Audit Office (2008) 'Young People's Attitudes to Mathematics: A Research Study among 11–13 Year Olds'. London: National Audit Office.

National Centre for Excellence in the Teaching of Mathematics (NCETM) (2008) 'Final Report – G070701 Developing Thinking Skills in Mathematics – Primary/Secondary Transition Project'. Online. Available from https://www.ncetm.org.uk/public/files/397299/Final_Report_G070701_Sir_James_Smith.pdf (accessed 28 March 2011).

National Centre for Excellence in the Teaching of Mathematics (NCETM) (2009) 'Final Report – G071217 Coventry Local Education Authority: Easing Transfer and Transition in Maths from KS2 to KS3'. Online. Available at https://www.ncetm.org.uk/public/files/501560/Final_Report_G071217_Coventry_Local_Education.pdf (accessed 28 March 2011).

Newstead, K. (1998) 'Investigating Children's Mathematics Anxiety: The Effect of Teaching Approaches'. *British Society for Research into Learning Mathematics: Informal Proceedings*, 13 (3): 49–55.

Nicholls, G. and Gardner, J. (1999) *Pupils in Transition*. London: Routledge.

Sutherland, R., Ching Yee, W., McNess, E. and Harris, R. (2010) 'Supporting Learning in the Transition from Primary to Secondary Schools'. University of Bristol. Online. Available from http://www.bristol.ac.uk/education/news/2010/transition-bristoluniversity.pdf (accessed 31 May 2010).

West, P., Sweeting, H. and Young. R. (2010) 'Transition Matters: Pupils' Experience of the Primary–Secondary School Transition in the West of Scotland and Consequences for Well-being and Attainment'. *Research Papers in Education*, 25 (1): 21–50.

# Children's reading choices

## Rethinking the curriculum

*Anny Northcote and Stephen Miles*

## Chapter summary

There is much debate concerning the different literacy practices that children encounter at home and in school. This chapter aims to investigate some of the issues around reading in the transition between Key Stage 2 (KS2) and Key Stage 3 (KS3). It will consider the range of literacy practices, literature and other texts and discourses that children may encounter at this age, and the relationship between children's choices in their reading and engagement with texts, alongside expectations of them as readers at home and in school. This discussion will be embedded in a brief overview of the changes in teaching reading in these two Key Stages in recent times, as well as some consideration as to what the future may hold. We will also consider how and whether teachers can work beyond those texts normally prescribed by the curriculum, particularly in KS3, and how a teacher can make informed choices about broadening children's reading experiences within the context of curriculum demands. We ask questions such as: What are the differences between the two Key Stages and what impact might they have on children as readers? Are the children inspired or disillusioned? The aim throughout this chapter is to investigate how young readers can have, and maintain, interest in such an important area of learning as they move from one Key Stage to the next.

## Introduction

It has been clear that, since the 1990s, in spite of a National Curriculum for English across all Key Stages, attainment in reading and writing is of particular concern. This stems, in part, from the numbers of children in Year 6 not achieving National Curriculum Level 4 in reading and writing in end of Key Stage Standard Assessments Tests (SATs). There is also a claim that, even after 15 years of national initiatives in the teaching of English, it has been found that:

> although England tends to perform at average or better in international league tables, we have *a long tail of underachievement*, with a significant minority of young

people failing to make good progress in their education; 16 per cent of children make no progress in English and maths between the age of 7 and 11, and 8 per cent of children leave primary school with levels of literacy and/or numeracy below those of the average 7-year-old.

(Sodha and Guglielmi 2009: 7)

The introduction of the Primary National Literacy Strategy (NLS) (DfES 1998) was an attempt to focus on teachers' understanding of the best ways to teach children to read and write. It was clearly identified as a 'Framework for Teaching', giving detailed objectives in what children were expected to learn and how the teacher was expected to achieve this, through a prescribed, though not compulsory, literacy hour, drawing on direct teaching strategies for children working as a whole class, in groups and independently.

There was a shift away from previously accepted pedagogies, which varied from school to school, to a more prescribed approach, which gave little room for allowing diverse teaching methods. The NLS established that all teachers needed a somewhat selective body of knowledge around the structure of language to inform skills and strategies that children needed to be taught, such as decoding and encoding, in order to be successful readers and writers. However, this raised many issues as to how children learn to read and write, in particular the role of the text; the link with spoken language in developing literacy competence; the needs of bilingual learners whose first language may not be English; children showing specific needs in language, which are not always identified, particularly in KS1; gender-specific issues; and the best way to include the new technologies in a predominantly traditional script-based learning environment.

There are two further components not specifically identified in the strategy but central to this chapter: first of all, recognition that literacy practices at home may be different to those of school, taking into consideration social, cultural and linguistic diversity, and, second, how these events should be considered alongside the school literacy practices in the classroom. It is evident that the reading materials children choose to engage with, at home or in the wider community, and those which are determined by the school curriculum can be very different. The potential shift in expectation between home and school, as well as between KS2 and KS3, needs to be considered if we believe in children as real readers not merely decoders of decontextualised scripts.

The demand for specific time and teaching strategies to be used, introduced into primary schools in the late 1990s through the NLS, was intended to be more in keeping with a KS3 or secondary school timetabled approach to English. However, although there were concessions to maintaining a primary pedagogy through flexibility in applying aspects of the framework and allowing more choice of texts than in KS3, it was quite confusing for primary teachers. The question as to whether this was useful for transition from primary to secondary was taken further, with a focus on how to teach literacy across the whole system rightly being promoted, with the intention of transforming the way we teach children to read and by blurring the distinctions between KS2 and KS3. It was considered appropriate to look at changes to the curriculum, pedagogy and organisation to ensure cohesion and continuity between the two Key Stages (Barber 1999).

The first initiative to reach secondary schools was a renewed emphasis on whole-school literacy, which followed closely the revision of the National Curriculum in 1999. This included an emphasis on 'Use of Language' across the curriculum, but this mainly meant another vain attempt to foist Standard English on children. This curriculum review also introduced the idea of 'writing triplets' – in which the complex conception of creativity was broken down into groups of supposedly similar skills, such as writing to inform, explain or describe, highlighting the government's obsession with rebranding English as a sterile view of literacy for a functional, secretarial, 'information age'.

Nobody could argue with the baseline of the Key Stage 3 National Strategy Framework for Teaching English that followed in 2001, which stated that 'Effective literacy is the key to raising standards across all subjects and equipping pupils with the skills and knowledge they need for life beyond school' (DfES 2001: 9). Transition was one of the key issues it was intended to address, along with boys' underachievement; it was also in some ways called forth by the lack of success delivered so far by the Primary Framework, as 'approximately a third of all children transferring to Key Stage 3 will be performing at Level 3 and below' and 'pupils' literacy development typically dips on school transfer' (DfES 2001: 7).

For children's reading, this whole initiative was a disaster. The emphasis was not on pleasure or quality in reading, but on abstract and unconnected lists of objectives, numerical targets and sterile functionality: 'It is hoped that teachers will use the objectives to translate numerical targets into curricular objectives, defining what pupils need to do to achieve the standards expected' (DfES 2001: 12). As a result, it came not to matter what text a child read, as long as objectives were met. Non-fiction came to dominate planning and exemplar materials, and even KS3 SATs, and students' reading of whole texts was replaced by bite-sized extracts from texts, not only at KS3 but even at GCSE, in which exam criteria favoured children who studied a chapter rather than a whole novel, or three poems in detail rather than a range of poetry. Philip Pullman analysed the situation astutely:

> Those who design this sort of thing seem to have completely forgotten the true purpose of literature, the everyday, humble, generous intention that lies behind every book, every story, every poem: to delight or to console, to help us enjoy life or endure it. That's the true reason we should be giving books to children. The false reason is to make them *analyse, review, comment* and so on.
>
> (Pullman 2003: 3)

Pullman might, arguably, be seen as not impartial or informed enough, despite having been a teacher and being an outstanding writer, but David Bell echoed his sentiments not long before he ceased to be HMI's Chief Inspector. In a speech made to mark World Book Day in 2005, he reflected boldly on the failures of the limiting strategy that both secondary and primary schools had been following in recent years:

When my inspectors visit schools, they frequently ask pupils why they think that reading is important. The answers are illuminating. Most pupils, even those in primary schools, will give essentially pragmatic answers. They will say that reading helps you to get a job. They will say that it helps you to do well in tests. They will say that it helps you to do well in school by teaching you good words to use or helping your spelling. All of these things are true but it is disappointing how few mention the joy of reading. Even more disappointing is how few will articulate the wider benefits of reading, how it contributes to our knowledge, understanding and wisdom.

(Bell 2005: 2)

These initiatives made it impossible for teachers to share common ground regarding reading in terms of breadth, depth or pleasure between KS2 and KS3.

Perhaps the authors of the framework needed to refer back to the Cox Report, in which it was stated that 'The best writing is vigorous, committed, honest and interesting. We have not included these qualities in our statements of attainment because they cannot be mapped onto levels' (DES 1988).

## Children as readers – expectations of school

By the end of KS2 children are assessed as being successful readers for their age if they achieve National Curriculum Level 4 in English SATs. Many secondary schools, however, quickly came to distrust the official KS2 SAT scores for reading and writing, partly because of well-recognised inconsistencies in marking, and partly because of primary teachers 'teaching to the test', but mostly because the SATs themselves test such narrow and arbitrary parts of what constitutes good reading and writing. Secondary schools therefore may retest children in the first few weeks at school, using Cognitive Abilities Tests, spelling age tests and similar judgements, before setting children or allocating reading support. Secondary schools are likely to pay close attention to the literacy skills of children arriving with a score below Level 4, however, as poor scores are rarely unreliable. Many schools offer catch-up support for these children, organised through the special educational needs co-ordinator, rather than through the English department, which involves the child being withdrawn from English lessons and taught in small groups; sometimes the withdrawal is from modern languages, following the questionable argument that a child who has not mastered their own language can hardly learn a second and sometimes they are withdrawn from a variety of subjects to minimise disruption. Whether a child with poor reading and writing skills is withdrawn to have additional support, or whether they join a normal English class, the change to secondary school is still massive. In primary school children study literacy as a subject or as part of cross-curricular themes or topics, but as they enter Year 7 literacy is either a catch-up skill taught separately to children with weak skills and understanding or embedded in whole-school cross-curricular initiatives. In place of literacy they now have English, which still differs in its scope from literacy, despite the shrinking and sterilising pressures of the English Framework and the Secondary Strategy, partly because of the love of literature among English specialists and partly because the National Curriculum still stands underneath the government's pedagogic guidance and objective-led advice, and that still requires a wide and challenging curriculum to some degree.

What is evident is that there is a range of testing, both formative and summative, in Year 6 and Year 7. Do tests, however, give us the full picture of children as real readers? There are many questions concerning motivation, enjoyment and imagination, which are hard to quantify, and reading certainly has its own dynamic. In a nutshell, learning to read well is hard. Writing is harder still. Unlike acquiring speech, reading and writing have to be learnt. There are skills that need careful instruction appropriate to the needs of the learner. This learning needs to take place in a social context for children to become successful readers. Although as literate adults we may read silently and privately, sharing what we read with others helps us make more sense of what it is we think we understand and develops our critical engagement with a text. We would therefore argue that reading is primarily a social activity, but as children go through the developmental stages of becoming a reader we clearly need to consider the linguistic processes that take place in the brain as well as in the social and cultural contexts. This is why any programme for teaching reading needs to identify strategies for supporting children's ability to make meaning central to developing their abilities to engage with texts, alongside decoding skills. The two processes do not exist in isolation but interact with each other.

By the end of KS2 children, for the most, are independent and fluent readers, able to make choices and express preferences with a degree of sophistication. Even those who may find reading difficult are able to express preferences if there is a choice to be had. However, there is something else central to learning to read. Just as acquiring language requires the presence of both a speaker and a listener, reading requires a text: a four-letter word with a multiplicity of meanings. Without a text, what can we interact *with*?

## Literacy practices at home and school

In our literate society we can choose what we read, at least when it comes to reading for pleasure. Whether this is fiction or non-fiction, in print format in the shape of a book or on a screen, with or without animated features, we are considered capable of making a judgement about what interests us. What motivates us to pick up a book from the shelf and take it to the checkout or library counter is in our hands. Is this the case with children? Very young children and beginner readers may need more guidance, but, as they become familiar with certain authors and illustrators, they are soon very capable of identifying the kind of books or texts they like best. As children become more experienced, the guidance might be reduced, although introducing children to new genres, media and technologies is an important part of the primary teacher's role. Then, just as the majority of young readers are becoming experienced and fluent and able to discriminate between books and texts for different purposes and interest, they move to 'big' school, where reading and writing is now called English and the choices they encounter in class must take them from children's literature to adult literature in 5 years. They may start Year 7 with author Michael Morpurgo (in the worst case, studying the same book as they encountered in Year 4 or 5) but must end with Steinbeck's *Of Mice and Men*, and even the poorest secondary English curriculum has to make that transition somehow. So, although most secondary schools treasure and encourage private and independent reading through library lessons, reading schemes, book weeks and the like, the class reader will become progressively narrowed by the demands of the awarding bodies at GCSE level.

This does not mean that the primary school has got it right, particularly in KS2. The demands of the National Curriculum, although 'streamlined' in 2000 (DfES/ QCA 1999), still leave little time for reading stories with children, browsing through books and that old-fashioned, yet worthy, pursuit of going to the library. Although children may engage with a range of written texts in different media in the course of their daily studies, the fascination of story has become somewhat diminished. The National Literacy Strategy (DfES 1998), by promoting a range of books, selected by schools, teachers and hopefully children, was useful in overruling the rather didactic use of reading schemes, but did not always recognise the value of reading whole stories, 'quality' children's literature and information texts for their own sake. The use of extracts has become common in teaching older primary children important textual and linguistic features, but often to the detriment of engaging them with the excitement of what a text has to offer. Eager and motivated readers and those with access to books may well go on to devour their favourite books in their own time, but for some children this is not necessarily an option, maybe because they find reading difficult or reading books may not be a common literacy practice in social contexts outside school, although they may be engaging in other practices of genuine worth. Is the child who spends time surfing the Web at home or swapping the latest collection cards in the playground, but who finds choosing a book and private reading difficult, deemed to be literate in the confines of the classroom? (Pahl and Rowsel 2005).

## Children's perceptions of what reading is 'for'

Reading for purpose and pleasure has long been the concern of many teachers and continues to be justified by many practitioners against the more skills-focused approach offered by the Literacy Strategies, which see reading as a means to an end in enabling the child access to knowledge and understanding of other subjects, as well as within English. The narrow focus on word- and sentence-level aspects, genre characteristics and other textual and linguistic features, taught through extracts rather than whole books, has limited children's engagement with reading for reading's sake. Clearly an important part of being a reader is to access information, whether it be interpreting a bus timetable, following written instructions to fix the washing machine or understanding the questions in a science A-level paper. Some might find this reading interesting and even enjoyable, but it is not really open to formal critical evaluation or informal discussion with others who have read the same text.

The debate around reading for pleasure and the role of literature within this is important when considering one of the key purposes of reading, which must be to stimulate the imagination and enjoy a good story. In 2001 the Progress in International Reading Literacy Study (PIRLS) of 150,000 9- to 10-year-olds in 35 countries found that in England pupils came joint first in terms of attainment in reading for literary purposes, but 27th in terms of attitudes towards reading. In 2006 pupils in England were 37th out of 45 countries, a significant worsening, with 15 per cent of English children having a poor attitude to reading, almost double the international average (PIRLS, cited in Lockwood 2008). Other surveys have revealed similar findings during the last 10 years. In particular, the Programme for International Student Assessment (PISA) survey of 15-year-olds' reading came to the conclusion that 'finding ways to engage students in reading may be one of the most effective ways to leverage social change' (Kirsch *et al.* 2002: 3). Sadly, the 2006 survey revealed a further decline in reading performance since 2000 amongst UK 15-year-olds relative to other countries in the survey (cited in Lockwood 2008).

The issues raised around reading and social class are considered further in Sodha and Guglielmi's (2009: 7) study, which found that 'Social background plays a stronger role in predicting attainment than in many other countries; at every level of our education system, children from deprived backgrounds with good prior attainment are less likely to make progress than their peers'.

Ofsted (2004), in a report entitled 'Reading for Purpose and Pleasure', found that even in those schools which were deemed to be successful in raising attainment in reading 'few were successfully engaging the interest of those who, though competent readers, did not read for pleasure. Schools seldom built on pupils' own reading interests and the range of reading materials they read outside school' (p. 4).

## So what motivates children to want to read?

This is always a hard question. We have high expectations of children in that being able to read is one of the first steps on a successful career path, but what kind of reading do we expect young people seeking employment to have? Can we be content with a functional literacy that enables those leaving school to complete application forms and communicate effectively enough in an interview? The reports and surveys (Sodha and Guglielmi 2009) into achievement, and the fact that in the UK there is a lack of interest shown in reading, may lead to the conclusion that there may well be a connection between motivation, reading and attainment.

Third-year undergraduates' questioning of young people about what 'being a reader' meant to them sheds some light on this. Josh, now 17 and a successful reader, talks about what reading was like for him when in primary school:

> I got bored easily and struggled to keep going . . . I read some school books and had to do book reviews, which I hated. I liked the library where my mum and I would choose together. I remember Dr. Seuss. All the children's books used to be stored in a wooden train that the children could sit in. There were about four or five carriages that kept different genres of books. I remember I used to pick what I wanted from a carriage and then sit in the driver's seat and read while my mum looked for her own books.

The differences between his memories are very striking. As a young child he clearly engaged with reading in many ways as he goes on to talk about his love of comics, making links to TV programmes and the pleasure he found in these home literacy events, which he was not getting from reading in school.

Rochelle, aged 11, has already switched off reading. An outgoing, friendly and talkative girl, she does not enjoy school, preferring outdoor activities:

> I read books at school because my teacher wants us to read, like loads. We have to take at least one book home a week and write about the book, like a summary of what's happened in it in our reading log. The more books you read, well whoever reads the most books in the term gets a prize, but I only ever take one book home so I've never actually won. I only read at home because I have to fill out my log book so I don't get into trouble at school, like literacy is important to my teacher and I don't want to look like I'm thick because I haven't read the book, because it's not like I can't read it, I just don't want to.

She goes on to reveal:

> I just can't be bothered with the effort of sitting down for ages and just reading. Reading is actually massively boring to me . . . All the books are quite girly really. The boys in my class read stuff like the Kernowland books, they seem quite good, like I think they're adventure books, but my friends, well me and my friends don't read them.

It is possible that Rochelle's lack of motivation stems from her lack of interest in the books she is expected to read. Reading in school has become a chore and the dominant force as literacy practices outside school are not discussed by her. Her perception of reading is already negative and not something she equates with pleasure. Clearly, in these cases, both participants are articulate and able to understand what is expected of them but have found reading at school unrewarding, yet both are capable of seeing that there must be more to it – there is something that might well draw them in, given the opportunity.

This begs the question as to how we are considering pupils as readers at a very crucial time of their reading development, particularly in terms of choice and preference between the ages of 10 and 12. The children and young people interviewed give us evidence that reading takes place in a social context, as they delve into sharing their memories in which reading, or lack of it, plays a central role in shaping their identities (Lockwood 2008). Also, although children with specific needs in reading are not the remit of this chapter, it is worth mentioning that those who may find reading more difficult than others often have similar reading interests to those of their peers, many of which will be rooted in shared cultural and literacy practices of friends, families and communities.

All discussion of what engages teenagers in reading rest on generalities, and, as Appleyard (1991: 99) nonchalantly asides, 'most teenagers do not voluntarily read much at all', which suggests that much of the articulate reflection gathered by researchers on the reading habits of teenagers will come from a minority for whom reading is a meaningful and valued activity. Therefore, to take one teenage girl, Hannah, and ask her to summarise her 'reading history' from earliest memory to date, and then discuss it with her, provides as interesting an option as any.

What counts as children's literature? One roll-call of 'classic' children's literature is provided by the Carnegie Award, presented annually since 1936 by the Library Association, and regarded as a prestigious recognition of excellence in children's literature. Such universally accepted key texts as *Watership Down* and *Tom's Midnight Garden* have received this award, which, in one sense, is a measure of the best in children's literature and a help to defining teenage fiction. Yet, at the same time, even a cursory glance at some of the names that do not appear, such as J. K. Rowling, R. L. Stine, Terry Pratchett, Roald Dahl and Jacqueline Wilson, shows that adult values rather than real reader popularity prevail. C. S. Lewis (a winner himself, of course) is quoted by Peter Hunt (2004: 3) as saying, 'I am almost inclined to set it up as a canon that a children's story which is enjoyed only by children is a bad children's story', which, by definition, excludes a very great deal of what children actually read. Thus, one of the issues in discussing children's literature is what qualifies as 'literature'. Even Hannah, discussing her own reading history, says dismissively, 'in between age 10 and 13 I did read a lot of trashy teenage girl books, none of which I really remember or are worth mentioning'.

Fortunately, for the future health of the nation, there are as many roads between a text and a reader as there are texts and readers; Hannah, throughout all of her contributions, remains a very practical reader. She reads for a (specified or unspecified) purpose and generally gets what she wants out of a text, rather than what another reader, particularly an adult one, expects. 'I think I try to read things which are going to help me, which are going to be interesting and relevant to what is going on in my life, and will help me make decisions and stuff'. The author's intentions, sacrosanct to literary critics of old, mean nothing to the autonomously reading adolescent. They read as much or as little as they want of a text and they read it in whatever way they wish, paying as much or as little attention to their reading as they determine.

Of course, it is changes in the reader that explain why books preferred at age 11 are often, but crucially not always, substantially different to those chosen by a 14-year-old. The knowledge, experience and desire that a reader brings to a text defines what they will derive from the experience of reading and how they will 'read' the text. As Hannah states:

> I don't think I would want to read it [a book in which she couldn't identify with the main characters] but it depends on the storyline because if there is other things going on in the plot or if the situation the character is in might make you want to read it.

She goes on to mention her all-time favourite book, *All Quiet On The Western Front*, and later her intention to read *The English Patient*: 'I find it better to read [books] with older people in it because I look up to them'.

It has been suggested that a preference for more 'difficult' literature follows from a literate teenager's growing acceptance that there are 'multiple versions' of the truth and from the teenager's predilection for a reality which stresses the 'dark themes' of life. Thus, although *River Boy* by Tim Bowler is arguably a somewhat old-fashioned rites of passage novel set in a partly timeless cultural context, and it is not surprising that the Carnegie judges liked it enough to award it their medal for 1998, in his acceptance speech Bowler struck a very modern note, discussing the perceived threat of other media to the written word and arguing with real feeling for the 'magic' of storytelling. 'Young people are the most complex creatures in the world . . . writing for them does not mean writing down, it means writing up', he said (Bowler 1998: 1). And on one further point he was adamant: 'We don't need to shield them from tough issues' (p. 2).

## Rethinking the curriculum

As the title of this chapter suggests, there is a need to rethink the curriculum offered to pupils at the end of their primary and beginning of their secondary years in terms of reading. A curriculum and resources that genuinely build on children's interests, lives and home literacy practices may go some way to reducing the tail of underachievement and engaging the competent, yet reluctant, reader.

If there is a need for a framework that is particularly appropriate to this transition age group, it needs to take into account the diverse home literacy events and practices of pupils. If we can accept that reading has a strong social and cultural dimension, a curriculum that puts the reader at the centre of their learning and draws on interest and background knowledge is essential. The original framework for both primary and secondary failed in this aspect:

> The framework itself atomised what it meant to be literate, for five to fourteen year olds, by listing around one hundred competencies a year for pupils to cover. In the main these lists comprised of items of knowledge, the implication being that pupils would know how to use them having been taught what they were. Each item was arranged under one of three headings – word, sentence and text level. The nature of the lists suggested that these items were discrete, acting independently of one another. The idea that the effectiveness of a sentence might be dependent not so much on its grammatical make-up but on the meaning of the words and the force of their communication, was absent from the document: so too was the context in which any given sentence or word might appear.
>
> (Marshall 2006: 69–70)

Although the primary framework has been streamlined, with more holistic 'strands' heading up the objectives in the Primary National Strategy, the focus is still very much on skills, with a particular emphasis on phonics at the early stages. However, it is not the purpose of this chapter to delve into the pros and cons of the 'Simple View of Reading' as a strategy, or to propose that schools and teachers simply abandon current teaching strategies or well-tried and tested resources, including those determined by National Curriculum assessment procedures and examination boards. These are in place to determine what is currently believed to be a good approach to supporting children to become readers in today's world. What we would argue is that these approaches should be scrutinised and questioned. The classroom is often a starting point for the children and therefore very influential in determining what reading is about.

The flow of information that pupils have access to is helping determine their interests and establish their understanding of the world, a crucial part of 'being a reader'. Such interaction and engagement through the current media culture is, of course, diverse and wide-ranging across the different pupils and families in any school or classroom. Similarly, how this is brought into the classroom is varied, as Ofsted's (2004) findings in primary schools and classrooms show and as David Bell commented himself in 2005:

> The Bullock Report famously concluded that, *'there is no one method, medium, approach, device, or philosophy that holds the key to the process of learning to read'* (HMSO 1975: 521). This principle is still ignored by some schools that continue to focus on a narrow range of approaches to teaching reading. Our evidence confirms Bullock's findings and shows that the most successful schools do indeed recognise the importance of introducing pupils to a broad range of strategies including the teaching of phonics.
>
> (Bell 2005: 3–4)

However, teachers are highly skilled professionals and are able to consider how to work with pupils in interacting with a range of texts and discourses beyond teaching a set of skills (Pahl and Rowsell 2005). The opportunities need to be created to allow them to understand and develop ways to meet the changing practices in a way that supports learners to engage with all types of texts: 'traditional', multimodal and radical.

Of course, if there is serious consideration of the interest and literacy practices of pupils, this must include an understanding of non-fiction. In secondary school, non-fiction reading and writing tends to reside predominantly in the subject areas. The KS3 strategy was developed to enable subject teachers to consider the language and literacy aspects alongside the subject discourse and not see the skills needed to access the material as solely being the job of the English teacher. The primary non-specialist KS2 teacher, working within the more recent Primary Framework (DfES 2006), is likely to consider the literacy aspects of a subject-based unit in the planning, under the guidance of both the literacy and the other subject co-ordinator. This is less likely, except in best practice, for non-English specialists at secondary level, but one consequence of the last 15 years of government guidance has been the prevalence of specific non-fiction units across all ages at secondary level in English departments. These are based on the same fundamental analysis of text types that the Primary Strategy employed, and, as Key Stage 3 SATs sometimes contained no prose or poetry at all, the incentive for schools to increase this aspect was strong. It is our view, however, that children learn little from such units, as the materials rarely engage with any of the passion or interest of fiction, and the extract-style texts that teachers use promote only very low-level skills that in truth rarely rise above primary levels of understanding, even in Year 9.

McCullagh and Jarman (2009: 143) argue that 'language, literacy and science learning are, or it is proposed should be, closely interlinked'. The discourse of any subject is part of engaging young learners to understand the subject itself. If scientific discourse is beyond the reach of the reader, the meaning is lost. It should be recognised that using the language of science is crucial to understanding, but how it is done should be as collaboration between specialists in both curriculum areas in primary and secondary schools and made accessible for all teachers to work with in their planning, teaching and assessment practices. This is not to say that the spoken and written scientific language has to be presented in the more familiar form of narrative, which most young children learn to access early in their 'talk', reading and writing, but there has to be some bridging between the familiar and the new, which should be carefully planned for in both Key Stages. The potential to assist pupils to make meaning and deepen their understanding through language activities based on the subject is a very powerful way to get pupils, particularly at this transition stage, to articulate their ideas and move them on from seeing certain subjects as difficult and intimidating at KS3. The primary teacher is familiar with ways of contextualising new language, as well as being aware of different learning styles and ways to engage pupils through visual and kinaesthetic learning opportunities to learn the new concepts and the language alongside, although this is not always as apparent in KS2 as in KS1. In KS3 teachers have the same skills, but see the end point for their pupils not unreasonably as being better scientific or geographical awareness; for them pupils' literacy is a means to their own subjects' ends.

Any good primary school should encompass a range of reading environments in the classroom, a library and prominent places around the school where reading and writing are displayed for all to see. This would include fiction, poetry and non-fiction by authors, children and their teachers and other adults. The range of books and other media should be extensive and, if there is a genuine belief in linking home and school, should include the diversity, cultural and literacy practices reflecting the lives and interests of the school community and that of the wider world.

In KS3 there is still the freedom to choose literature, although writing in 2010 with a recently elected coalition government it is uncertain what the future holds. The expected new National Curriculum for English and the demise of the Secondary Strategy suggest an opportunity for reading to resume its central place in English teaching at secondary level, but this will need support not only from government, but also from teachers, who must grasp the opportunity to aim high. As Hirsch (1987: 32) suggests, 'We will be able to achieve a just and prosperous society only when our schools ensure that everyone commands enough shared background knowledge to be able to communicate effectively with everyone else'.

To achieve such a curriculum and a testing system that encourages the breadth, depth and deep thinking there needs to be some reassessment of learning and teaching of the English curriculum and teaching frameworks. Between KS2 and KS3 consideration needs to be given to an overarching commitment to the nature of 'English' and what children need to know. A revised curriculum needs to establish rigour and excellence at the heart of passionate teaching of reading in both sectors. This means shared practices and developing teachers as readers, particularly in primary, and a selection and coherent sequence of the best of the literature that exists. Challenging opportunities to extend knowledge and thinking, including a requirement to secure reading outside the curriculum, are part of this. This needs to go further in providing opportunities for experience of the adaptation of a work of literature into another medium, or, for example, live theatre and performance poetry. Young readers need to learn how to choose more difficult reading for themselves as well as have opportunities to discuss literature informally with their peers. As Pullman (2003: 15) says,

> when you're telling a story, you need to let the story take its own time. Never mind these programmes and units and Key Stages; to hell with them. If the children want to go on listening, then go on telling.

## Questions to consider

- What in your experience are the main curriculum and pedagogical differences between the teaching of reading in primary and secondary schools?
- How do you think each sector learns from and supports each other to create a good learning environment in which pupils learn to read across the curriculum?
- Would closer attention to pupils' home literacy practices help them to become more motivated and successful readers at school?

## Suggested further reading

Marshall, B. (1998) 'English Teachers and the Third Way'. In *Literacy is Not Enough: Essays on the Importance of Reading*, ed. B. Cox. Manchester: Manchester University Press.

An insightful critique of the ways in which the Cox Report questioned issues around 'cultural' heritage, but considered how the 'crisis' in teaching reading led to an endorsement of such a heritage, which then informed the literacy strategy's closing doors on children's own reading choices. This is one chapter within this excellent book addressing a range of ways to approach reading.

Bearne, E. and Marsh, J. (eds) (2007) *Literacy and Social Inclusion: Closing the Gap.* Stoke-on-Trent: Trentham Books.

This book brings together a selection of readings by renowned authors to address the issue of social inclusion in relation to children's literacy. Gender, bilingualism, race and sexuality are explored in this enlightening text.

Wyse, D., Andrews, R. and Hoffman, J. (eds) (2010) *The Routledge International Handbook of English, Language, and Literacy Teaching*. London: Routledge.

A very thorough and weighty exploration of issues surrounding the reading and literacy debate with international perspectives from research and classroom practice.

## References

Appleyard, J. A. (1991) *Becoming a Reader*. Cambridge: Cambridge University Press.

Barber, M. (1999) 'Taking the Tide at the Flood: Transforming Education in the Middle Years'. Paper presented at the Middle Years of Schooling Conference, Melbourne, 28 March 1999.

Bell, D. (2005) 'A Good Read'. Speech by David Bell, Her Majesty's Chief Inspector of Schools, Ofsted, to mark World Book Day, 2 March 2005.

Bowler, T. (1998) 'Acceptance Speech', Carnegie Award. Online. Available from http://www.timbowler.co.uk/carnegiespeech.html (accessed 14 October 2010).

DES (1988) 'English for Age 5–11: Proposals of the Secretary of State for Education and Science and the Secretary of State for Wales'. London: HMSO.

DfEE/QCA (1999) *The National Curriculum.* Nottingham: DfEE.

DfES (1998) 'The National Literacy Strategy: A Framework for Teaching'. London: DfES.

DfES (2001) 'Framework for Teaching English'. London: DfES.

DfES (2006) 'Primary National Strategy: Primary Framework for Literacy and Mathematics'. London: DfES.

Hirsch, E. D., Jr (1987) *Cultural Literacy: What Every American Needs to Know.* Boston: Houghton Mifflin.

HMSO (1975) *A Language for Life.* London: HMSO.

Hunt, P. (2004) *An Introduction to Children's Literature.* Oxford: Oxford University Press.

Kirsch, I., de Jong, J., McQueen, J., Mendelovits, J., Monseur, C. and Lafontaine, D. (2002) *Reading for Change: Performance and Engagement across Countries. Results From PISA 2000.* Paris: OECD.

Lockwood, M. (2008) *Promoting Reading for Pleasure in the Primary School.* London: Sage.

McCullagh, J. and Jarman, R. (2009) 'Climate Change? A Comparison of Language and Literacy Practices Relating to the Teaching of Science across the KS2/3 Interface in Two School Clusters'. *Literacy*, 43 (3): 143–151.

Marshall, B. (1998) 'English Teachers and the Third Way'. In *Literacy is Not Enough: Essays on the Importance of Reading*, ed. B. Cox. Manchester: Manchester University Press.

Marshall, B. (2006) 'The Future of English'. *Forum*, 48 (1), 69–78.

Mullis I. V. S., Martin M. O. and Gonzalez E. J. (2001) *International Achievement in the Processes of Reading Comprehension: Results From Progress in International Reading Literacy Study 2001 in 35 Countries.* Boston: PIRLS.

OECD (2007) *The Programme for International Student Assessment (PISA).* Paris: OECD.

Ofsted (2004) 'Reading for Purpose and Pleasure: An Evaluation of the Teaching of Reading in Primary Schools'. London: DfES.

Pahl, K. and Rowsell, J. (2005) *Literacy and Education: Understanding the New Literacy Studies in the Classroom.* London: Paul Chapman.

Pullman, P. (2003) 'Isis Lecture'. Online. Available from https://docs.google.com/viewer?url=http://www.philip-pullman.com/assets_cm/files/PDF/isis_lecture.pdf (accessed 14 October 2010).

Sodha, S. and Guglielmi, S. (2009) 'A Stitch in Time: Tackling Educational Disengagement'. Interim report. Online. Available at www.demos.co.ukm (accessed 25 October 2010).

Twist, L., Schagen, I. and Hodgson, C. (2007). *Readers and Reading: National Report for England 2006.* Slough: NFER.

# The Fundamental Movement Skills programme (Steps PD)[1]

## Physical development challenges and opportunities in the primary school context

*Rachael Jefferson-Buchanan*

## Chapter summary

There is little direct investigation of the links between children's transition experiences from primary to secondary education and their motor competence, but this chapter suggests that the sometimes demanding and disorienting journey through adolescence might be facilitated by ensuring that pre-pubescent children have maximised their movement potential during the primary school years. Indeed, if Year 6 pupils left their primary schools as proficient movers, this could support their physically active adolescent years ahead, concurrently improving their future health and well-being. High-quality, research-led movement programmes, such as Fundamental Movement Skills (FMS), could therefore be valuable tools within the primary school, particularly for their potential to pervade the classroom and the entire school curriculum during a critical motor development period in young children. Proficient fundamental movement skills can be developed with opportunities for focused practice, encouragement, and effective teaching, learning and assessment strategies in the primary school context. If children entered secondary school with high movement proficiency levels, there could be less demand for traditional 'skill drill' tasks in the early stages of the secondary physical education context, with an ensuing positive effect on adolescent attitude and participation in physical activity. Accordingly, the FMS programme might prove to be one of the most cost-effective health insurances on the market, particularly as it is ideally placed in the early stages of compulsory schooling when physical activity and appropriate long-term health behaviours can easily be nurtured.

## Introduction

'The transition from primary to secondary school is probably the greatest source of discontinuity in the education of pupils' (Katene 2000: 188), but it can also often coincide with a steep decline in children's physical activity levels (Caspersen *et al.* 2000; Kimm *et al.* 2002). Indeed, many children and adolescents fail to meet physical activity guidelines (Riddoch *et al.* 2004; Jago *et al.* 2005), from which it might be deduced that the final years of primary school are potentially pivotal periods of change and influence. As regular participation in physical activity is related to short- and long-term physical, emotional, cognitive and social health benefits for both children and adolescents (Sallis *et al.* 2000; Yang *et al.* 2006), the importance of nurturing positive attitudes towards physical activity in the primary school environment is recognised. Children entering adolescence should have experienced a range of enjoyable, rich and progressive physical activities designed to facilitate the development of their movement skills throughout their primary school years. Positive, physical experiences in children's formative years can help ease their passage to the more specialised secondary physical education context, perhaps even encouraging their lifelong participation in physical activity, as there is some evidence to suggest that active children are more likely to become active adults (Boreham and Riddoch 2001). However, in the primary school context, physical activity time should not be limited to the physical education lesson; there is much potential to integrate subject areas and embed movement within the school curriculum through thematic approaches that can simultaneously address children's needs for '60 active minutes' per day (NHS 2010). The Fundamental Movement Skills programme (Hands *et al.* 2004a,b) supports this symbiotic relationship between movement and other subject areas, guiding teachers to underpin existing curriculum content with highly focused physical activities.

## Motor development and physical activity levels

Previous literature examining motor development and related performance standards of children has considered movement patterns, such as how fast they can run or how far they can throw by a certain age (Shephard 1982; Cratty 1986). Within physical development debates, there is often reference to critical periods of learning and children's neurological 'readiness' to learn something. Clearly, this derives from a maturational concept of children's development, in which children are believed to mature in similar progressive ways. Indeed, maturationalists (Gesell 1928; McGraw 1935) maintain that each child is born with biological processes that result in a universal sequence of movement skill acquisition, with maturation of the central nervous system being the trigger for the appearance of new skills. However, more recent research (Clark *et al.* 1988, 1989; Thelen and Ulrich 1991) confirms that children mature at very different rates, with complex interactions in their socio-cultural environments affecting their motor behaviour. Thus, 'development is seen as a discontinuous process with new patterns of movement replacing old ones' throughout the life cycle (Gallahue and Ozmun 2006: 8). This highlights the importance of fostering appropriate physical development opportunities early in the educational context, to ensure that the process and products of motor development are positively influenced in a key setting at a critical time.

It is unlikely that all children at the end of Key Stage 2 will have fully refined their fundamental movement skills such as catching, throwing, running, jumping and rolling, owing to a range of complex factors that will have impinged on the physical development process. However, the majority of children at this age do seem to have strong perceptions about their individual proficiency levels in physical education and sports activities, readily comparing these with those of their peers. Although it has been acknowledged elsewhere that 'children acquire self-confidence and self-esteem as a result of successful experiences, particularly in the motor domain' (Bunker 1991: 467), self-perceptions that err on the side of negativity – an apparent familiar trend in children with low motor skill levels (Hands *et al.* 2004a: 40) – mean that they tend to avoid and eventually drop out of physical activities, fearing 'public failure' or ridicule from peers (Rose *et al.* 1994). Because adolescent girls' attitudes towards physical education deteriorate as they progress through their secondary schooling (Bailey *et al.* 2005; Subramaniam and Silverman 2007), it would therefore seem particularly important to develop girls' motor skill proficiency well before this transition point. Moreover, low self-image or self-esteem has been linked to low preparedness for transfer to secondary school and subsequent poorer transition (McGee *et al.* 2003); the issue of children's motor skill development is thus more complex than at first sight if the relation between a child's physical and affective progress is accepted.

Evidently the foundations of proficient movement need to be acquired by the final years of primary school to minimise associated feelings of frustration, along with difficulties in learning more advanced skills, both of which could adversely affect a child's enjoyment levels and reduce the probability of them becoming a physically active adolescent. Because mastery of motor skills in childhood is likely to be a key determinant of later adolescent motor skill mastery (Branta *et al.* 1984; Burton and Miller 1998), early intervention would seem to be essential. Motor skill level and perceived physical activity competence also have associations with increased levels of physical activity in children, as, among 8- to 10-year-olds, not only is motor proficiency positively associated with physical activity levels, but also self-perception and preference for physical activity correlate strongly with motor proficiency amongst boys in particular (Wrotniak *et al.* 2006). If studies such as these are taken into account, the need for primary teachers to regularly review the content and processes of their physical education lessons is clear, particularly when a child begins to employ 'avoidance strategies' such as 'feigning illness or injury . . . going to the toilet . . . [or] forgetting appropriate clothes' (Hands *et al.* 2004a: 40). This type of avoidance behaviour could be symptomatic of a child's motor skill deficits, illuminating the need to provide them with individualised movement enhancement programmes before they commence a more specialised secondary school physical education programme.

## Primary versus secondary physical education

In relation to the physical development debate, what appears to be crucial for educators is how they present physical activities to children in the primary school and what form these activities might take if they are to promote motor skill learning. To help clarify such issues, the primary physical education curriculum warrants brief consideration in relation to its secondary successor. When a review of National Curriculum content is undertaken, there are visible links between primary and secondary physical education. Indeed, the primary physical education curriculum has a similar activity-based content to the secondary physical education curriculum, with its focus on dance, gymnastics, games, athletics, outdoor and adventurous activities (OAA), and swimming. The rationale behind adopting these types of activities across the age ranges was to encourage greater balance, whilst simultaneously moving away from a traditional games-dominated curriculum (Penney and Evans 1999: 44). However, at Key Stage 1, only three activities eventually became compulsory (dance, gymnastics, games), with swimming and water safety denoted an optional activity area. The number of activities is increased at Key Stage 2, when two activity areas from athletics, OAA, and swimming and water safety are added.[2] Unfortunately, because of the breadth of activities offered, primary teachers have tended to deliver National Curriculum physical education 'as a set of discrete experiences' (Griggs 2007: 61), rather than developing a curriculum with pupil learning at its centre that is strongly underpinned by the four aspects of the programme of study: acquiring and developing skills; selecting and applying skills, tactics and compositional ideas; evaluating and improving performance; and knowledge and understanding of fitness and health.

Within the Key Stage 3 and 4 physical education programmes of study (QCA 2007), the 'range and content' sections reveal the six primary curriculum activity areas once more, although only four of these at Key Stage 3, and two at Key Stage 4, are currently obligatory. The inclusion of 'fitness and health activities' at this level signifies a minor amendment to the general activity content of physical education since its primary roots. This gives an impression of continuity between primary and secondary programmes at the level of activity content. However, there were greater similarities when the four aspects spanned the primary–secondary programme, until these were replaced by 'key concepts' and 'key processes' in successive reviews of secondary physical education (QCA 2007). Surprisingly, despite ongoing criticism of the physical education programme of study for being a 'top-down' model, the more recent Primary Review (Rose 2009) failed to provide a similar framework of 'key concepts' and 'key processes' for primary physical education. It should be mentioned here that physical education was also renamed in the Primary Review (Rose 2009: 52) as 'understanding physical development, health and wellbeing'. It proposed a curriculum based on 'essential knowledge', 'key skills' and 'cross-curricular studies' (Rose 2009: 17), which would have been rather a missed opportunity to raise the profile of the process of learning in tandem with central concepts of physical education had an incoming government not aborted proposed changes. There is still clearly a need to forge a stronger primary–secondary curriculum bridge so that primary teachers might gain a clearer conception of the purpose of physical education, which could empower them to do what they do best: teach the children in their care (Carney and Bailey 2005).

The previous discussion implies that National Curriculum physical education at both primary and secondary levels advocates a focus on skills, knowledge and understanding that are specific to the activity context, as opposed to an emphasis on learning and teaching linked to broader educational aims and agendas. Indeed, at first sight the subject appears to be little more than a list of activities in which pupils participate, leading some to conclude that 'There seems an inherent danger of diminishing, or perhaps losing sight of altogether, the "education" in "physical education"' (Penney and Evans 1999: 22). It is thus questionable as to whether motor development in the primary school could ever be a priority at all while activity areas remain at the heart of the physical education programme of study. Although it might be argued that since the four aspects of physical education were added they have provided a clearer framework for the primary curriculum, or that the secondary key concepts and key processes have offered a stronger educational underpinning, misunderstandings of physical education as a subject still prevail at institutional and national level. The absence of a clear definition, together with a general lack of consensus, has contributed to long-standing disputes over the inherent nature and purposes of physical education per se (Kirk and Tinning 1990; Talbot 1995; Penney 1998; Doll-Tepper 2005; McNamee 2005). Despite this, it is still widely recognised that primary physical education is the most appropriate context for fostering the development of fundamental movement skills (Marsden and Weston 2007; Pickup *et al.* 2007; Stork and Sanders 2008).

## Notions of integration and holism

Although the first two aspects of the primary physical education programme of study emphasise acquiring and developing skills, and selecting and applying these, it is clear that there is still some way to go before the notions of education *in* and education *through* movement are valued, and indeed visible, in the day-to-day practice of every primary school teacher. Education *in* and *through* movement are components of the triumvirate model of physical education comprising education *about, in* and *through* movement (Arnold 1979; Bailey 1999). Within an activity-based physical education curriculum, education *about* movement can be fostered when children are introduced to a broad and balanced range of movement experiences such as dance, gymnastics and games. However, it is education *in* and *through* movement that presents the primary school teacher with a greater challenge, requiring them to help children understand the intrinsic value of physical education as 'insiders' (education *in*), simultaneously considering how physical education might contribute to other educational goals and areas of the curriculum (education *through*). In this manner, a more integrated, holistic conception of physical education would be developed, encouraging departure from the current activity-driven physical education programme of study. This would facilitate the dissolution of hierarchical boundaries between primary core and foundation subjects,[3] enabling the primary classroom to become a cross-curricular, developmental movement haven for young children. Without doubt, this would impact on the continuity between primary and secondary physical education, but it is debatable whether activities should be the threads that bind primary and secondary physical education together. As mentioned previously, learning processes and fundamental concepts of physical education could instead become the bridge, thereby easing the transition to secondary school physical education for Year 6 children.

Despite the fact that physical education is viewed as the principal societal institution for promoting physical activity in primary school children (Cale and Harris 2006), there is clearly an ideal opportunity for movement to be embedded throughout the school day if pedagogy and practice become more holistic and integrated in nature. Accordingly, motor development opportunities could be maximised during the primary school years, ensuring that children enter secondary school with a strong foundation in all of the FMS, ready and eager to taste the menu of specialist physical education activities. In so doing, the teacher would need to venture beyond the confines of traditional subjects, placing more emphasis on active, interactive learning in an effort to nurture and embrace movement whenever possible in the primary classroom. Davies (2003: 1) warns that it is easy to take movement for granted and neglect its importance in education because 'movement is seen to be a part and parcel of their [young children's] everyday lives'. However, the need to develop movement proficiency in young children cannot be underestimated, as the physical aspects affect all areas of development and learning.

The notion of integration therefore extends beyond the four walls of a primary classroom to a child's holistic development, even though many educational theories focus solely on the cognitive components of child development. However, 'the ability to think, reason, understand and learn also involves perceptual and sensory skills – and these cannot be separated from the physical development of children' (Marsden and Weston 2007: 386). Piaget (1952) seems to confirm this in his analysis of sensorimotor activities (those involving sensory perceptions and motor activities) during infancy (0–2 years), for he believes these physical explorations help provide the foundations of children's intelligence. Movement therefore becomes a vital component in the acquisition of increased cognitive structures, especially for infants and preschool children. Other theorists maintain that action, play and movement constitute the 'culture of childhood' (Bruner 1983: 121), with movement providing a meaningful context for children's learning. It is also widely recognised that neural pathways between the brain and body are strengthened by movement (above all if it is repetitive), and that movement plays an important role in shaping a child's personality, emotions and achievements (Lamb and Campos 1982; Williams 1983; Goddard Blythe 2005; Hannaford 2005). Schemas (generic knowledge) in movement thus merit recognition alongside other aspects of children's learning. Davies (2003: 102) suggests, for example, that vertical schemas are used as children repeatedly climb up and down, whereas dynamic schemas are visible when a tricycle is energetically pedalled. Movement experiences might also constitute some of the first opportunities that young children have to develop social interactions, problem-solving abilities and their self-esteem. Bearing these points in mind, it could be construed that physical activity should not merely be limited to the physical education lesson, for movement truly engages the whole child and has the potential to enhance and integrate all aspects of children's development.

## Fundamental Movement Skills programme

Notions of integration and holism are central to the FMS programme, constituting one of its two aims: 'The Resource emphasises the importance of integration and valuing the social, emotional, linguistic, creative, spiritual and cognitive needs of children as well as their movement skills' (Hands *et al.* 2004a: 1). Integration and holism also manifest themselves through the programme's six key understandings:

FMS are important in the development of the 'whole child'; FMS, like all learning, is best supported when the school, family and community work together; FMS can be embedded in everyday classroom activities; FMS can be learned through play; movement skill development is age related not age dependent; and early childhood is the optimal time to teach and learn FMS.

(Hands *et al.* 2004a: 19–20)

These key understandings emphasise that developing proficiency in FMS can support the child's all-round development, and that physical activity should be an intrinsic and integral part of the primary school curriculum. Moreover, they illuminate the need for a holistic approach to the learning of FMS with shared practice between the home and school community, which should be underpinned by the motivating context of play. The importance of children 'moving to learn' and 'learning to move' is also apparent, as it is believed that, when they become actively involved in their own physical development processes, children gain positive early attitudes towards physical activity with resultant positive effects on self-image, self-confidence, and health and well-being.

Although the process of learning, teaching and assessing FMS is recognised as being interwoven and interdependent, the FMS resource does provide a planning cycle with six sequential steps: identify children's interests, strengths and needs; choose focus skill or skills and identify possible learning outcomes; assess each child's level of FMS achievement; plan and implement appropriate learning experiences; continue to assess each child's level of FMS achievement; and share the information gathered (Hands *et al.* 2004a: 9). As the teacher gains confidence in their teaching of FMS, this planning cycle can be separated out and used more creatively because of its fluid, multiple entry point structure. Reflection points for each of the six steps help promote teacher understanding and are framed by the six key understandings. Within the first step it is acknowledged that children's interests, strengths and needs are situated in the context of their family, community and school. Ways in which learning programmes might develop these are suggested through such strategies as talking to the children, families, community, other teachers, as well as considering how certain skills might support school topics and the whole-school plan (Hands *et al.* 2004a: 26). When considering the choice of focus skill, it is through the second step of the planning cycle that the need for up to 10 hours of quality teaching to develop proficiency in any FMS is revealed (Kelly 1989). A suggested order for teaching the 22 FMS[4] is given for children aged 4–8 years, comprising four or five body management, locomotor and object control skills per school year. These three FMS categories were determined in collaboration with a number of teachers who were directly involved in the FMS programme development, in an endeavour to facilitate their individual planning processes.

During the assessment of a child's achievement of FMS (Step 3 of the planning cycle), it is imperative that information is gathered from a range of experiences over time. In this manner, a comprehensive profile of the child's learning in FMS can be constructed, through an assessment process that endeavours to be fair, valid, explicit and educative (Hands *et al.* 2004a: 30). It is through two different 'Tools' in FMS Book 2 that an insight into a broad range of assessment strategies is gained. 'Tools 1' provides a detailed review of each of the 22 FMS with guidance on the importance of each skill criterion, successful teaching strategies, and an Observation Record for teachers to record their skill observations. The Observation Records detail the three different types of movement, thereby aiming to scaffold a systematic analysis of continuous, explosive and receptive skills. However, they are merely one of many assessment strategies that might be utilised by the teacher, and in 'Tools 2' a number of alternatives are offered: learning stories, rubrics, profiles, teaching cards, photographs, images, drawings, video, talks with children, audio, self-reflection and peer reflection.

Children can learn and apply FMS in many different ways, and Step 4 of the planning cycle focuses on the planning and implementing of learning experiences. These have been grouped under the headings of child-structured and teacher-structured learning experiences (Hands *et al.* 2004b: Tools 3), with detailed examples given to encourage different ways of using them to nurture FMS development. Child-structured learning experiences include playground play, invented games, movement to music, and dramatic play. Within teacher-structured experiences there are obstacle courses, circuits, learning centres, play stations, skill practices, problem-solving, task sheets, contracts, peer teaching, long walk or run, games (simple, co-operative, modified), poems, rhymes and songs, aerobics, dance, gymnastics, sports, outdoor pursuits and performance tasks. It is recognised that some learning experiences might be initially led by the teacher but subsequently structured by the children, and there is an emphasis at all times on experiences being both relevant and meaningful. The need to differentiate learning experiences to cater for children's individual needs is also considered essential, and ways to achieve this are deliberated to ensure that participation levels are maximised.

As teachers will continue to gather information about children's movement proficiency levels during learning experiences, Step 5 of the planning cycle recommends ongoing assessment of children's achievement of FMS. It is acknowledged here that teachers, despite their efforts to differentiate, may still be concerned about a child's skill performance and so further reading of the 'Children with Movement Difficulties' section is suggested. In the final step of the planning cycle, the importance of sharing information about the children and their skill development is highlighted. The need to include children, other teachers, the school, other adults and the community is emphasised, in keeping with the FMS key understanding that the learning of FMS is accelerated and enhanced when the school, family and community collaborate and support one another. A wide range of strategies for sharing information are proposed, some of which include postcards, class lists, letters, newsletters, certificates, portfolios, reports, parent–child–teacher conferences, school assemblies, carnivals (events that show children's learning and development) and school–community displays (Hands *et al.* 2004b: Tools 4).

## Challenges and opportunities

There are challenges and opportunities within the primary physical education context for the FMS programme, as well as for physical development in terms of its status and prominence. Challenges include the diversionary effect of a plethora of initiatives in all sectors of education introduced since physical education became compulsory in the National Curriculum. These have impacted on policy and practices in the subject, contributing to its marginalisation as one of several foundation subjects, and a subsequent reduction of physical education hours in primary Initial Teacher Education (ITE) (Pickup and Price 2007). In conjunction with this, there has been a complete restructuring of the Association for Physical Education (afPE), and the birth of a national continuing professional development (CPD) programme for primary physical education. Movement programmes have emerged during this period, perhaps as a result of neo-liberalism that has contributed to a 'market philosophy in education, schools and HPE [Health and Physical Education]' (Macdonald *et al.* 2008: 6). This phenomenon, together with political and socio-cultural educational reform, seems to have led to a commodification of primary physical education that involves the buying and selling of professionals, physical education hours and movement programmes. In contrast, secondary physical education does not seem to have experienced such rapid transformation over a relatively short period of time; this could be due to the high number of specialists at this level, who have more in-depth subject knowledge than the generalist primary teacher.

Notwithstanding this, the claimed link between physical education and health dominates physical education pedagogy in the UK at all levels of education (Armstrong and Sparkes 1991; Capel and Piotrowski 2000; Kirk *et al.* 2006; Griggs 2007; Bailey and Kirk 2009). This health focus is reminiscent of the context in which the FMS programme was originally developed during 1995–1997 in Western Australia. The Western Australia Department of Education initially funded the 'Physical Steps' initiative, with one of the outcomes being the development of a FMS support package for teachers of children aged 4–8 years. Follow-up research continued to emphasise the importance of developing proficiency in FMS to ensure long-term health benefits for children and adolescents, and a number of subsequent reports on FMS (Senate Standing Committee on Environment, Recreation and the Arts 1992; Report on the Review of Physical Education in Western Australian Schools 1994) recommended increased support for early childhood teachers to help them plan, deliver and evaluate quality teaching and learning programmes that maximise children's learning of FMS. Such support is consistent with the second aim of the FMS programme: 'The Resource supports early childhood teachers, assistants, workers and community helpers in designing learning and teaching programmes that incorporate the development of children's fundamental movement skills' (Hands *et al.* 2004a: 1). In contrast, the current Youth Sport Trust national primary physical education CPD programme in the UK is largely activity driven and subject bound, rather than having an integrated development of FMS at its core. This is problematic for primary teachers, whose knowledge of motor skill development in young children can be limited because of the nominal amount of physical education provided at ITE level. Furthermore, it is challenging to engage teachers (and indeed parents) in their children's physical development if negative biographical experiences of physical education are relied on, for these will inevitably influence beliefs and self-efficacy during the teaching process (Morgan *et al.* 2001).

In spite of these stumbling blocks, there is enormous potential within primary physical education to positively influence children's attitudes towards physical activity and its importance throughout the lifespan. With around 500 hours of physical education taught during the primary age phase, the physical education lesson should remain an essential means of enhancing physical activity. Notwithstanding this, there is a also a window of opportunity to develop effective learning experiences that incorporate appropriate levels of physical activity throughout the day if the FMS programme were adopted by committed schools. This might help counter Ofsted's (2009: 20) criticism that 'Fewer than a fifth of the schools visited made strong connections between physical education and other subjects to help pupils understand the context of their learning better'. It could simultaneously reduce the amount of time children spend statically practising skills or learning National Curriculum activities that are too generic in content. A further issue that has been highlighted by several researchers is the underutilisation of break times and lunchtimes as contexts for promoting physical activity (Sleap *et al.* 2000; Ridgers and Stratton 2005). This situation could be improved by adopting the FMS whole-school approach, thereby raising the profile of motor skill development across the entire school day.

Perhaps the most significant aspect of physical education that the FMS programme could support is assessment. Ofsted (2009: 16) cited this as the weakest area of physical education in both primary and secondary schools, commenting that procedures were not robust enough to monitor and analyse the achievements of all pupils. Indeed, 'Less than a third of the primary schools shared records of pupils' achievements in PE with their partner secondary schools' (Ofsted 2009: 16). The procedure for gathering information about primary pupils' achievement levels in physical education is managed in a relatively ad hoc way from school to school, and it is predominantly a 'bottom-up' approach from the primary to the secondary school during transition. Some 20 years ago, there were calls for secondary school physical education specialists to 'embrace the complete 5–18 age range . . . and to contribute, in conjunction with primary school teachers, to the continuity and progression that are so essential' (Murdoch 1990: 73). Clearly, there are still lessons to be learned, and evident scope for a more coherent assessment system in which the primary pupils' strengths, interests and needs in the physical domain are taken into account, with primary teachers also being given feedback by secondary teachers on their pupils' physical progress during the later stages of their education. Sutherland *et al.* (2010: 64) suggest that this type of 'two-way communication' would help support primary teachers to reflect on their teaching, learning and assessment approaches in all subject areas, which constitutes a central component of the FMS programme's content and philosophy.

Evidently, the FMS programme could only attempt to resolve some of the aforementioned issues within primary physical education in the UK if it were given adequate curriculum time, and were led by practitioners who were convinced of the importance of children's holistic development. There are, then, both challenges and opportunities in the primary school context for this type of child-centred movement programme, but the enhancement of children's physical development through integrated teaching–learning approaches should be high on the list of priorities for every primary teacher with an understanding of young children's love and need of movement.

## Questions to consider

- What structures and procedures do you consider are in place to aid teaching–learning–assessment progression in physical education between Key Stage 2 and Key Stage 3?

- Is it possible to positively influence children's physical activity levels in the primary school environment, and, if so, how do we involve parents and the wider community in this process?

- Can continuing professional development in primary physical education make up for the current deficit model of primary physical education training within UK Initial Teacher Education?

- What steps other than movement programmes such as FMS could be taken by primary schools to ensure that the development of children's movement skills is prioritised?

## Notes

1. Fundamental Movement Skills is a resource developed by the Western Australia Education Department to provide access to high-quality professional development, support materials and strategies for all primary school teachers, enabling them to develop teaching, learning and assessment approaches that maximise children's proficiency levels in 22 fundamental movement skills. Steps PD (UK) is a not-for-profit company owned by Edith Cowan University, Perth, Western Australia. Website: http://www.steps-pd.co.uk/fms.htm.
2. Out of these three activities, swimming is compulsory unless pupils have completed the full Key Stage 2 teaching requirements in relation to swimming activities and water safety during Key Stage 1.
3. Core subjects in the UK National Curriculum (1999) are English, mathematics and science. Foundation subjects are physical education, information and communication technology, design and technology, music, geography, art and design, history and religious education.
4. The 22 FMS are categorised as follows – *body management skills*: balance on one foot, line or beam walk, climb, forward roll; *locomotor skills*: sprint run, hop, jump for distance, jump for height, skip, gallop, side gallop, dodge, continuous leap; *object control skills*: catch, overhand throw, underhand throw, chest pass, kick, punt, two-handed strike, hand dribble, foot dribble.

## Suggested further reading

Davies, M. (2003) *Movement and Dance in Early Childhood*, 2nd edn, London: Paul Chapman.
This book provides a focus on movement and dance development in children from birth to 8 years, highlighting the importance of learning in and through movement. There are also detailed links given between movement and early childhood theories of education and care. Chapter 2 relates particularly well to the FMS programme, with an investigation of motor skill development in a clear, accessible format.

Goddard Blythe, S. (2005) *The Well Balanced Child. Movement and Early Learning*, 2nd edn, Gloucestershire: Hawthorn Press.
An exploration of the physical basis for learning is central to this book, and the vital functions of early reflexes are illuminated. Various sections on the potential effects

that these reflexes can have on other aspects of development such as posture, balance, motor skills and emotional development connect well with the holistic underpinning of the FMS programme and previous reflection on motor skill progression in young children.

Hands, B., Martin, M. and Lynch, P. (2004a) *Fundamental Movement Skills. Book 1: Learning, Teaching and Assessment*, Perth: Western Australian Minister for Education.

Hands, B., Martin, M. and Lynch, P. (2004b) *Fundamental Movement Skills. Book 2: The Tools for Learning, Teaching and Assessment*, Perth: Western Australian Minister for Education.

These two books constitute the key texts that accompany the 12-hour FMS professional development; they are therefore essential reading for a better understanding of both FMS theory and practice. Book 1 gives an overview of learning, teaching and assessment, offering a theoretical foundation for FMS and an insight into associated case stories. In Book 2, five detailed sets of ideas and strategies in the form of practical tools for learning, teaching and assessment of FMS are provided.

# References

Armstrong, N. and Sparkes, A. (eds) (1991) *Issues in Physical Education*, London: Cassell.

Arnold, P. J. (1979) *Meaning in Movement, Sport and Physical Education*, London: Heinemann.

Bailey, R. P. (1999) 'Physical education: Action, play, movement', in Riley, J. and Prentice, R. (eds) *The Primary Curriculum 7–11*, London: Paul Chapman.

Bailey, R. P. and Kirk, D. (eds) (2009) *The Routledge Reader of Physical Education*, London: RoutledgeFalmer.

Bailey, R. P., Wellard, I. and Dismore, H. (2005) 'Girls and physical activities: A summary review', *Education and Health*, 23 (1): 3–5.

Boreham, C. and Riddoch, C. (2001) 'The physical activity, fitness and health of children', *Journal of Sports Science*, 19: 915–929.

Branta, C., Haubenstricker, J. and Seefeldt, V. (1984) 'Age changes in motor skills during childhood and adolescence', *Exercise and Sport Sciences Reviews*, 12: 467–520.

Bruner, J. (1983) *Child's Talk: Learning to Use Language*, Oxford: Oxford University Press.

Bunker, L.K. (1991) 'The role of play and motor skill development in building children's self-confidence and self-esteem', *The Elementary School Journal*, 91 (5): 467–471.

Burton, A. W. and Miller, D. E. (1998) *Movement Skill Assessment,* Champaign, IL: Human Kinetics.

Cale, L. and Harris, J. (2006) 'School-based physical activity interventions: Effectiveness, trends, issues, implications and recommendations for practice', *Sport, Education and Society*, 11 (4): 401–420.

Capel, S. and Piotrowski, S. (eds) (2000) *Issues in Physical Education*, London: RoutledgeFalmer.

Carney, P. and Bailey, R. (2005) 'Teachers' perspectives on talent development in primary physical education', BERA Conference Paper, University of Glamorgan, September 2005.

Caspersen, C. J., Pereira, M. A. and Curran, K. M. (2000) 'Changes in physical activity patterns in the United States, by sex and cross-sectional age', *Medicine & Science in Sports & Exercise*, 32 (9): 1601–1609.

Clark, J. E., Whittal, J. and Phillips, S. J. (1988) 'Human interlimb coordination: The first 6 months of independent walking', *Developmental Psychology*, 21: 445–456.

Clark, J. E., Phillips, S. J. and Petersen, R. (1989) 'Developmental stability in jumping', *Developmental Psychology*, 25: 929–935.

Cratty, B. J. (1986) *Perceptual and Motor Development in Infants and Children*, 3rd edn, Englewood Cliffs, NJ: Prentice Hall.

Davies, M. (2003) *Movement and Dance in Early Childhood*, 2nd edn, London: Paul Chapman.

Doll-Tepper, G. (2005) 'The UK in the world of physical education', *British Journal of Teaching Physical Education*, 36 (1): 41–43.

Gallahue, D. L. and Ozmun, J. C. (2006) *Understanding Motor Development. Infants, Children, Adolescents, Adults*, 6th edn, New York: McGraw-Hill.

Gessell, A. (1928) *Infancy and Human Growth*, New York: Macmillan.

Goddard Blythe, S. (2005) *The Well Balanced Child. Movement and Early Learning*, 2nd edn, Gloucestershire: Hawthorn Press.

Griggs, G. (2007) 'Physical education: Primary matters, secondary importance', *Education 3–13*, 35 (1): 59–69.

Hands, B., Martin, M. and Lynch, P. (2004a) *Fundamental Movement Skills. Book 1: Learning, Teaching and Assessment*, Perth: Western Australian Minister for Education.

Hands, B., Martin, M. and Lynch, P. (2004b) *Book 2: The Tools for Learning, Teaching and Assessment*, Perth: Western Australian Minister for Education.

Hannaford, C. (2005) *Smart Moves. Why Learning Is Not All in Your Head*, 2nd edn, Salt Lake City, UT: Great River Books.

Jago, R., Anderson, C., Baranowski, T. and Watson, K. (2005) 'Adolescent patterns of physical activity: Differences by gender, day and time of day', *American Journal of Preventive Medicine*, 28 (5): 447–452.

Katene, W. (2000) 'Progression and continuity in physical education between primary and secondary school', in Capel, S. and Piotrowski, S. (eds) *Issues in Physical Education*, London: Routledge.

Kelly, L. E. (1989) 'Instructional time', *Journal of Physical Education, Recreation and Dance*, August, 29–32.

Kimm, S. Y., Glynn, N. W., Kriska, A., Barton, B. A., Kronsberg, S. S., Daniels, S. R., Crawford, P. B., Sabry, Z. I. and Liu, K. (2002) 'Decline in physical activity in black girls and white girls during adolescence', *New England Journal of Medicine*, 347 (10): 709–715.

Kirk, D. and Tinning, R. (1990) *Physical Education, Curriculum and Culture: Critical Issues in Contemporary Crisis*, London: Falmer.

Kirk, D., Macdonald, D. and O'Sullivan, M. (eds) (2006) *Handbook of Physical Education*, London: Sage.

Lamb, M. and Campos, J. (1982) *Development in Infancy*, New York: Random House.

Macdonald, D., Hay, P. and Williams, B. (2008) 'Should you buy? Neo-liberalism, neo-HPE, and your neo-job', *New Zealand Physical Educator*, 41 (3): 6–13.

McGee, C. R., Ward, R., Gibbons, J. and McCarthy, K. A. (2003) 'Transition to secondary school: A literature review', Report to the Ministry of Education, Hamilton: University of Waikato, New Zealand.

McGraw, M. B. (1935) *Growth: A Study of Johnny and Jimmy*, New York: Appleton-Century.

McNamee, M. J. (2005) 'The nature and values of physical education', London: Sage. Online. Available from http://www.uk.sagepub.com/upm-data/9756_036313Ch1.pdf (accessed 2 June 2009).

Marsden, E. and Weston, C. (2007) 'Locating quality physical education in early years pedagogy', *Sport, Education and Society*, 12 (4): 383–398.

Morgan, P., Bourke, S. and Thompson, K. (2001) 'The influence of personal school physical education experiences on non-specialist attitudes and beliefs about physical education'. Paper presented at the annual conference of the Australian Association for Research in Education, Fremantle, Western Australia, December 2001.

Murdoch, E. (1990) 'Physical education and sport: The interface', in Armstrong, N. (ed.) *New Directions in Physical Education*, Volume 1, Champaign, IL: Human Kinetics.

NHS (2010) 'Change4Life'. Online. Available from http://www.nhs.uk/change4life/Pages/Default.aspx (accessed 16 June 2010).

Ofsted (2009) 'Physical education in schools 2005/08. Working towards 2012 and beyond', London: Ofsted.

Penney, D. (1998) 'Positioning and defining physical education, sport and health in the curriculum', *European Physical Education Review*, 4 (2): 117–126.

Penney, D. and Evans, J. (1999) *Politics, Policy and Practice in Physical Education*, London: E. & F. N. Spon.

Piaget, J. (1952) *The Origins of Intelligence in Children*, New York: International Universities Press.

Pickup, I. and Price, L. (2007) *Teaching Physical Education in the Primary School: A Developmental Approach*, London: Continuum.

Pickup, I., Haydn-Davis, D. and Jess, M. (2007) 'The importance of primary physical education', *Physical Education Matters*, 2 (1): 9–11.

QCA (2007) 'Physical Education. Programme of Study for Key Stage 3 and Attainment Target', London: QCA.

Report on the Review of Physical Education in Western Australian Schools (1994) Perth, Western Australia: Office of the Minister for Education.

Riddoch, C., Andersen, L. B., Wedderkopp, N., Harro, M., Klasson-Heggebo, L., Sardinha, L. B., Cooper, A. R. and Ekelund, U. (2004) 'Physical activity levels and patterns of 9- and 15-yr-old European children', *Medicine & Science in Sports & Exercise*, 36 (1): 86–92.

Ridgers, N. D. and Stratton, G. (2005) 'Children's physical activity levels during school playtime', *Journal of Sports Sciences*, 23 (2): 134.

Rose, B., Larkin, D. and Berger, B. (1994) 'Perceptions of social support in children of low, moderate and high levels of coordination', *ACHPER Healthy Lifestyles Journal*, 41 (4): 18–21.

Rose, J. (2009) 'Independent Review of the Primary Curriculum: Final Report', Nottingham: DCSF.

Sallis, J. F., Prochaska, J. J. and Taylor, W. C. (2000) 'A review of correlates of physical activity of children and adolescents', *Medicine & Science in Sports & Exercise*, 32: 963–975.

Senate Standing Committee on Environment, Recreation and the Arts (1992) *Physical and Sport Education*, Canberra: Commonwealth Government.

Shephard, R. J. (1982) *Physical Activity and Growth*, London: Year Book Medical Publishers.

Sleap, M., Warburton, P. and Waring, M. (2000) 'Couch potato kids: Lazy layabouts – the role of primary schools in relation to physical activity among children in primary school', in Williams, A. (ed.) *Primary School Physical Education: Research into Practice*, London: David Fulton.

Stork, S. and Sanders, S. W. (2008) 'Physical education in early childhood', *The Elementary School Journal*, 108 (3): 197–206.

Subramaniam, P. and Silverman, S. (2007) 'Middle school students' attitudes towards physical education', *Teaching and Teacher Education*, 23 (5): 602–611.

Sutherland, R., Chin Yee, W. and McNess, E. (2010) 'Supporting learning in the transition from primary to secondary schools', University of Bristol. Online. Available from http://www.bris.ac.uk/education/news/2010/transition-bristoluniversity.pdf (accessed 1 February 2010).

Talbot, M. (1995) 'The politics of sport and physical education', in Armstrong, N. (ed.) *New Directions in Physical Education*, Champaign, IL: Human Kinetics.

Thelen, E. and Ulrich, B. D. (1991) 'Hidden skills: A dynamic systems analysis of treadmill stepping during the first year', *Monographs of the Society for Research in Child Development*, 56 (1): 1–104.

Williams, H. (1983) *Perceptual and Motor Development*, Englewood Cliffs, NJ: Prentice Hall.

Wrotniak, B. H., Epstein, L. H., Dorn, J. M., Jones, K. E. and Kondilis, V. A. (2006) 'The relationship between motor proficiency and physical activity in children', *Pediatrics*, 118: 1758–1765.

Yang, X., Telama, R., Viikari, J. and Raitakari, O. T. (2006) 'Risk of obesity in relation to physical activity tracking from youth to adulthood', *Medicine & Science in Sports & Exercise*, 38: 919–925.

# Becoming a global citizen

## Cultural strategies for community cohesion at Key Stage 2–3 transition

*June Bianchi*

## Chapter summary

The key points in this chapter are:

- Children progress through the primary–secondary transitional stage within a culturally diverse society.

- Understanding global perspectives equips children at the transitional stage to take their place as citizens within local, national and international contexts.

- Sharing cultural experience fosters appreciation of pluralist values, facilitating tolerance and cultural inclusion.

- Participation in arts and cultural education at transition effectively promotes social cohesion and global citizenship.

## Introduction

Recovering from the trauma of international war, which polarised populations on both an ethnic and a cultural basis, the United Nations Educational, Scientific and Cultural Organization (UNESCO), founded in 1945, recognised the significance of shared experience in contributing to 'the building of peace, the eradication of poverty, sustainable development and intercultural dialogue through education, the sciences, culture, communication and information' (UNESCO n.d.).

In his Director's Report of 1947, UNESCO's first director, Sir Julian Huxley, encouraged countries to 'share in the riches of a single diversified world culture' (Stenou 2007: 82), reifying cultural participation within an optimistic and developmental vision of the future. UNESCO's Declaration of Cultural Diversity, in the aftermath of 9/11, again advocated sharing of culture to foster global understanding, tolerance, economic stability, social cohesion and intellectual, emotional and spiritual fulfilment. Education is viewed by UNESCO as a significant factor in promoting 'the positive value of cultural diversity', and the declaration exhorts dissemination of pluralist cultural experiences as a means to raise educational standards, 'improving both curriculum design and teacher education' (UNESCO 2002).

This chapter uses UNESCO's notion of cultural transmission as a basis for developing global citizenship, investigating the extent to which children in Key Stage 2–3 transition can participate in socially inclusive activities benefiting themselves and the wider community. It will survey a range of social policies on community cohesion in the light of current educational initiatives, exploring their relevance at the transitional stage of education. Referring to relevant third sector organisations, networks and resources, as well as mainstream educational implementation, the chapter will synthesise theory and practice, presenting two focal Key Stage 2–3 transitional case studies that demonstrate the significance of cultural strategies in addressing community cohesion. Through participation in arts-based initiatives, children, including those potentially vulnerable at primary–secondary stage transition, can be supported in engagement within their local community, as well as encouraged to become citizens of the wider international community.

## Community cohesion and Key Stage 2–3 transition

Within the UK children's and young people's progress towards adulthood takes place within a complex pluralist society, described by the Parekh Report (2000: Preface) as a 'community of communities'. A key challenge identified by the report lies in balancing sometimes competing requirements of unity and diversity within a culturally diverse society. Whether despite of or because of centuries of colonialist history and decades of black and minority ethnic (BME) immigration supplying essential services within the UK's economy, 'the notion of racial hierarchies has not altogether disappeared and stereotypes still abound in society' (DfES 2007: 6).

There is both a moral and a legal imperative for educationalists to recognise these societal challenges, acknowledging the multiplicity of perspectives, ideologies and values held by individuals and ethnic and cultural groups within the greater community, with inevitable areas of shared values and dissent. The 2000 Race Relations Amendment Act reinforced schools' responsibilities 'to eliminate unlawful racial discrimination and to promote equality of opportunity and good relations between people of different groups' (DCSF 2007: 1).

Community cohesion is a prevalent aim and Alan Johnson, the then Secretary of State for Education and Skills, speaking in Parliament on 2 November 2006, outlined the importance of establishing:

> a common vision and sense of belonging by all communities; a society in which the diversity of people's backgrounds and circumstances is appreciated and valued; a society in which similar life opportunities are available to all; and a society in which strong and positive relationships exist and continue to be developed in the workplace, in schools and in the wider community.

> (DCSF 2007: 3)

Schools within the state sector are required to address these aims through a curriculum promoting children's spiritual, moral, cultural, mental and physical development in conjunction with their academic needs (DCSF 2007). Discussing the notion of five 'learning bridges', Professor Michael Barber comments on the importance of creating a conducive environment for children to learn, which effectively links social, curriculum and pedagogic bridges. He raises the need to address social factors preventing effective learning, both intrinsic issues such as individuals' self-esteem and extrinsic issues of bullying, racism or family and community breakdown, emphasising the importance of meeting students' aspirations alongside their immediate needs (Barber 1999a). Barber references American philosopher Martha Nussbaum in advocating education to develop empathy and foster citizenship 'of the world, showing respect for human beings whatever their background' (Barber 1999b: 18). Such a directive informs the recommendations of the Diversity and Citizenship Curriculum Review (DfES 2007: 1), which states that 'we passionately believe that it is the duty of all schools to address issues of how we live together'.

Primary schools' ethos and pedagogical practice may more readily encompass pastoral issues, with a more intimate community offering an environment that can potentially support individuals' needs. The University of Bristol's investigation into transition from primary to secondary school suggested that the 'culture and ethos of a school is inextricably related to both pupil learning and approaches to teaching and learning' (Sutherland et al. 2010: 71). Although some children may experience the move into a wider sphere of experience as liberating, with commensurate extension of academic and social opportunities, others perceive the shift as threatening to emotional well-being, a cause of 'serious disaffection and disengagement from formal schooling and, ultimately, from social norms' (Sutherland et al. 2010: 12); transition may potentially act as a precursor to social exclusion.

Underachievement is a key indication of disaffection, and the Bristol study quotes a National Strategy paper from the Department for Children, Schools and Families (DCSF 2008a) evidencing diminished motivation at primary–secondary transition across a range of learning contexts. Current policy and practice emphasise the role of pastoral education in eliciting successful transition for students across the spectrum of academic ability, socio-cultural backgrounds and learning needs, and statistical evidence generates a persuasive case for urgency in preventing alienation from the educational process and mainstream society at this stage. The notion of community cohesion is a powerful one with the Diversity and Citizenship Curriculum Review (DfES 2007) identifying the school community and families it serves as a significant dimension alongside the community of the school's locality, the UK community and the global community. For children experiencing instability within this community network, the transitional stage can be a period when fragile self-esteem and reduction of feelings of self-worth negatively impact upon learning. Gulati and King's (2009) report on transition amongst vulnerable young people emphasises the importance of psychological, emotional and spiritual development, alongside the fostering of mutually satisfying relationships, and the ability to empathise with others.

Effective achievement of the five outcomes of 'Every Child Matters' (ECM) – be healthy; stay safe; enjoy and achieve; make a positive contribution; and achieve economic well-being (DCSF 2008b) – can be viewed as indices of effective provision for children's welfare, and a barometer of social inclusion. When baseline health and welfare needs are met, children's potential to enjoy, achieve and contribute within their lives becomes a factor in provision, and DCSF seeks to promote participation in culture, sport and play for young people, facilitating participation and developing talent. Policy-makers and educational practitioners recognise the wider benefits of such activities for both individuals and their communities in 'promoting diversity, fostering creative partnerships between a range of trusts and agencies and enabling young people to participate in creative and inspiring activities within and beyond the school curriculum' (Bianchi 2008: 173).

Despite the prevailing emphasis on measuring achievement through quantifiable performance indicators or Standard Assessment Testing across the western world, there is a growing sense that education separates 'enjoy' from 'achieve' at the peril of children's well-being and ultimately that of society. As creativity consultant Sir Ken Robinson argues: 'The future for education is not in standardizing but in customizing, not in promoting groupthink and "deindividuation" but in cultivating the real depth and dynamism of human abilities of every sort' (Robinson 2009: 250).

## Community cohesion and cultural education initiatives

> Another way in which inequality directly affects educational achievement is through its impact on the aspirations, norms and values of people who find themselves lower down the social hierarchy . . . in more unequal countries we found a larger gap between aspirations and actual opportunities and expectations.
>
> (Wilkinson and Pickett 2009: 115–117)

In *The Spirit Level*, Wilkinson and Pickett (2009) compare international indices of health and well-being in relation to relative levels of equity across a range of societies. Using research data covering a multiplicity of societal factors, including mental and physical health, crime, social relations and social mobility, teenage birth rate and educational opportunities and achievement, they draw far-reaching conclusions on the significance of levels of equality within both individual societies and the global community. The writers conclude that levels of equity not only impact upon domestic policy and practice within nation-states but also significantly affect the attitude and approaches that countries bring to the world stage: 'Inequality is related to worse scores on the Global Peace Index, which combines measures of militarization with measures of domestic and international conflict and measures of security, human rights and stability' (Wilkinson and Pickett 2010: 235).

Wilkinson and Pickett's statistical data indicate that both the UK and the US have unprecedented widening gaps between the incomes of the richest and those of the poorest 10 per cent of citizens, gaps that increased exponentially in Britain during the 1980s, and that have remained largely unchallenged during the last decade. Likewise, Bourdieu and Darbel's 1969 research analysing international cultural consumerism (Bourdieu and Darbel 1997) indicated that access to cultural experience also provides a signifier of quality of life, with cultural capital denoting both levels of educational achievement and also affluence. Recent commensurate research studies conducted in the UK have confirmed that cultural access remains largely unchanged, demonstrating that patterns of cultural access remain a relevant indicator of inequity within a society. Arguably, education should therefore facilitate parity of access to economic, social and cultural capital, providing a model of global citizenship that aims to ameliorate and challenge inequities in order to address social and community cohesion on both a domestic and an international level.

The Social Exclusion Task Force's 2009 analysis of risks of social exclusion amongst families (Oroyemi *et al.* 2009) used ECM outcomes as focal areas of research into children's and families' well-being. The families identified as most at risk of social exclusion were 'more likely to be lone parents; young mothers; families with younger children; social and private tenants; and families with mothers from Black and Asian ethnic groups'. They were also more likely to 'live in urban areas and in the bottom 20% of the most deprived areas' (Oroyemi *et al.* 2009: 33). The 2007 Bristol study of social exclusion by Levitas and colleagues discussed the multi-dimensional factors involved, recognising exclusion as involving denial of both goods and services alongside:

the inability to participate in the normal relationships and activities available to the majority of people in a society, whether in economic, social, cultural or political arenas. It affects both the quality of life of individuals and the equity and cohesion of society as a whole.

(Levitas *et al.* 2007: 25)

The Bristol Social Exclusion Matrix, developed from the study by Levitas *et al.*, focused on three measureable domains indicating social exclusion – resources, participation and standard of living – and their research audits sections of the community's access to these entitlements, demonstrating pockets of need within a relatively affluent society. Like *The Spirit Level*, the findings from the Bristol-based research provide an imperative towards development of community cohesion strategies for both the individual's well-being and that of the macrocosm. Extensive research cited on the significance of maintaining motivational levels amongst children moving through primary to secondary transition would suggest that addressing these factors at this stage is a necessity not a choice.

## Case study: building esteem and aspiration through cultural strategies

Bristol Children and Young People's Services operate within a city where a survey carried out in 2007 indicated that 12.8 per cent of children aged from 5 to 15 were being educated within the private sector. As the national average for private education was then 6.4 per cent, Bristol can be regarded as relatively affluent (My Society 2010), yet like any major city Bristol also harbours educational disaffection and demotivation, frequently concentrated in areas of social deprivation across the city. Socio-cultural groupings are not consistent throughout the city, with National Health Service statistics for the area commenting that:

The BME population of Bristol is not evenly distributed throughout the city. The inner city wards of Lawrence Hill, Ashley and Easton have the highest percentage of BME residents – 32%, 26% and 25% respectively. This compares to some wards where the BME population is as low as just 2%.

(NHS Bristol, Public Health 2010)

Social exclusion cannot be attributable to a single specific cause as different wards have pockets of socially excluded children and families with a range of characteristics, as 'Our Shared Future', the Commission on Integration and Cohesion's report on social cohesion, noted:

> The commitment to social justice and tackling poverty and inequality is as much about addressing the low levels of achievement amongst some white working class boys or white adults without qualifications as it is about dealing with lack of advancement of some members of Black and minority ethnic communities.
>
> (Commission on Integration and Cohesion 2007: 4)

Across the range of Bristol wards, issues to be addressed included those noted earlier with attendant implications of vulnerability to racism, bullying, substance abuse, school exclusion and such factors as 'grooming' of underage girls by older boys with consequences of early pregnancy, prostitution and exclusion from mainstream society. Drawing on the findings of the Cabinet Office's research (Social Exclusion Task Force 2008) Bristol Children and Young People's Services are committed to providing learning opportunities, experiences and course options that enhance children's and young people's self-esteem, engendering wider aspirations and improved potential across the socio-economic spectrum (Thomas 2010). This is best initiated at the primary–secondary transition stage as studies such as the Avon Longitudinal Study of Parents and Children by Indices of Multiple Deprivation (ESDS 2010) indicate that children as young as 8 years hold levels of beliefs about their abilities that suggest social deprivation as a key determinant. Children who could be described as experiencing social exclusion believe not only that they are less able but also that they have little control over their future. The Bristol Children and Young People's Services noted that 'children between the ages of 8–14 years from more deprived areas tend to have an external locus of control and believe outcomes are determined by external forces rather than themselves' (Thomas 2010: 1). As well as children from reduced income families, this group incorporates students with special educational needs, students with less fluency in English and students from some ethnic groups (Galton et al. 1999).

As part of its ongoing 'Every Child Matters' initiative, DSCF has funded a national Career Related Learning programme aimed at Key Stage 2 transition; its key focus is 'extending horizons and raising aspirations' (DCSF 2010a). Bristol Children and Young People's Services have been one of six successful regions bidding for funding; all areas have been targeted as holding a high proportion of 'NEETs' – young people not in employment, education or training (DCFS 2010b). Bristol's response places significant emphasis on cultural participation in encouraging community and social inclusion. The programme has been managed by Hugh Thomas, Investors in Learning leader, who draws on his own background in performance arts and art and design education in co-ordinating a programme generating vibrant links between educational, business and cultural communities within the city, 'creating social and cultural bridges to widen experience' (Thomas 2010). The overall project, entitled 'My Future My Choice' (MFMC), comprises a progressive three-stage programme stimulating broader cultural and economic access to children across the transitional phase:

- Phase 1: 'Imagine My Future' (IMF), at Year 5, integrates business and media professionals into the curriculum, with guidance materials including a 'Top Trumps' game and stage show designed to widen career aspirations at Key Stage 2. The stage show integrates business volunteers, film clips and a time travelling student reflecting back upon career choice decisions made at Year 5.

- Phase 2: 'Explore my Future' (EMF), at Year 6, introduces activities beyond the school, including visits to business and cultural settings such as museums, galleries, performance venues, festivals and neighbouring cities. The programme engages students, parents, schools and participating host centres in fostering independent learners with the capacity to thrive through transition, recognising the relevance of secondary school in facilitating future success. Discussing the projects, Thomas commented on the significance of organising the visits to the cultural centres as Year 6 students did not always utilise them otherwise, and he believed them to be a free and accessible resource which could potentially provide a stimulating and worthwhile focus for learning. As research has indicated, acquisition of confidence in accessing such institutions, characterised as 'cultural capital' (Bourdieu 1984), bestows social confidence and self-esteem.

- Phase 3: 'Vision My Future' (VMF), at Years 8 and 9, continues to build self-esteem, impacting on aspirations and life expectations at Key Stage 3. Using the format of a 'soap opera' DVD, the programme provides students with tools to vision a broader future, enabling them to set higher goals based on wider options, which impact upon their choices at Key Stage 4.

Surveys reviewing MFMC have indicated that the Bristol scheme is popular with educational, cultural and business partners. Research data gathered from the 2008 Year 5 pilot and subsequent years' events indicated that 40 per cent of children attending IMF events broadened their career aspirations: 'This is an inspiration to me because I can do lots of different things and I don't have to join the army' (Year 6 boy, Bank Leaze Primary School).

Teachers also responded positively, with some schools reporting significant increases in attainment for literacy, numeracy and science. At the time of writing, participation in the scheme is open to all Bristol schools, and the creative, enjoyable and accessible format is honed by individual schools according to the specific socio-economic, cultural, ethnic and linguistic needs of their communities. Recognition of MFMC's potential to fuse synergy between educational, business and cultural institutions was conferred when Thomas received the 2009 Sieff Award for community-based activity that 'collaborated with business to benefit society' (Business in the Community 2010), an acknowledgement that the project provided reciprocal benefits in social cohesion benefitting the wider community.

The success of MFMC can be attributed to its widening social participation agenda, re-engaging students with their own community, and broadening their aspirational horizons. In the words of Ken Robinson, it also lies with the opportunity it affords young people to 'find their Element . . . the distinctive talents and passions that can inspire us to achieve far more than we imagine' (Robinson 2009: 8).

## Case study: celebrating cultural diversity at transition

The shift from primary to secondary schooling can sometimes be regarded as a 'fresh start' (Galton *et al.* 1999: 6), yet key values and issues progress across phases with ongoing development of active citizenship of local, national and global communities. The importance of intercultural learning experiences during the transitional stages from childhood into young adulthood is promoted within the UK by educational and third sector organisations, with empirical evidence supporting the claim that arts and culture can effectively promote awareness of global citizenship issues. Within the National Curriculum the incorporation of a framework of eight key concepts is advocated: global citizenship, conflict resolution, diversity, human rights, interdependence, social justice, sustainable development and values and perceptions.

The new primary curriculum promotes the arts as a means to engage with 'children's personal, social and emotional development' as well enabling them 'to participate in and respond to the creative and cultural life of their communities and to gain insights into different viewpoints, identities, traditions and cultures' (QCA 2010).

The citizenship and cross-curricular dimensions of the secondary curriculum emphasise the pluralist nature of British society and that of the wider community, with young people encouraged to understand the 'influences on and the development of identity and the sense of community, multiple identities and national identity – including Britishness' (Huddleston 2007). Learners are also required to be aware of global issues for their personal development and their participation as active citizens in a changing world: 'By exploring the connections between the local and the global, they can also realise that it is possible to play a part in working towards solutions to challenges, such as climate change and global poverty' (DEA 2009).

The Development Education Association promotes learning about 'global interconnections' to make sense of countries' relationships with each other and their impact upon people and environments; it can 'counter the sense of helplessness in the face of "global forces"' (DEA 2010). As advocated in the community cohesion agenda, students need 'skills that will enable them to combat injustice, prejudice and discrimination' (DfES 2005: 2), enabling them to recognise shared values and the distinctiveness of diverse socio-cultural and ethnic groups. Such qualities can be appreciated through experience of the arts; art, dance, drama and music convey the uniqueness of their cultural context as well as personal and universal values, political meanings and stories in communicating 'the ways individuals, communities and cultures shape and are shaped by others locally and globally' (DEA 2006: 2). The arts can generate intercultural creative collaborations between artists, teachers and students across a range of contexts, fostering wider understanding and cohesion within local, national and international communities. The Runnymede Trust, the 'non-party political charity working to end racism' (Runnymede Trust 2010), commented on the

Parekh Report: 'the arts and heritage sectors have moved a long way in developing initiatives to recognise the ethnic diversity of British societies' (Runnymede Trust 2004: 3).

Launching the Global Learning Charter alongside charities, councils, businesses and schools, Malcolm Bruce MP remarked that his 'visits to developing countries have reinforced how important it is that people in this country learn about global issues' (DEA 2010). Such commitment to promoting cultural pluralism is a feature of education at St Gregory's Catholic College, Bath, a co-educational, 11–16, voluntary-aided school with Specialist Status in the Performing Arts that addresses global issues through citizenship and the wider curriculum with a particular emphasis on the arts. The College's arts achievements have been recognised by awards such as Gold Arts Mark, Artswork National Awards and the British Council International School award featuring links to six European countries and Nepal.

St Gregory's Catholic College has the largest proportion of BME students in the Bath area, with 20 per cent of students coming from diverse backgrounds, including Chinese, Afro-Caribbean, Philippine, Polish and other Europeans, compared with the local average of 2.8 per cent at the last census in 2001 (Bath & North East Somerset Race Equality Scheme Review 2010).

International connections are characteristic of students' arts experiences, and the annual Key Stage 3 Arts Week features input from international performers linked to the World of Music and Dance (WOMAD) festival, including performers from six of the seven continents. Citizenship issues of equity and diversity are taught across subject curricula and pastoral and extra-curricular activities. The significance of this agenda is echoed by students' website statements affirming that:

There are no boundaries between the different cultures and races here.

Respect and equality are the foundations of our school.

(St Gregory's Catholic College 2010)

Celebrating cultural diversity through the arts is pivotal in the college's programme for Key Stage 2–3 transition. Year 6 students from local feeder primary schools begin their autumn term with an intercultural arts day at the college, an event encouraging transitional students to 'critically examine their own values and attitudes; appreciate the similarities between peoples everywhere, and value diversity' (DfES 2005). The day includes workshops, performances and presentations by international theatre companies with opportunities for students to engage in reflection and produce arts outcomes based on the focal culture. The Keralan Kathakali Company 'Centre Ocean Stream' has featured as guest performers; the company disseminates the culture, history and meaning of Kathakali culture, enabling students to appreciate the role of the arts within a Hindu context, recognising unique and common elements of the spiritual tradition. Kathakali exponent Vijayakumar performs women's roles with consummate grace, leading workshops in the mimetic tradition of performance, conveying subtlety of gesture, facial expression and movement in narrating stories of India's heroes, heroines and demons. The African Iroko Theatre Company has also performed and run workshops for students during the school's transition event;

its aim is to 'nurture and uphold African culture' and to 'educate and enhance the creative potential, self-confidence and self-esteem of children and young people from varied backgrounds and abilities' (Iroko Theatre Company n.d.). The transitional arts and culture workshops, held during the final primary year, prepare students for addressing wider citizenship issues of pluralism and inclusion within the secondary curriculum. Key points raised at the workshops are initially followed up within cross-curricular sessions in their primary schools, with students then re-visiting core issues throughout their secondary religious education, humanities, citizenship and arts curricula at St Gregory's Catholic College.

Such an intercultural transition event contributes to the holistic focus at St Gregory's Catholic College, commended in its 2008 Ofsted report, which praised community cohesion as a strength of its work, noting students' 'opportunities to increase their understanding of global, national and local citizenship' (Ofsted 2008), alongside fostering diversity through a range of strategies including the arts, community projects and language lessons for the developing Polish community. Ofsted praised the contribution of the arts events at transition:

> Cultural and spiritual development is exceptionally strong and students put into practice in their day-to-day work the values they learn in college. For example, they develop their spirituality through the outstanding chaplaincy sessions and their awareness of other cultures through events such as a recent Kathakali workshop.
>
> (Ofsted 2008)

The head of the Arts faculty, Andrew Jackson, has been instrumental in establishing a wide range of arts-based projects such as the Arts Council-funded Creativity Action Research Award (CARA), now funded by the college, providing cultural workshops with practitioners such as dancers, musicians and cartoonists for BME students representing a dozen different heritages; arts outcomes and experiences such as sharing of food culture are then disseminated throughout the college. In his discussion with the author, Jackson expressed his belief that both at the transitional stage and across the secondary phase the universal frequently non-verbal language of the arts provides a vital tool enabling children to express, share and celebrate their diverse cultures within the community.

## Conclusion

Students at primary–secondary transition are balanced at a crucial stage in their lives when attitudes, values and aspirations are potentially extended or diminished. Experiences that enrich experience of the world and build understanding of their place within a wider local, national and international community can enhance their capacity to learn, increasing students' potential for a successful future. Global citizenship can be explored across the whole curriculum but the case studies presented demonstrate the success of arts and cultural strategies in promoting key issues in an enjoyable and accessible way across a range of abilities and contexts. The success of such strategies in all cases will be the result of committed practitioners able to plan appropriately to inspire students at pivotal life transitions:

Teachers, with their knowledge of the young people they work with, have an important role in reflecting on how to support critical global thinking whilst enabling young people to feel sufficiently optimistic and aware of their power for change to take their chosen action in a complex world.

(Brown and Shah 2010)

## Questions to consider

- What key issues do children need to address in order to take their place within a pluralist society?

- In what ways are arts and cultural experiences significant in contributing to children's development as global citizens?

- Discuss with a fellow educationalist the impact of arts and cultural education you have participated in, or observed, in promoting pluralism and socio-cultural equity.

- Plan an arts and culture event within a chosen setting to promote children's understanding of global development issues.

## Acknowledgements

Thanks for assistance, support and contributions from Michelle Farmer, Service Manager, Learning Partnerships and Collaborations; Annie Hudson, Strategic Director; and Hugh Thomas, Investors in Learning Leader, all of Bristol Children and Young People's Services; and from Andrew Jackson, head of the Arts faculty, St Gregory's Catholic College, Bath.

## Suggested further reading

Wilkinson, R. and Pickett, K. (2010) *The Spirit Level: Why Equality is Better for Everyone*, 2nd edn, London: Penguin.
The book provides an overview of levels of global equity and inequality and a context for challenging attitudes and assumptions within UK society.

DEA website: http://www.dea.org.uk/ (accessed 10 June 2010).
The website provides a regularly updated resource for interrogating and understanding the relationship between societies, and the global challenges to be addressed in order to create a fairer, more sustainable, world.

UNESCO website education pages: http://www.unesco.org/en/education (accessed 12 June 2010).
An excellent resource for finding our about educational developments around the globe. The website is constantly updated and features many case studies of cultural educational projects and links.

## References

Barber, M. (1999a) 'Taking the Tide at the Flood: Transforming the Middle Years of Schooling', *Education Today*, 49 (4): 3–17.

Barber, M. (1999b) 'Taking the Tide at the Flood: Transforming Education in the Middle Years'. Paper presented at the Middle Years of Schooling Conference, Melbourne, Australia. Online. Available from http://www.ict-tutors.co.uk/documents/Barber_The_Five_Bridges.pdf (accessed March 2011).

Bath & North East Somerset Race Equality Scheme Review. (2010) Online. Available from http://www.bathnes.gov.uk/BathNES/communityandliving/equality/Race+Equality+Scheme+Review+2005.htm (accessed 10 June 2010).

Bianchi, J. (2008) 'Cultural Connections in Learning', in Ward, S. (ed.) *A Student's Guide to Education Studies*, London: Routledge.

Bourdieu, P. (1984) *Distinction: A Social Critique of the Judgement of Taste*, trans. R. Nice, London: Routledge and Kegan Paul.

Bourdieu, P. and Darbel, A. (1997) *The Love of Art: European Art Museums and Their Public*, Cambridge: Polity Press.

Brown, K. and Shah, H. (2010) 'DEA Thinkpiece: Critical Thinking in the Context of Global Learning'. Online. Available from http://clients.squareeye.com/uploads/dea/documents/dea_thinkpiece_shah_brown_3.pdf (accessed 10 June 2010).

Business in the Community (2010) Online. Available from http://www.bitc.org.uk/awards_for_excellence/awards_for_excellence_2010_winners/award_winners_2009/sieff.html (accessed 8 August 2010).

Commission on Integration and Cohesion (2007) 'Our Shared Future'. Online. Available from http://image.guardian.co.uk/sys-files/Education/documents/2007/06/14/oursharedfuture.pdf (accessed February 2011).

DCSF (2007) 'Guidance on the Duty to Promote Community Cohesion', Nottingham: DCSF.

DCSF (2008a) 'The National Strategies, Strengthening Transfer and Transitions: Partnerships for Progress'. Online. Available from http://nationalstrategies.dcsf.gov.uk/node/85276.

DCSF (2008b) 'Every Child Matters: Revised ECM Outcomes Framework'. Online. Available from http://www.everychildmatters.gov.uk/aims/outcomes/(accessed 12 June 2010).

DCSF (2010a) 'Key Stage 2 Career Related Learning Pathfinder Grant'. Online. Available from http://www.dcsf.gov.uk/everychildmatters/news-and-communications/local-authority-circulars-2008–2011/lac0510090005/ (accessed 12 June 2010).

DCSF (2010b) 'Every Child Matters: Young People not in Education, Employment or Training (NEET)'. Online. Available from http://www.dcsf.gov.uk/everychildmatters/Youth/ypnieet/neet/ (accessed 12 June 2010).

DEA (2006) 'The Arts: The Global Dimension'. Online. Available from http://www.dea.org.uk/page.asp?p=3860 (accessed 14 June 2010).

DEA (2009) 'Exploring Together: A Global Dimension to the Secondary Curriculum'. Online. Available from http://www.globaldimension.org.uk/uploadedfiles/Whats_New/exploring_gd_folder.pdf (accessed 23 March 2011).

DEA (2010) 'Global Charter'. Online. Available from http://www.dea.org.uk/news/item.asp?n=7125 (accessed 12 June 2010).

DfES (2007) 'Curriculum Review: Diversity and Citizenship', Nottingham: DfES.

DfES (2005) 'Developing the Global Dimension in the School Curriculum', Glasgow: DFID.

ESDS Longitudinal (2010) 'An ESDS Guide'. Online. Available from http://www.esds.ac.uk/longitudinal/access/lsype/L5545.asp (accessed 15 June 2010).

Galton, M., Gray, J. and Ruddock, J. (eds) (1999) 'The Impact of School Transitions and Transfers on Pupil Progress and Attainment', Research Report RR131, Nottingham: DfEE.

Gulati, A. and King, A. (2009) 'Supporting Vulnerable Young People in Transition: Addressing the

Poverty of Wellbeing', final report to Quartet Community Foundation for the West of England, Bristol: Quartet.

Huddleston, T. (2007) 'Identity, Diversity and Citizenship: A Critical Review of Educational Resources'. Online. Available from http://www.citizenshipfoundation.org.uk/lib_res_pdf/0747.pdf (accessed 17 March 2011).

Iroko Theatre Company (n.d.). Online. Available from http://www.irokotheatre.org.uk/ (accessed June 2010).

Levitas, R., Pantazis, C., Fahmy, E., Gordon, D., Lloyd, E. and Patsios, D. (2007) 'The Multidimensional Analysis of Social Exclusion', London: Social Exclusion Task Force. Online. Available from http://tna.europarchive.org/20080305150514/http://www.cabinetoffice.gov.uk/social_exclusion_task_force/publications/multidimensional.aspx (accessed April 2010).

My Society: They Work for You (2010) Online. Available from http://www.theyworkforyou.com/wrans/?id=2007–07–03b.147349.h (accessed June 2010).

NHS Bristol, Public Health (2010) Online. Available from http://www.bristolpct.nhs.uk/PublicHealth/healthofbristol/about_the_population/black_minority_ethnic_pop_electoral_ward.asp (accessed 10 June 2010).

Ofsted (2008) 'St Gregory's Catholic College Ofsted Report'. Online. Available from http://www.st-gregorys.bathnes.sch.uk/docs/OfstedReportSept2008.pdf (accessed 10 June 2010).

Oroyemi, P., Damioli, G., Barnes, M. and Crosier, T. (2009) 'Understanding the Risks of Social Exclusion across the Life Course: Families with Children: A Research Report for the Social Exclusion Task Force', London: Cabinet Office

Parekh Report (2000) *The Future of Multi-Ethnic Britain*, London: Profile Books.

QCA (2010) 'The Primary Curriculum'. Online. Available from http://ufa.org.uk/uploaded_media/resources/1272541790-New_primary_curriculum_handbook_tagged_tcm8-16333.pdf (accessed 17 March 2011).

Robinson, K. (2009) *The Element: How finding Your Passion Changes Everything*, London: Penguin.

Runnymede Trust (2004) 'Realising the Vision: The Report of the Commission on the Future of Multi-Ethnic Britain (2000) Revisited in 2004'. Online. Available from http://www.runnymedetrust.org/uploads/publications/pdfs/RealisingTheVision (accessed 7 August 2010).

Runnymede Trust (2010) Online. Available from http://www.runnymedetrust.org/ (accessed 7 August 2010).

St Gregory's Catholic College (2010) Online. Available from http://www.st-gregorys.bathnes.sch.uk/default.asp (accessed 10 June 2010).

Social Exclusion Task Force (2008) 'Think Family: Improving the Life Chances of Families at Risk'. Online. Available from http://tna.europarchive.org/20080521201536/http://www.cabinetoffice.gov.uk/social_exclusion_task_force/~/media/assets/www.cabinetoffice.gov.uk/social_exclusion_task_force/think_families/think_family_life_chances_report%20pdf.ashx (accessed 17 March 2011).

Stenou, K. (ed.) (2007) 'UNESCO and the Question of Cultural Diversity 1946–2007. Review and Strategy'. Online. Available from http://unesdoc.unesco.org/images/0015/001543/15431mo.pdf (accessed 23 March 2011)

Sutherland, R., Ching Yee, W., McNess, E. and Harris, R. (2010) 'Supporting Learning in the Transition from Primary to Secondary Schools'. University of Bristol. Online. Available from http://www.bristol.ac.uk/education/news/2010/transition-bristoluniversity.pdf (accessed 10 June 2010).

Thomas, H. (2010) 'C4EO Submission: My Future My Choice', unpublished.

UNESCO (n.d.) 'Introducing UNESCO: What We Are'. Online. Available from http://www.unesco.org/new/en/unesco/about-us/who-we-are/introducing-unesco/ (accessed 14 April 2010).

UNESCO (2002) 'Declaration of Cultural Diversity'. Online. Available from http://unesdoc.unesco.org/images/0012/001271/127160m.pdf (accessed June 2009).

Wilkinson, R. and Pickett, K. (2010) *The Spirit Level: Why Equality is Better for Everyone*, 2nd edn, London: Penguin.

# Managing learning

## An ecological perspective on childhood

*Mim Hutchings and Tilly Mortimore*

## Chapter summary

This chapter aims to provide the voice and story of a real adolescent, Ashley, and consider, through his eyes and experiences, some of the questions posed by the theoretical frameworks, policy and practices presented here and in other chapters. We will examine how the individual's emotional and developmental differences can emerge at the Key Stage 2/3 transition time to challenge vulnerable children, such as Ashley, and explore some typical provision and interactions between the child, his or her family, the school and the wider community. This will raise questions about the extent to which such children can be helped to develop their resilience and reduce the risk of their becoming disaffected or excluded.

## Introduction

This chapter begins with a narrative of personal experience: Ashley's story of his school life. It is a case story compiled from the recollections of children we have met. The aim is to investigate Ashley's story and explore how his experience is significant to understanding transition for vulnerable children. Why narrative? First, narrative is based on people's views of their real-life experiences. Narrative offers cases for the reader to explore, investigate, relate to theory and learn from. They are concrete practical knowledge, open to interpretation and critical reflection. Second, narrative is a way in which humans make sense of their lives and the world (Bruner 1990). Every day we tell stories of our lives. Narrative research is rooted in stories of how people experience the world. For example, Xu *et al.* (2007) tell of the transitions in the educational experience of Yang Yang, a newcomer to Toronto. The stories we tell of our lives always carry traces of our past, present and future selves and worlds. As we go through life each experience, good, bad or just usual, influences us in some way and becomes part of us.

In our stories there are always ideas about who I am, where I am, what I am doing here and how I got here. Ashley, now aged 15, tells his real-life story. By looking back with him on his transitions we are aiming to address three issues:

1   How can personal accounts bring alive broader patterns of inequalities and injustice – for problem-solving/thinking anew?

2   How can personal accounts help us understand wider public and political issues?

3   What conceptual and theoretical frameworks can be explored?

## Part 1: Ashley

Today was school open day. I had to stand up in front of 200 people and collect the Year 9 prize for English – even more to the point, I picked up my national bronze medal for swimming 200 metres. My Mum was embarrassing – she cried. Can't think why. Then later on when my friends came up and said well done – she went all red again. Maybe it was because she was more used to people calling me names than shaking my hand and saying 'well done, Ashley, mate'.

That's me – Ashley – what's to tell about me? I can swim faster than anyone in this school, and in lots of schools actually. I make and fly wicked aeroplanes. I don't hit people in the dinner queues any more . . . mostly. I have a best mate here called Barney. We fall out from time to time, I'm not sure why sometimes, but we usually make it up. What else? I like playing with numbers. I'm in the school football team when I'm not training for swimming. I'm 14 years old – I've got dyslexia, which means I find writing what I think really hard. And I've got what people call Asperger's syndrome, which means I really like and really hate certain things and don't always know how to get on with people or say the right things.

I've been at this special boarding school since the end of Year 7, when my Dad left us and Mum finally persuaded the local authority at home that the bullying in my secondary school wasn't going to stop. It would have done actually, because I've got bigger and I've been using weights to build up my muscles and I'd just grab those kids by the throat and throttle them. But it's good I don't have to do that now. I was really sad when I first came here but it's OK at this school.

What sort of school is it? Well it's small and most of us board and it's specially for boys – and a few girls – who have dyslexia but lots of us have other things to deal with. Barney's got dyspraxia, which means he's a bit clumsy and his writing's just dreadful. Some kids are really hopeless at maths and others can't find the right words to say – or always find the wrong ones! Some kids come here so angry and get into fights and shout at the teachers but they usually calm down once they feel OK here. The classes are really small and we spend lots of time on reading, writing and maths but we still get to pass quite a few other subjects at GCSE and there's lots of chances to do all kinds of sport and art and drama – I don't do drama but some people really like it and they do great shows at the end of term. There are always people here to talk to you and try and help you to get out of trouble.

It's been good for me. Most of the teachers understand there's things I can't take and other things I won't do and I've got mates here and my reading and writing has come on loads. It helps that I'm actually here every day because I used to stay off school a lot before. I do sometimes wish, however, that I could go to school at home because the holidays can be a bit lonely when you don't have any mates around and you don't know what to do. I suppose I'll be at this school till I finish my GCSEs. I like computers and I really like maths – but I don't know what will happen then, maybe college. I sometimes wonder how I've got here, what would have happened if I'd stayed in my school at home and what the future's going to bring. Mostly I'm looking forward to it but not all of the time . . . I get scared sometimes, because I don't really like change.

Ashley does not like change – or as termed in this book 'transition'. He has experienced a fair amount of it in his young life and little has been smooth or easy. If you have a knowledge of Asperger's syndrome, you will know that routine and familiarity can be vital to children with Asperger's syndrome, and this tends also to be the case for many children made vulnerable by learning differences or social exclusion.

Looking back at Ashley's journey so far, and at the choices made for him, particularly at the KS2/3 transition, should help to make some of these theories and dilemmas come alive and highlight the impact that these decisions can have on real people. We will also look at his story through the lenses of two theoretical frameworks to see how we might conceptualise and explore some of the real events that a child might experience during the process of transition.

## Part 2: conceptual frameworks – risk and triggers

It is sometimes difficult to make the connections between the real lives of individuals and the theoretical frameworks and paradigms discussed within an academic context. These frameworks, however, can provide opportunities for critical appraisal and comparisons across groups, time, space or culture, which allow judgements to underpin action.

The first conceptual framework is particularly accessible. It emerged from the Equalities Review (2006). It illustrates how combinations of aspects within the lives of particular groups of people can be a trigger for increasing vulnerability. The review suggests that there are two measurable dimensions of vulnerability:

- first, social groups such as race, class, disability and gender, in which membership is associated with disproportionate, persistent and unjust inequalities;

- second, the impact of trigger episodes within a domain or field, such as education, employment or health, which lead to increased vulnerability and further loss of opportunities and hence to social and/or educational exclusion.

This framework successfully highlights the interaction between both individual factors and social forces in understanding responses to specific contexts. Traditionally inequalities tend to be analysed through comparison of average outcomes for large social groups, in respect of gender, disability or ethnicity, against those of society more widely. This broad-brush approach overlooks the ways in which individuals can belong to many groups, both simultaneously and at varying stages in their lives. Considering the role played by specific triggers adds a further more subtle distinction to this analysis. Thus we can explore how, for example, one student with a disability, such as dyslexia or Asperger's syndrome, may thrive in an education setting, whereas a second, faced with a series of trigger episodes, struggles to survive or succeed.

> We may by choice and talent, travel life's road more quickly or slowly than others. Somewhere along the way, however, some individuals, and some groups disproportionately, are forced along a tougher, less direct path, from which it becomes hard to rejoin the main road.
>
> (Equalities Review 2006: 10)

Figures 11.1 and 11.2 illustrate how this two-dimensional framework might provide a way of analysing and understanding Ashley's story.

The 2010 review carried out by the Centre for Excellence and Outcomes in Children and Young People's Services (NFER 2010) cites numerous policy initiatives,

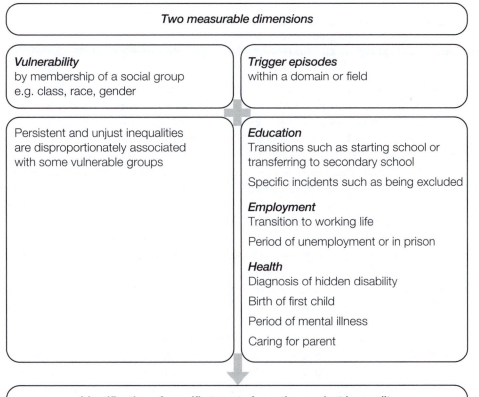

**FIGURE 11.1** Dimensions of vulnerability.

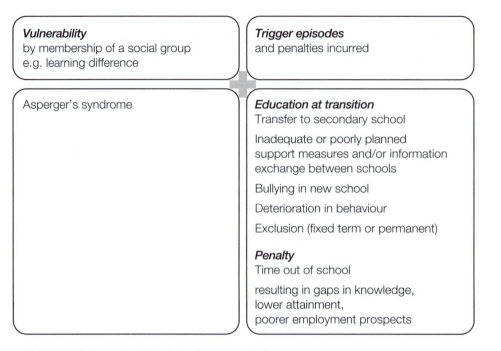

**FIGURE 11.2** Two measurable dimensions: an example.

stimulated by the 'Every Child Matters' agenda (DCSF 2003), that aim to improve children's experiences of transition and ensure that the five outcomes of the Every Child Matters agenda are met. The majority of young people successfully negotiate the risks (Evangelou *et al.* 2008), but transition is clearly a trigger towards a tougher pathway for those vulnerable groups who experience pressures such as economic deprivation or disability. Chapters 2, 3 and 4 in this book have explored the nature of the changes all children go through during the transition from Key Stage 2 to Key Stage 3 and how these can have a traumatic impact upon emotional development, self-identity and learning, regardless of group membership. Studies from the UK and America confirm the suggestion that children from deprived backgrounds, or with additional support needs, may be more likely to experience difficulties during the transition from primary to secondary school, to be at risk of bullying or to make less progress than their peers (Evangelou *et al.* 2008; Carlson *et al.* 2009; DCSF 2009a,b). How might this be represented within the vulnerabilities and triggers framework? How might this apply to a child with Asperger's syndrome (Figure 11.2)?

Ashley's learning differences place him within a vulnerable group for whom transition can be a real trigger for risk. Mackay (2009: 208) discusses the 'transition dip' experienced by dyslexic learners. Ashley mentions his experiences of bullying and admits that his school attendance was dropping. Children with behavioural, emotional and social difficulties and those on School Action Plus (i.e. those for whom school-based additional support has proved ineffective) are disproportionately represented amongst the 9.5 per cent of secondary school students who are persistent absentees, that is, absent for more than 6 weeks in any one year (DCSF 2009b). These 'absent' children have a high risk of choosing to disengage with learning and dominate the not in employment, education or training (NEET) group with its higher levels of economic and social deprivation. However, outcomes are not inevitable. Although employment figures for adults with Asperger's syndrome vary according to the source, many successfully complete higher education and are found in a range of types of employment (http://www.aspergersysndrome.org; accessed 13 July 2010). Hence the vulnerabilities and triggers framework can be used to predict and explain risk and to suggest targets that might be put in place to increase resilience, but only the individual learner's story can tease out the subtle factors that make the difference between success and failure.

Ashley is a student with complex and hidden learning differences. Asperger's syndrome is a type of high-functioning autism that has only recently begun to be recognised and supported appropriately. Children with Asperger's syndrome experience the triad of impairment typical of autism – communication impairments, social impairments and impairment of interests, activity and behaviours (NIASA Working Group 2003). They are less vulnerable than autistic children in that they frequently have broad vocabularies but they may have difficulty understanding the perspectives of others and with establishing the social use of language necessary for smooth relations. They often depend upon set routines and obsessive interests, showing rigidity of behaviour and inability to adapt to change (Atwood 2001). Ashley's learning differences are exacerbated by his severe dyslexia, with the result that, by transition time at the age of 11, although seemingly articulate, his reading and spelling ages were 4 years behind his chronological age and he had been consistently failing in the classroom. These differences affect every aspect of his life at school. His literacy difficulties have made it hard for him to access the curriculum – even in a subject he likes, such as maths, his self-esteem and concept of himself as a learner have plummeted and his poor social skills have prevented him from being accepted in his peer group and have singled him out as a candidate for bullying. These are just some of the factors that have made him vulnerable.

Earlier chapters have highlighted challenges posed by transition – these challenges are particularly acute for children with learning differences (Crombie and Reid 2009). To summarise, the move from primary to secondary school imposes many demands upon all children. For vulnerable survivors of primary school, already affected by classroom failure, the transfer to a larger alien environment where they must cope with new people, routines and rules coincides with the insecurity of the physical and emotional changes associated with puberty and with the changing priorities of adolescence, when family influence may be eclipsed by the values and judgements of the peer group. Children may have moved from the security of a single classroom with one teacher and a small group of peers to separate areas and many teachers. Curriculum delivery and teaching style frequently change from experience-based multi-sensory modes to more verbal and auditory modes, demanding sustained periods of attention and listening skills and employing more complex academic language (Galton and Willcocks 1983). This is frequently the point at which difficulties with literacy translate into a frustrating inability to access the curriculum (Mortimore and Dupree 2008). Combining these pressures with the child's increased size and strength and the complex relationships within the Key Stage 3 classroom means that behaviour frequently becomes harder for teaching staff to handle as learners reach adolescence.

## Activity for the reader: Hunt the trigger

Consider how this information links back to people, events and decisions from Ashley's story. Certain critical episodes may well have triggered choices that cast a long shadow through Ashley's journey.

For example, Ashley's aunt, who worked as a cleaner in his primary school, reported seeing Ashley when in Year 2 screaming and being dragged by the arm by a teacher who left him in a corridor. The conflict between the aunt's role as an employee and her role as one of Ashley's family left her unable to decide what to do. He later slipped unnoticed out of the unlocked school front door and ran home.

This incident will have had an impact on all those involved with him – teaching and support staff, parents, wider family, peers, parents of peers, school governors and the wider community. How might different people respond? What a terrible naughty child? Has he got problems at home? Does he need a special needs label? How can the school security have been so poor? How can we protect him? What sort of impact might an incident such as this have had upon the decisions made later at transition stage?

Look again at Ashley's story and select an event that you consider to be an important trigger. Consider what the options might have been at transition stage and what might have influenced the choices made.

You have now focused on an event you consider to be a key trigger but may not be aware of the processes or options in place at KS2/3, or the stakeholders who might be involved in the decision-making. Legislation and government policy, enshrined in such documents as the Special Educational Needs Code of Practice (DfES 2001), establishes clear principles for the support of a child with a learning difference, making the process explicit. A child's progress through primary school is closely monitored. There are three stages to the Code: 1, School Action; 2, School Action Plus; and 3, the Statement. If a child is causing concern, or failing to meet the expected targets for each year, he or she will be flagged up by the class teacher and placed upon the first stage, School Action, at which point the SENCO will liaise with teaching staff, teaching assistants, parents and the child to set up and monitor an Individual Educational Plan (IEP) containing targets that they will help the child to achieve within the classroom. There will be regular monitoring meetings to chart progress and, should the child still be struggling, the next stage – School Action Plus – would involve consulting specialist teams within the local authority for support and suggestions. The final stage is the issuing of a Statement of Special Educational Needs and the laying down of the clear procedures of the Common Assessment Framework (CAF). Evidence is gathered from a multi-disciplinary team of professionals who take account of the opinions of all stakeholders, including the family and the child, and set appropriate targets, provision, strategies and placements and decide how they are to be reviewed (Frederickson and Cline 2009). It is at this stage that the decision was made to place Ashley in a special school rather than supporting him in his local school and community. The existence of special schools and the ways in which they are integrated and utilised is controversial. Was this the right decision to make for Ashley at his KS2/3 transfer? What do you think Ashley's feelings were? How much power do you think he had to determine his own pathway?

In listening to Ashley's voice and exploring his experiences, the temptation is to focus upon him as an individual and to see his differences or difficulties as the problem that others must solve. This has been criticised as a 'medical' perspective, which describes disability as rooted in the individual's personal biological or cognitive impairments, placing an emphasis upon personal tragedy, diagnosis by experts and, frequently, as in Ashley's case, specialised separate facilities (Booth and Ainscow 2002). A more recent social perspective, driven by the move towards inclusive practices, removes the 'problem' from the impaired individual and locates it firmly within the ways in which society establishes physical and conceptual barriers that oppress disabled people.

The Disability Discrimination Act 2005 has challenged schools to ensure that adjustments are made to attitudes and contexts to dismantle any physical and conceptual barriers that might prevent full inclusion. It is possible to interpret the Common Assessment Framework described above as a process that focuses upon the child and his individual profile as a 'medical' perspective. However, the onus upon all involved is to ensure that the child has equal access to all aspects of the educational field and this has been evidenced by such initiatives as the Dyslexia Friendly Schools programme (Mackay 2006). The CAF acknowledges that the child stands at the centre of a complex network of people, organisations and policy that affect how society views the child and the decisions made. The second conceptual framework provides a way to explore the ways in which these networks around Ashley interact.

## Bronfenbrenner's ecological systems framework

Bronfenbrenner's (1979, 2005) ecological systems theory suggests that learning and development are all embedded within an interconnected series of layers. These layers are called micro-, meso-, exo- and macrosystems (Figure 11.3). As one experience leads onto another there is movement within the ecosystem. At the heart of the ecosystem is an individual, in our example Ashley, whose life world is influenced by all the layers within these ecological systems. Most of the examples in each system are connected with the field of education and provide an opportunity to explore the influences relevant to transition for children with learning differences and disabilities.

All systems are embedded within the 'macrosystem', which is linked to political, economic, social and cultural contexts and changes. For example, international, European and UK agreements on human rights (Unicef 1990) established a framework on children's rights. This includes UK policy and legislation (Special Educational Needs and Disability Act 2001) and sets out guidance (DCSF 2001) for local authorities and schools emphasising the rights of children to be included in decision-making in their lives. Specifically relevant for Ashley would be the good practice guidance on autistic spectrum disorders (DfES 2002). Services for children with learning differences and disabilities are also part of this network of policy, legislation and practice. All of these influence what happens throughout the ecology. The attitudes and principles enshrined in government policy affect all levels, and changes of government in a country can shift education fields. In short, changes in

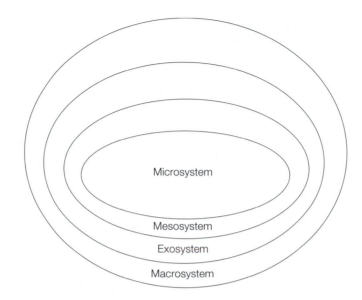

**FIGURE 11.3** Bronfenbrenner's ecological systems framework.

political and economic priorities affect how individuals, such as Ashley and his family, experience the field of education.

The next layer, the 'exosystem', is composed of a variety of influences, relationships and places that are not directly a part of a child's experience but which have an indirect influence. For example, how effective is Ashley's school at implementing the legislation and policy guidance stemming from macro influences, such as the Code of Practice for Special Educational Needs? How does the school interpret responsibilities stemming from the Disability Discrimination Act? Other obvious examples of the impact of the exosystem are the nature of parental or carers' working lives. Are they in stressful jobs with long working hours, which can influence a child's home life? Another example could be whether local authorities prioritise safe play environments or clubs for children so that they can socialise safely with friends away from home or whether high-quality respite placements for children with disabilities and their families are accessible. Decisions at the macro level of government policy will influence priorities for funding, which can have a direct effect on a child's life and opportunities. The influence of the exosystem on a child can be strong but it is not directly experienced.

The 'mesosystem' is part of the interactions between a person's different microsystems, such as home and school. In the mesosystem it is the interactions and the kinds of influence they have that are crucial, for example establishing and maintaining home/school relations for children with disabilities and learning differences; including children in making decisions about their education. Another example could be how safe parents feel their local neighbourhood to be and how this will affect their child's independence and socialising with their friends. The relations between different microsystems can be directly linked or there can be multiple links. If systems are working collaboratively rather than in tension, the risks and triggers for a child can be diminished.

Centrally placed is an individual, in this case Ashley, living within microsystems that are made up of different people and places in which he lives and spends time. For example, for a Year 6 child this would be likely to include at least home, family, school and social settings (clubs, play areas). By age 11, it is likely that a child will inhabit a number of microsystems that extend beyond school and home and which become increasingly linked to friendship groups (Schlegel and Barry 1991).

Initially ecological systems theory appears complicated; however, the idea of nested systems allows for recognition of connections across (lateral) systems and through time (temporal). As a child approaches or goes through transition from primary to secondary school there are shifts in the ecology, but, at the same time, as political, economic and social worlds shift, so does the experience of the individual.

This systems theory offers a way of mapping networks of influence on vulnerability and opening up for evaluation the risks present at transition. Like the vulnerabilities and triggers framework, it helps us to see Ashley's story through a theoretical lens, which enables us to generalise from his individual experience to the broader canvas. As we reflect back on Ashley's journey to his placement in an independent specialist setting it then becomes possible to think not only about Ashley, his vulnerability and the risks, but also about the effectiveness of systems that should include, support and protect him. Most crucially it offers space to reconsider how interaction between individual factors and social forces constructs a view of the issues around transition.

## Conclusions

Ashley is looking back on his experience of transition and forward to his next transition – from secondary school to the outside world – with mixed feelings. You have examined his experiences, the specific pressures of transition and how these will be exacerbated for a child with the complex learning and social needs linked with Asperger's syndrome and dyslexia. Other chapters in this book have identified some of the processes at work during transition and the people involved in the planning and decision-making and you have applied this information to Ashley's life. You have been shown how to place this child's journey within theoretical frameworks which confirm that risks are systemic as well as personal.

Ashley, a member of a vulnerable group, had been though the standard UK education system – primary to secondary – then particular triggers sent him down the path to the segregated residential school. Were the right choices made for him? Where and by whom were these choices made? How were people constrained by current systems, social and political? Transition involves three partners – the young person, parents/carers and the professionals; early planning, co-operation and communication across the two educational fields is essential but it can be fraught with anxiety and all three partners can have conflicting agendas and priorities.

An inclusive approach and the 'Every Child Matters' agenda would suggest that, at KS2/3 transition, adaptations should have been made in Ashley's local secondary school to ensure that he was safe there with access to the full curriculum and his community. What constraints were at play? Whose voice was heard? Continuing in the local context might have led to absenteeism, academic underachievement and eventually social exclusion. What are the penalties he has paid, however, for being removed from the local school and his peers? Ecological systems theory might suggest that this has split his micro worlds into home world and school world and disrupted his ecosystems. He is able to manage and states that he is happy, is making progress with his learning and has found 'mates' in one world – his current school – but remains vulnerable in the home world that he will return to.

How do you see Ashley's future? Will he become one of the successful students with Asperger's syndrome who graduates with a degree in maths or history or IT and finds a niche in the world of work, or will he be one of the unemployed and potentially troubled? What might the impact of the last 4 years be for his next transition – to further or higher education or employment? Will his time in the residential school have resulted in dependence or learned helplessness, and separated him from his community, or helped him to develop coping strategies and to become more resilient? How would a different way of thinking about both the here and now and the future have changed Ashley's story at KS2/3 transition?.

There are no easy answers to these questions. What values, theory or priorities might have driven decisions? It is possible to argue that there are no such things as 'right' choices, that the rigidity of the current UK education system, which reflects the beliefs and values of those groups currently in power, forces choice at particular stages in a child's learning journey. Ashley's choices are constrained by the opportunities available in systems. Some alternative, more fluid, systems are beginning to take hold in the field of education. You might like to explore what is currently developing and consider how these options, such as a learning campus containing all levels of school and college, plus residential facilities, might have helped to solve the dilemmas evident in Ashley's story. Might these new approaches help to make the process of state system education more just and equitable and develop the resilience of a learner such as Ashley?

Ashley is mostly looking forward to his future but he sometimes feels scared and he still finds it hard to cope with change.

## Questions to consider

- Think back to earlier chapters and pull out what you have learned about the cognitive, social and educational pressures of transition. Now re-read Ashley's story. Which social groups might claim him as a member? Thinking about the field of education, what might have made him particularly vulnerable at the KS2/3 transition stage?

- Think about the particular issues around transition described in this book. Which might present real risks for Ashley?

- Re-read Ashley's story and select some events that you consider to be important triggers. Consider what the options might have been at transition stage and what might have influenced the choices made.

- Using the ecological systems framework (Figure 11.3) map all the different influences on Ashley's transition from primary to secondary school.

- Critically reflect on what you have learned from this chapter; concentrate on the three questions in the introduction to the chapter.

## Suggested further reading

Brunswick, N. (2009) *Dyslexia: A Beginner's Guide*. Oxford: One World.
An accessible overview of theoretical and practical issues around special learning difficulties/dyslexia.

Frederickson, N. and Cline, T. (2009) *Special Educational Needs, Inclusion and Diversity*, 2nd edn. Maidenhead: Open University Press. Chapter 3, 'Concepts of Special Educational Needs' and Chapter 4, 'Inclusion'.
A recent exploration of the systems and processes that affect the choices and outcomes for individual learners with additional support needs.

Haddon, M. (2003) *The Curious Incident of the Dog in the Night Time*. London: Jonathan Cape.
This offers a compelling insight into the world of a boy with Asperger's syndrome.

## References

Atwood, T. (2001) *Asperger's Syndrome – A Guide for Parents and Professionals*. London: Jessica Kingsley.

Booth, T. and Ainscow, M. (2002) *Index for Inclusion: Developing Learning and Participation in Schools*. Bristol: Centre for Studies in Inclusive Education (CSIE).

Bronfenbrenner, U. (1979) *The Ecology of Human Development: Experiments by Nature and Design*. Cambridge, MA: Harvard University Press.

Bronfenbrenner, U. (2005) *Making Human Beings Human: Bioecological Perspectives on Human Development*. London: Sage.

Bruner, J. (1990) *Acts of Meaning*. Cambridge, MA: Harvard University Press.

Carlson, E., Daley, T., Bitterman, A., Heinzen, H., Keller, B., Markowitz, J. and Riley, J. (2009) 'Early School Transitions and the Social Behavior of Children with Disabilities: Selected Findings from the Pre-Elementary Education Longitudinal Study: Wave 3 Overview Report from the Pre-Elementary Education Longitudinal Study (PEELS)'. Washington, DC: Institute of Education Sciences. Online. Available from http://ies.ed.gov/ncser/pdf/20093016.pdf (accessed 20 January 2010).

Crombie, M. and Reid, G. (2009) 'The Role of Early Identification: Models from Research and Practice'. In Reid, G. (ed.) *The Routledge Companion to Dyslexia*. London: Routledge.

Department for Children, Schools and Families (DCSF) (2001) *Special Educational Needs Code of Practice*. London: DCSF.

Department for Children, Schools and Families (DCSF) (2003) 'Every Child Matters'. Online. Available from http://.everychildmatters.gov.uk/deliveringservice s/integratedworking/training (accessed 15 July 2010).

Department for Children, Schools and Families (DCSF) (2009a) 'Deprivation and Education: The Evidence on Pupils in England, Foundation Stage to Key Stage 4'. London: DCSF. Online. Available from http://www.dcsf.gov.uk/research/data/uploadfiles/DCSF-RTP-09-01.pdf (accessed 28 January 2010).

Department for Children, Schools and Families (DCSF) (2009b) 'Post-16 Progression Measure'. London: DCSF. Online. Available from http://www.dcsf.gov.uk/14-19/index.cfm?sid=42&pid=355&ctype=TEXT&ptype=Single (accessed 15 March 2010).

Department for Education and Skills (DfES) (2002) *Autistic Spectrum Disorders: Good Practice Guidance*. London: DfES.

Equalities Review (2006) 'The Equalities Review: Interim Report for Consultation'. London: Cabinet Office.

Evangelou, M., Taggart, B., Sylva, K., Melhuish, E. and Sammons, P. (2008) 'What Makes a Successful Transition from Primary to Secondary School? (Effective Pre-School, Primary and Secondary Education 3–14 Project)'. DCSF Research Report 019. London: DCSF. Online. Available from http://www.dcsf.gov.uk/research/data/uploadfiles/DCSF-RR019.pdf (accessed 20 January 2010).

Frederickson, N. and Cline, T. (2009) *Special Educational Needs, Inclusion and Diversity*, 2nd edn. Maidenhead: Open University Press.

Galton, M. and Willcocks, J. (eds) (1983) *Moving from the Primary Classroom*. London: Routledge and Kegan Paul.

Mackay, N. (2006) *Removing Dyslexia as a Barrier to Achievement: The Dyslexia Friendly Schools Toolkit*. Wakefield: SEN Marketing.

Mortimore, T. and Dupree, J. (2008) *Dyslexia-Friendly Practice in the Secondary Classroom*. Exeter: Learning Matters.

NFER (2010) 'All Children and Young People Make Sustained Progress and Remain Fully Engaged through All Transitions between Key Stages: A Research Review on behalf of Centre for Excellence and Outcomes in Children and Young People's Services'. Online. Available from http://www.c4eo.org.uk/themes/schools (accessed 15 March 2011).

NIASA (National Institute for Autism: Screening and Assessment) Working Group (2003) *National Autism Plan for Children*. London: National Autistic Society.

Schlegel, A. and Barry, H., III (1991) *Adolescence: An Anthropological Enquiry*. New York: Free Press.

Special Educational Needs and Disability Act (2001) London: HMSO.

The National Autistic Society (n.d.) Online. Available from http://www.autism.org.uk (accessed 13 July 2010).

Unicef (1989) 'Convention on the Rights of the Child'. Online. Available from http://www.unicef.org/rightsite (accessed 15 March 2011).

Xu, S., Connelly, F. M., He, M. F. and Phillion, J. (2007) 'Immigrant Students' Experience of Echooling: A Narrative Inquiry Theoretical Framework'. *Journal of Curriculum Studies*, 39 (4): 399–422.

# Managing primary–secondary transfer

## Lessons learned?

*Alan Howe*

## Chapter summary

This chapter addresses those who take, or will take, responsibility for transition and transfer arrangements or those who wish to develop a dialogue with such senior managers and policy-makers. It will:

- summarise the challenges that the transfer of children presents for schools;
- discuss what we have learned about the management of primary–secondary transition by drawing on the previous chapters and other reports and published sources and identify where there is a consensus on the direction of future 'good' practice;
- consider what can be learned from practice elsewhere in the world, including those education systems that do not have a primary–secondary divide;
- identify some radical alternatives to the current structure of the education system in the UK.

## Partnerships and relationships

As we have seen, particularly in Chapters 2, 4 and 11 of this book, how children make meaning during transition is crucial to their progress. This is succinctly summed up by a DCFS (2008: 5) report: 'Effective transfers and transitions happen inside the minds of pupils'. Galton (2010) reports on a review of 24 UK studies in which pupils' pre- and post-transition concerns are identified. It gives us some insight about matters on children's minds. Most could be classified under six headings:

    i)    Personal adaptability: Mainly concerns about being the youngest and smallest and about fitting in with older pupils;

    ii)   Work: Coping with different subjects and doing homework on time;

iii)    Size: Getting lost, not using authorised routes, etc.;

iv)    Teachers: adjusting to several teachers (particularly how strict they were);

v)    Friendships: Making new friends and keeping old ones; and

vi)    Moving: Getting to school on time, learning the rules, bringing the right books and equipment, buying school dinners, getting a locker.

(Galton 2010: 111)

Although the adults around the child might try to allay these fears, or even see them as unfounded and likely to 'go away', once the 'reality' of the situation is experienced it is a child's *perceptions*, Pietarinen *et al.* (2010) argue, that will influence their ability to cope. Pietarinen *et al.* identify pupils' *active learning agency* as a key concept within the process of transition. They suggest that learning agency regulates one's ability and 'will' to participate in pedagogical practices and can therefore be considered as an individual's capacity for management of new learning. For example, 'a fragmented, dogmatic and narrow perception' (p. 149) of a new school is likely to result in a passive agency and hence a limited capacity to manage new learning. In other words, if a child develops a negative view of a secondary school during the transition period, they are unlikely to be ready to learn in their new classrooms. Pietarinen *et al.* submit that learning agency is regulated by *perceptions* of what goes on in a school, which in turn are generated by interactions that the child has with peers, family, teachers and other staff associated with transitional arrangements. We have seen in Chapter 2 how *attachment* can give a child emotional resilience to cope with change. On the other hand, 'unsolved disagreements and perceived detachments are likely to cause frictions, feelings of alienation, and inequality and hence undermine the pupils active learning agency' (Pietarinen *et al.* 2010: 149).

So how can primary and secondary schools cooperate to ensure that, in the mind of the pupil, transition is perceived as an opportunity, rather than a threat? Previous chapters have discussed the 'bridges' that need to be built between primary and secondary schools to facilitate this effective transition. This chapter will draw together the themes and issues explored previously and, with reference to recent official reports and other research, reach conclusions about the actions that schools need to consider to manage transition arrangements for the benefit of all stakeholders. Bore and Fuller (2007: 17) describe this *administrative bridge* as being

> a formal liaison between schools, usually at senior management level, in order to establish effective and robust administrative arrangements to support transition, such as pupil records transfer, including performance data management, administrative meetings between key school staff and common procedures.

It is clear that a good relationship between primary and secondary schools is at the heart of the matter. There is a consensus within recent research and reports (Evangelou *et al.* 2008; DCFS 2008; Sutherland *et al.* 2010; Jindal-Snape 2010) that both institutions must take responsibility for, and contribute to, transition arrangements throughout the transition phase. Akos (2010) suggests that this phase must be considered a year-long process. He also suggests that a needs assessment should be carried out in order to review the effectiveness of existing arrangements. Later in the chapter, *evaluation* of transition programmes will be discussed.

Evangelou *et al.* (2008: 8) offer school managers some questions to consider that highlight the possible ways to stimulate good liaison:

- How can you encourage your colleagues to work more closely with the teachers from local primary/secondary schools and learn about each other's schools?
- Are there any networking opportunities or joint CPD activities for different phase teachers in your area?

They seem sensible starting points, but Sutherland *et al.* (2010) suggest that cooperation between schools may be difficult to achieve because of the different cultures, characterised by their depiction as 'two tribes' within the primary and secondary sectors. On the one hand, they find, there seems to be 'a great willingness' of teachers to work across the divide, yet, on the other hand, there are 'tensions and lack of understanding' between them (Sutherland *et al.* 2010: 74). Depending on the phase they will work in, teachers are immersed in different 'pedagogical subcultures' (Pietarinen *et al.* 2010), often from the moment they begin initial teacher training. The 2008 DCSF report 'Strengthening Transfers and Transitions' recommends that institutional communication and cooperation is essential for effective transitions and that effective partnerships are built on common vision, shared responsibility and trust. It would seem that school managers will need to be aware of the potential for tensions to exist between school staff and should plan to engender a sense of common purpose and professional trust. This mutual understanding, the report suggests, requires shared experiences and a common language. It warns that 'there can be no sense of hierarchy' between partners (DCSF 2008: 5). In the medium term teachers could be brought together through structured, shared staff development. This, as we have seen in Chapter 6, can operate effectively at subject level, where teachers can have the opportunity to develop a mutual understanding of subject pedagogies and perhaps realise that they are not too far apart in either their fundamental values or pedagogical approaches. Curriculum 'bridging units' do, however, present particular challenges to schools and, although it seems that they are widely considered a good idea, the implementation of them has presented particular challenges for school managers.

Galton (2010) reports how primary staff are sometimes resentful of spending 'even more time' on core subjects, on which bridging units tend to focus. These units usually follow end of Key Stage assessments in the core subjects, which tend to dominate curriculum time for most of Year 6 in many schools. This suggests that cross-curricular bridging units may be better received, at least by primary teachers. Managing and collating the mixed responses from the variety of primary schools with which the secondary school interacts also presents a considerable challenge for secondary staff – some children will not have done the units. Galton also reports on how the function of the units is not always seen as curriculum focused by teachers; rather they are seen as somewhat related to the child's social transition. If there is a difference of perception between primary and secondary colleagues, the unit is unlikely to seem coherent to the pupils concerned.

Assessment information is usually exchanged between primary and secondary schools. This can be a useful exchange, but also a source of tension. Sutherland *et al.* (2010: 63) found a lack of trust between the 17 secondary schools and their feeders:

> In general we found that secondary schools do not trust Key Stage 2 SATs results and use their own forms of assessment when students enter secondary school, a result that is consistent with the findings of previous research [see, for example, Galton *et al.* 2003 and Evangelou *et al.* 2008]. This is probably one of the major factors that contribute to a lack of trust between primary and secondary schools.

Local authorities may have a role in ensuring that opportunities exist for collaboration between phases and that continuing professional development includes opportunities for cross-phase activity. Akos (2010) recommends that transitional teams are established. These teams should include school managers, key teachers, support staff, parents and pupils from receiving and feeder schools. Curriculum planning, assessment and record keeping could all be areas for joint development. In the long term initial teacher training also has a role to play in developing every teacher's professional values and challenging, at the outset, any notion that a trainee is about to join a discrete community of either primary or secondary teachers. Sutherland *et al.* (2010: 30) also warn of 'unintended barriers' that may be created by close partnership between particular schools. It is possible, they suggest, that partnerships could perpetuate social divisions. Those outside a partnership may view it as an exclusive arrangement favouring transfers from particular schools at the expense of others. Receiving schools will need to be aware of how they are perceived in the local community.

The shared vision and values of partnerships will be reflected in the actions and activities they organise for pupils and their parents. These can be considered in terms of pre-transition and post-transition arrangements. Pre-transition activities can include:

- Presentations to students and parents on selecting a secondary school, which include information on how the schools cooperate to manage transition arrangements; it is a reassuring message to suggest that there is no 'gap' to negotiate and the 'journey' will not be undertaken alone.

- Information packs/online material that reiterate presentation messages and inform those unable to make meetings.

- An open-door policy or internet forum for parents and children to ask questions and discuss their worries about transition.

- A Year 6 curriculum that includes social and emotional aspects of learning relevant to the needs and anxieties elicited from the pupils (see also Chapter 2), for example:
  - discussions and 'circle times' (Mosley 2005) during Year 6, such as discuss 'How are you feeling about going to your new school?', 'What are your hopes and fears for the next year?', 'Are there questions you would like to ask your new teachers about being at secondary school?';

- subject-specific or cross-curricular 'bridging units' co-planned by primary and secondary staff (see Chapters 6 and 7).

- Visits from receiving school staff and/or pupil teams to feeder primary schools. Activities could include:
  - small group meetings with transferring pupils;
  - 'Getting to Know You' activities, for example completion of 'All About Me' activity, which is retained by receiving staff and added to in Year 7;
  - team teaching of lessons by primary/secondary staff;
  - liaison meetings/joint staff development;
  - curriculum 'articulation' to explain to pupils the kinds of activities and learning that will take place under the subject headings used by the secondary school.

- Visits to receiving schools by pupils and staff. Activities could include:
  - shadowing programmes – involving staff and pupils of primary schools shadowing peers during a secondary school day;
  - school tours, conducted by older pupils;
  - mixed extra-curricular activities, such as cultural or sporting events (see Chapter 11);
  - the assignment of 'learning buddies' or mentors, with regular meetings between them.

- Communication between pupils and receiving staff, for example e-mails/letters, question and answer exchanges.

Post-transition events can include:

- Time in the secondary school when only Year 7 pupils attend – to allow them to experience the space without older pupils crowding the halls, canteens, etc.
- Peer mentor programmes with Year 7 children supported by older pupils.
- Tutor group team building events such as:
  - residential trips and outdoor challenges;
  - group and pair work and planned seating arrangements to help children make new friends;
  - 'speed meetings' – each child to talk to every other during a session.
- Systematic identification procedures for vulnerable children and focused support for all, for example individual tutorials, pupil review meetings.
- Completion of bridging units started in primary school.
- A pedagogy that explicitly values primary school learning, for example:
  - class discussions on 'things I learned in primary school', 'good things about my primary school';
  - explicit reference to the primary curriculum as experienced in feeder schools;

 – team teaching with visiting Year 6 teachers.

■ A curriculum that actively links to the KS2 curriculum in subject and cross-curricular teaching.

The above recommendations have been synthesised from Akos (2010), Evangelou *et al.* (2008), DCFS (2008), Sutherland *et al.* (2010), Galton *et al.* (1999, 2003) and many other informal sources.

Many of the points listed above are exemplified in this short case study from Ralph Allen School, Bath. The school is an 11–18 co-educational, non-denominational comprehensive that has developed a multi-faceted approach to transition:

> Underpinning [our approach] is our growing understanding of the ordering principles that affect the well-being and cohesion of people when they form a group. Groups are human systems. Operating within these systems are dynamics – often hard to detect – that help shape behaviours. The fundamental need of human beings to 'belong' underpins these dynamics . . . We believe that healthy peer grouping will be more likely to be created if we have attended to the dynamics and supported them mindfully.
>
> We organise visits to the primary schools to meet the year 6 children – not only the ones coming to our school. The year 7 team – the Head of Year and the Pastoral Manager – spend time with each child individually talking about their forthcoming transition . . . there is also a chance for the class teachers and SENCO to exchange important information with out team.
>
> Each child produces a photomontage . . . showing their family members, hobbies, pets and favourite things. On the other side, the children collect autographs and positive statements from friends, family members and their teachers . . . The card encapsulates year 6 experiences and contains messages that the students can look back on with pride. They then provide us with a really valuable insight into each child . . . they can also be used as a resource in subjects such as English . . . and in PSHE.
>
> In the latter part of the summer term I write a letter to each of the 175 children who will be joining us in September. Aside from simply welcoming the new students, we want to model an important aspect of our culture from the outset. I am making authentic contact – as one human to another. I tell them about me . . . I invite them each to write back . . . I receive many replies.
>
> (Lee and James 2010: 3–4)

## Evaluation of transition arrangements

Schools will wish to evaluate current transition arrangements and evaluate any changes that they implement. Analysis by Evangelou *et al.* (2008) revealed five aspects of a successful transition. These aspects suggest a framework for the evaluation of provision (Figure 12.1).

| INDICATORS OF SUCCESSFUL TRANSITION (AFTER EVANGELOU *ET AL.* 2008) | RELEVANT DATA SOURCES AND EVALUATIVE QUESTIONS (EXAMPLES) |
| --- | --- |
| Children are developing new friendships and improving their self-esteem and confidence once at secondary school | *To pupils*:<br>Which of these statements do you agree with:<br>I have more friends in secondary school than in primary school<br>I have fewer friends in secondary school<br>I have about the same number of friends<br>I am more confident than I was in primary school, etc. |
| Children are settled so well in school life that they cause no concerns to their parents | *To parents*:<br>To what extent are you/were you concerned about the transition from primary to secondary school?<br>*To pupils*:<br>What have you told you parent(s) about your transition from primary to secondary school? |
| Children are showing an increasing interest in school and school work | *To pupils*:<br>Do you think you have made good progress in your subjects this year? If so, in which ones? If not, in which ones and why do you think that is?<br>Do you think you contribute to class as much as you did in your primary school? If not, why do you think that is?<br>*To staff*:<br>Is there evidence that your pupils are making the progress expected of them? |
| Children are getting used to their new routines and school organisation with great ease | *To staff*:<br>What are your observations regarding pupils' familiarity with school routines? Are there changes that the school could make to simplify our organisation?<br>*To pupils*:<br>How do you feel about having different teachers for different subjects? Does this make a difference to how you learn? |
| Children are experiencing curriculum continuity, i.e. they find work completed in Year 6 to be very useful for the work they are doing in Year 7 | *To pupils*:<br>Are some lessons or subjects easier or harder than in primary school?<br>Is the type of work you do in lessons here the same as in primary? How is it different?<br>Can you think of examples of how something you did in Year 6 helped in Year 7?<br>*To staff*:<br>Can you give an example of how your planning has been informed by the Year 6 curriculum? |

**FIGURE 12.1** Suggestions for the evaluation of transition arrangements.

## An international perspective

Much of this book has focused on the education system in the UK, particularly England. An appraisal of 'our' system – its strengths and weaknesses – can be enhanced when we have some understanding of other ways that systems can be organised. We know from recent international surveys that the UK education system is not the best in the world (Edwards 2009). That accolade might be awarded to Finland. The skills of Finnish students (aged 15) were among the best in all domains assessed in the Programme for International Student Assessment (PISA) surveys of 2000, 2003 and 2006. Although there is no evidence that any single factor has contributed to the excellent reputation of Finland's education system, it is worth noting that Finnish schools are 'all-through' comprehensives from grades 1 to 9 (ages 6/7–15/16). Unlike in the UK, this structure is a result of reform that abolished the division of comprehensive school into lower and upper stages because of the negative effect that such a divide had on children's progress (Eurydice 2009). There are four types of teachers in basic education, namely class teachers (lower-grade specialists), subject teachers (mostly teaching grades 7–9), special needs teachers and guidance counsellors. The first three categories of teacher are educated to master's level. What might be relevant to note is that generalist and specialist teachers all work in the same school. There is no evidence of a 'two tribes' culture that has been identified in the UK.

An analysis of the PISA 2006 results (OECD 2007) has shown that streaming of students at an early stage tends to increase the impact of socio-economic background on student performance. In other words, the earlier the students are stratified into separate institutions or programmes, the stronger the impact the school's average socio-economic background has on performance. This is a significant finding for the UK where, as we have seen, children are selected or streamed 'early' (at age 11) in some regions, there is considerable variation between the attainment of children even in non-selective schools and the society is relatively unequal, with children coming from a wide range of socio-economic circumstances (Wilkinson and Pickett 2009). The OECD finding therefore suggests that any selection of children into different schools at age 11 may well be counter-productive in relation to later attainment.

Finland is a very different country from the UK. It is small and relatively uniform in culture, language and wealth distribution (Wilkinson and Pickett 2009; Edwards 2009) and it is therefore difficult to make direct comparisons. At this point it is simply conjecture that an all-through comprehensive school contributes to a first-class education system. It is worth noting that Denmark has an all-through schooling structure similar to that of Finland yet achieves more modestly in international 'league tables'.

## Some radical alternatives to the current structure of the education system in the UK

Emerging from the discussion above are some possible alternatives to the current two-tier system we find in the UK:

1. establishment of 'all-through' schools;
2. dismantling of the divide between primary and secondary curriculum and pedagogy.

## All-through schools: slow progress

There has been a long tradition of radical educators setting up independent all-through schools. One of the most well known is Summerhill, set up by progressive educator A. S. Neill. Summerhill educates children from 5 to 18 years. The school states that:

> all the inhabitants are considered equal members of the community. All are equally entitled to citizenship of the school – teachers, big kids, and little kids alike – and this is reflected in their interactions with each other. There is an ease of manner between equals that cannot exist in a hierarchy, however friendly and informal.
>
> (Summerhill 2010)

Another example is the Acorn School, Gloucestershire, also all-through, independent and co-educational, 'known for its unique approach to providing outstanding holistic education' (Acorn School 2010). The school accepts children from the age of 7 and continues to age 18 or 19, when the majority of students go on to university. These schools represent a tiny fraction of the independent sector. In the state sector, all-through schools are similarly rare.

In 2008 the *Independent* newspaper published an article entitled 'An Academy for All Ages: Why "All-Through" State Schools are Booming' (Wilce 2008). The article suggested that academies and their sponsors are very keen on all-through schooling and an increasing number are coming up with proposals. The then schools minister Andrew Adonis was quoted as saying:

> [Sponsors] see the advantages of getting children at a younger age. And we are receptive to such proposals, although we are not saying they should become the standard that everyone should follow. They may have implications for how schools work, but we will have to wait and see how they do.
>
> (Wilce 2008)

A publication from the government's 'innovation unit' around that time suggested that there are two main all-age models:

(i) All-age school federation – this comprises two or more schools which share a degree of governance and pedagogical programmes, but remain funded as separate institutions. They may or may not share one site/campus.

(ii) All-age school – this is one school comprising all or multiple phases with one governing body and is funded as a single institution. It often occupies a single site/campus or is combining its previously separate institutional sites into a new build.

(DfES Innovation Unit n.d.: 3)

The document sets out five 'principles' to guide those considering setting up such a school, which are summarised here:

- Leadership, management and governance – effective management is crucial for the successful development of all-age institutions.

- Curriculum – the concept of all-age schooling can become increasingly meaningful to staff as they recognise the many opportunities it offers for curriculum development.

- Resources – an important benefit of all-age schooling is being able to achieve greater cost-effectiveness through the sharing of resources in a variety of ways.

- Ethos – the desire to develop or maintain a common ethos is often a major factor driving the development of an all-age institution.

- Community – an all-age institution can also offer the opportunity to enhance all aspects of community development, both within and beyond the boundaries of the school(s), in line with the 'Every Child Matters' agenda of the Department for Education.

Two years on and, at the time of writing, government priorities have changed. There is little evidence of the 'boom' in all-through schooling identified by the *Independent*. In September 2010 the new Conservative government published a list of academies opening for the new school year. Of 98 academies listed, one was an all-through school (Department for Education 2010).

## Dismantling of the divide between primary and secondary curriculum and pedagogy

In the first chapter of this book we saw how the divide between primary and secondary schools has a long history, and that there is no strong educational rationale for its existence. Yet it also seems there is little chance that there will be a radical reorganisation of schooling in the near future; at the time of writing we await news on government plans for the curriculum and there is no evidence to suggest that the curriculum at Key Stages 2 and 3 will be reviewed or revised in tandem. There has been considerable development, evident in many schools, of the excellent management of the transfer of children, which has led to the majority taking the event in their stride. We have also seen, however, that there still exists a fundamental divide within the teaching profession and perceived divides within the curriculum (Chapters 1, 4 and 6–8). Sutherland *et al.* (2010: 6) make a number of recommendations in their report, including a demand for joint training, development and support of primary and secondary teachers, especially those who work with pupils around transition from primary to secondary school. They also suggest that the proposed Masters in Teaching and Learning should incorporate elements that allow primary and secondary teachers to work together on issues of academic transition between primary and secondary school. In England, there is a low baseline on which to build such programmes. There are currently 'middle years' or KS2/3 initial training courses offered in England by

17 providers (universities). The number of students on these courses is probably a small proportion of the 33,350 who gained qualified teacher status in 2009 (General Teaching Council 2010) (The General Teaching Council does not distinguish between 'middle years' and 'secondary' students in their figures.) 'Middle years' courses are designed for trainee teachers to gain an in-depth understanding of the issues discussed in this book. Canterbury Christ Church University offers a course for trainees who:

> have a strong interest in their specialist subject, but also like the idea of working with primary children; are concerned about smoothing the transition of pupils from primary to secondary education; are interested in working across this age group such as in innovative state models of schooling; continental or independent schools.
>
> (Canterbury Christ Church University 2010)

It is these kinds of 'enlightened' courses that may help satisfy such calls for a better understanding between the 'two tribes' discussed throughout this book. After qualification, joint professional development could also provide opportunities for collaboration. The General Teaching Council survey of teachers published in 2006 identified that around 40 per cent of teachers had experienced some sort of collaborative or network professional development, although figures do not show how many of these events were primary–secondary focused (Hutchings *et al.* 2006). These data suggest that there is considerable work to do if the teaching profession is to bring together the two pedagogic cultures that currently exist.

Throughout this book there is a great deal of evidence to suggest that many schools are taking transition and transfer seriously. What we have learned from the authors in this book is that each 'bridge' we build for children is important, although some bridges seem to receive more investment than others. Most children manage the journey although structures may be faulty or incomplete. Vulnerable learners are less well equipped to cope. An alternative is to reject the concept of 'bridging' and work instead on reforming the landscape.

## Questions to consider

- Is the 'administrative bridge' between schools the most important of our 'five bridges'?
- What might be the disadvantages of an 'all-through' school system, such as that in Denmark?
- How can teacher training contribute to challenging the difference between primary and secondary teachers?

## Suggested further reading

Jindal-Snape, D. (2010) *Educational transitions.* London: Routledge.
This volume explores transitions at all stages of educational progression, that

is, nursery to primary, primary to secondary, and secondary to post school. It also examines these transitions across a variety of countries and types of schools.

## References

Acorn School (2010) Online. Available from http://theacornschool.com/ (accessed 11 September 2010).

Akos, P. (2010) 'Moving through elementary, middle, and high schools: The primary to secondary shift in the United States'. In Jindal-Snape, D. (ed.) *Educational transitions.* London: Routledge.

Bore, K. and Fuller, K. (2007) 'Crossing bridges: Ready for transfer'. *CB*, 5 (3): 17–20, 64–65.

Canterbury Christ Church University (2010) 'PGCE 7–14 Structure and Subject'. Online. Available from http://www.canterbury.ac.uk/courses/prospectus/pgce/7-14-structure-and-subject.asp (accessed 23 September 2010).

Department for Children, Schools and Families (DCSF) (2008) 'The National Strategies. Strengthening transfers and transitions: Partnerships for progress'. Online. Available from http://nationalstrategies.standards.dcsf.gov.uk/node/85276 (accessed 20 July 2010).

Department for Education (2010) 'List of academies opened at the start of September 2010'. Online. Available from http://www.education.gov.uk/academies/Open%20academies (accessed 14 September 2010).

Department for Education and Schools Innovations Unit (n.d.) 'All through schooling: A resource'. Online. Available from http://www.innovationunit.org/images/stories/files/pdf/allage_booklet2.pdf (accessed 14 September 2010).

Edwards, A. (2009) 'High schools and high stakes assessments'. In Bignold, W. and Gayton, L. (eds) *Global issues and comparative education.* Exeter: Learning Matters.

Eurydice (2009) 'Organisation of the education system in Finland 2008/09'. Online. Available from http://eacea.ec.europa.eu/education/eurydice/documents/eurybase/eurybase_full_reports/FI_EN.pdf (accessed 14 September 2010).

Evangelou, M., Taggart, B., Sylva, K., Melhuish, E., Sammons, P. and Siraj-Blatchford, I. (eds) (2008) 'What makes a successful transition from primary to secondary school?' London: DCSF.

Galton, M. (2010) 'Moving to secondary school: What do pupils in England say about the experience?' In Jindal-Snape, D. (ed.) *Educational transitions.* London: Routledge.

Galton, M., Gray, J. and Ruddock, J. (eds) (1999) 'The impact of school transitions and transfers on pupil progress and attainment'. Research Report RR131. Nottingham: DfEE.

Galton, M., Gray, J. and Ruddock, J. (eds) (2003) Transfer and transitions in the middle years of schooling (7–14): Continuities and discontinuities in learning. Nottingham: Department for Education and Science.

General Teaching Council (2010) 'Annual digest of statistics 2009–10: Profiles of registered teachers in England'. London: GTC. Online. Available from http://www.gtce.org.uk/documents/publicationpdfs/digest_of_statistics0910.pdf (accessed 23 September 2010).

Hutchings, M., Smart, S., James, K. and Williams, K. (2006) 'General Teaching Council for England survey of teachers Appendix E: Frequency tables: 2004/2005/2006 comparison'. London: GTC. Online. Available from http://www.gtce.org.uk/documents/publicationpdfs/research_survey06appe.pdf (accessed 23 September 2010).

Jindal-Snape, D. (ed.) (2010) *Educational transitions.* London: Routledge.

Lee, L. and James, J. (2010) *Helping transition: A systemic perspective.* Derby: Nowhere Foundation.

Mosley, J. (2005) *The circle book.* Trowbridge: Positive Press.

OECD (2007) 'OECD's PISA survey shows some countries making significant gains in learning outcomes'. Online. Available from http://www.oecd.org/document/22/0,3343,en_2649_35845621_39713238_1_1_1_1,00.html (accessed 14 September 2010).

Pietarinen, J., Soini, T. and Pyhalto, K. (2010) 'Learning and well-being in transitions: How to promote pupils' active learning agency'. In Jindal-Snape, D. (ed.) *Educational transitions.* London: Routledge.

Summerhill (2010) 'Introduction to Summerhill'. Online. Available from http://www.summerhillschool.co.uk/pages/index_continued.html (accessed 11 September 2010).

Sutherland, R., Ching Yee, W., McNess, E. and Harris, R. (2010) 'Supporting learning in the transition from primary to secondary schools'. University of Bristol. Online. Available from http://www.bristol.ac.uk/education/news/2010/transition-bristoluniversity.pdf (accessed 10 June 2010).

*Wilce, H. (2008)* 'An academy for all ages: Why 'all-through' state schools are booming'. Online. Available from http://www.independent.co.uk/news/education/schools/an-academy-for-all-ages-why-allthrough-state-schools-are-booming-947912.html (accessed 14 September 2010).

Wilkinson, R. and Pickett, K. (2009) *The spirit level: Why more equal societies almost always do better*. London: Allen Lane.

# Index